Leeds Metropolitan University

D0337067

People Management
Challenges and opportunities

Edited by

David Rees
and
Richard McBain

Selection and editorial matter © David Rees and Richard McBain 2004
Individual chapters © individual contributors 2004

All rights reserved. No reproduction, copy or transmission of this
publication may be made without written permission.

No paragraph of this publication may be reproduced, copied or transmitted
save with written permission or in accordance with the provisions of the
Copyright, Designs and Patents Act 1988, or under the terms of any licence
permitting limited copying issued by the Copyright Licensing Agency,
90 Tottenham Court Road, London W1T 4LP.

Any person who does any unauthorised act in relation to this publication
may be liable to criminal prosecution and civil claims for damages.

The authors have asserted their rights to be identified
as the authors of this work in accordance with the Copyright,
Designs and Patents Act 1988.

First published 2004 by
PALGRAVE MACMILLAN
Houndmills, Basingstoke, Hampshire RG21 6XS and
175 Fifth Avenue, New York, N.Y. 10010
Companies and representatives throughout the world

PALGRAVE MACMILLAN is the global academic imprint of the Palgrave
Macmillan division of St. Martin's Press, LLC and of Palgrave Macmillan Ltd.
Macmillan® is a registered trademark in the United States, United Kingdom
and other countries. Palgrave is a registered trademark in the European
Union and other countries.

ISBN 0–333–92030–9

This book is printed on paper suitable for recycling and made from fully
managed and sustained forest sources.

A catalogue record for this book is available from the British Library.

Library of Congress Cataloging-in-Publication Data
People management : challenges and opportunities / edited by David Rees and
    Richard McBain.
      p.   cm.
Includes bibliographical references and index.
ISBN 0–333–92030–9 (pbk.)
1. Personnel management.   I. Rees, David, 1952–   II. McBain, Richard.

HF5549.P415 2004
658.3—dc22   2004054821

10   9   8   7   6   5   4   3   2   1
13 12 11 10 09 08 07 06 05 04

Printed and bound in China

LEEDS METROPOLITAN
UNIVERSITY
LIBRARY
1706361176
YFF-B HEV
HC-63853
14.6.05
658.3 REE

Contents

List of figures

List of tables

Foreword

There is no doubt that human resource practitioners and academics stand at a crossroads concerning the way people will be managed in the future. The global business environment is increasingly competitive, driving market players to gain advantage over their rivals. Huge pressures are exerted from both inside and outside the organisation to deliver the necessary performance for success – success that will inevitably be based on the effective management of people. Dramatic changes in technology, social preferences and lifestyle choices across the world are stretching organisations in their thinking about what people management philosophies, strategies, tactics, methods and techniques to adopt.

A number of questions need to be considered as we search for the 'right approach' to the management of people.

Is there a new path that we can follow, leading us to an 'ultimate' model of people management? If so, do we retrace our steps and see if we have missed a turning? Or do we pursue the existing route? Or is there a way forward that is simply a figment of our imagination?

Whatever way we choose, how easy will our journey be? Is this a fairly straight road, or is it full of twists and turns? Can we predict the obstacles that may lie ahead, or are there so many unknowns that we just have to address novel situations as best we can? What capacity does the organisation have to deal with such unpredictabilities? Do businesses have the people management capabilities to perform effectively in environments of uncertainty and complexity?

This book is intended to place a number of key topics on the agenda of managers who have a responsibility for getting things done through other people. The issues raised over the following chapters are intended to alert managers to the challenges ahead. Some of these are already confronting managers and human resource specialists.

Our contributions are not intended to be speculative, neither are they intended to be deeply philosophical. Each chapter heading has been selected on the basis of indicative evidence, practitioner experience, previous and current research. There have been a number of influences on the authors who are drawn from a variety of backgrounds. Some writers have had extended careers in academia, particularly the international business school environment. Others are recognised consultancy specialists, human resource management professionals, or management developers. Many have continuing managerial roles and responsibilities. They do have a common link, however, through their association with Henley Management College, UK.

The editors have been responsible for designing the framework of the book and instituting linkages between sections and chapters. Further, the editors have advised and facilitated contributors in terms of content and focus. However, we have decided to allow individual writing talents to flourish by not imposing a consistent house style. We believe that the key messages our writers wish to emphasise are best conveyed in a balanced environment of a guiding framework and personal style. Our framework is described in the next section.

The stimulus for this publication came from the team who designed and produced the Managing People module for the Henley MBA programme in the late 1990s. Acting upon feedback from course participants and clients from executive programmes, it became apparent that the world of people management was moving faster than we realised. Course members were ideal sources of opinion and information, providing a genuinely broad overview of people management in action. Module assignments required learners to take a look into the future of their organisations and propose new people management strategies. These produced a fountain of ideas, challenges and issues that deserved a wide audience. This book has attempted to capture the key debates with contributions containing a balance between theory and practice.

The editors acknowledge that our agenda is probably incomplete and many issues that we have not addressed specifically here deserve attention. However, we believe that the agenda offered is a reasoned choice that will provoke managers to engage in the development of appropriate people management strategies and develop the competencies needed to be effective future people managers.

DAVID REES AND RICHARD MCBAIN
AUGUST 2004

Notes on contributors

Victor Dulewicz has worked at Henley Management College since 1986 and is currently Head of the Human Resource Management and Organisational Behaviour Faculty, Director of Assessment Services and Governor of the College. He lectures on Personality, Team Roles, Emotional Intelligence and Management Assessment & Development on most courses, and acts as a syndicate and individual advisor on executive programmes. He led a major government-funded project investigating competences for boards of directors and is currently researching board and company performance, and leadership.

In the past, Victor worked as an occupational psychologist for Rank Xerox and the Civil Service Selection Board, and was Manager of Assessment and Occupational Psychology for the STC Group (now Nortel) for nine years.

Since 1986, Victor has advised many large international companies on management assessment and development, specifically on competences, psychological testing, emotional intelligence and assessment centres. He has written over 100 articles and presented at numerous national and international conferences on these subjects. He was a section editor of the handbook *Assessment and Selection in Organisations* (1989) and co-author, with Professor Malcolm Higgs, of Making sense of *Emotional Intelligence* (2002).

Victor is a chartered occupational psychologist, a Fellow of both the British Psychological Society and the Chartered Institute of Personnel & Development, and a member of the Institute of Directors. Further details appear at www.dulewicz.com.

Malcolm Higgs is the Academic Dean of Henley Management College and a member of the Human Resource and Organisational Behaviour Faculty. He moved to Henley from his role as Principal Partner in Towers Perrin's European Human Resource Management practice. Prior to this he had eight years consulting experience with the Hay Group and Arthur Young. In 1987 he undertook a research programme into the human resource implications of the major changes in the UK financial markets and in 1988 published a book on the subject. He has also published extensively in the areas of leadership, change management, team development and executive assessment. More recently he has published and co-authored a number of papers and a book on Emotional Intelligence, together with a number of related psychometric instruments.

Malcolm is a member of the British Psychological Society and a Chartered Psychologist and, as a consultant, works with organisations on leadership assessment, development and change management.

Elizabeth Houldsworth a member of the HR/OB faculty and Head of Connected Management Learning at Henley Management College. She teaches across a range of qualification and client programmes as well as managing a number of funded research projects. Her individual research interests are varied and include aspects of HR, particularly performance management and adult/management learning – particularly through the application of technology. She previously worked for a number of years as an HR consultant specialising in performance management.

Shawn Ireland is the Managing Director of HRC group, a global learning and organisation development company, and a psychologist with a practice based in London. He works with organisations on the effective utilisation of virtual teams, project leadership, performance management and leadership for change. His research examines the implications of critical self-reflection in fostering transformative learning in organisations, and his clinical research had produced innovative treatment models for work families.

Shawn has worked extensively with international Fortune 500 companies including AT&T, Cable and Wireless, DOW and Schlumberger, and diversely with organisations such as US Department of Defence (Europe) NATO, the Fulbright and Pew Trust for International Management Development Institute (IMDI). He has also worked as a learning and development advisor to governments in the Middle East, Africa and Europe.

Shawn is also an approved supervisor for DBA students at Henley Management College.

Tim Osborn-Jones, following personnel appointments in the construction industry, undertook a series of executive appointments focusing on change management in the housing/community care and business/continuing professional education sectors. Being a member of the Human Resources and Organisational Behaviour Faculty Group at Henley Management College, Tim works with Open Executive and Corporate Qualification programmes and conducts research in the field of talent management and employment relations, focusing especially on the psychological contract. Tim is an NLP Practitioner and a Board Member of the South Oxfordshire Housing Association.

Jason Leonard has worked for a variety of international blue-chip companies in utilities, pharmaceuticals, healthcare, Oil and FMCG manufacturing industries for the last 14 years as well as in a consultancy. With an enthusiasm for learning Jason has, during this time, followed up his first degree in Human Biological Sciences with an MSc in Ergonomics, professional qualifications in health, safety and environmental areas, and an MBA from Henley Management College (with a dissertation looking at cultural due diligence in mergers and acquisitions). He has published in various areas in relation to his work which have focused around work design, culture, risk management, corporate social responsibility and management systems.

Richard McBain is currently Director of Studies for the MBA by Distance Learning at Henley Management College and also a member of the Human Resource Management and Organisational Behaviour Faculty at the College. His principal areas of professional interest are in the fields of e-learning and assessment strategies. Richard teaches on the Managing People and Dissertation modules of the Henley MBA programme. In addition he is actively researching in the areas of mentoring, emotional intelligence, self-efficacy and academic progression. He is a regular contributor to 'Manager Update', a quarterly review of current management research. Prior to joining Henley Management College, Richard had 17 years experience in the financial services industry, which included the management of a corporate training and development function. His interest in mentoring stems from experience in managing a formal mentoring programme and has continued at Henley as a mentor on executive development programmes and with doctoral research.

Helen Murlis has spent over 25 years working, researching, writing and consulting in the fields of reward strategy and performance management. Early experience in the aerospace industry was followed by senior research, advisory and editorial roles at the British Institute of Management and Incomes Data Services. Her consulting career started in 1985 and she has worked with a very wide range of public and private sector clients both in the UK and internationally. For the last 13 years at the Hay Group, Helen has played leading roles in the reward, performance management and Central Government practices, and she is now Director there.

With Michael Armstrong she is co-author of *Reward Management: A Handbook of Remuneration Strategy and practice* (fourth edition, 1998/fifth edition Autumn 2004). Helen was the Chair of the CIPD Compensation Forum in the past and former Vice President of Pay and Employment Conditions. Helen continues to teach, write and publish regularly on total reward and performance issues, notably on 'Engaged Performance'. She also trained for people and works actively as an executive coach.

David Rees is the Director and Principal Consultant at Cultural Fluency Training and Development Ltd. David was appointed as Visiting Teaching Fellow at Henley Management College in 1988 and has been a member of the College Associate Faculty since then.

Business career in the telecommunications sector and following professional training as work-study analyst with Australian consultants, W.D. Scott, took up posts in management services. He moved into a lecturing career at Guildford College of Technology before forming a partnership with the Belgian organisation, *Séjours Educatifs*, to deliver language training programmes. He launched his own enterprise in 1983, focusing on language and culture training, international management consultancy and translations/interpreting.

He is currently researching and developing models of human capital and cultural due diligence. He trains and consults on an international basis for many large public and private sector organisations. His previous publications have been in the fields of European people management, international project management and cultural due diligence.

Book overview and structure

Our book is built around a framework that categorises the influences on human resource management policy, strategy and tactics under four main headings. This framework is shown as Figure 1, with examples under each heading.

Figure 1 Influences on people management policy, strategy and tactics

The framework indicates the functional activities that need to be undertaken. These activities such as recruiting, developing and retaining people, may be the responsibility of a central HR department, or they may be carried out by local line managers.

There are a range of influences from outside the organisation's direct control – government policies, social trends, technological, development and competitor behaviour. Corporate performance can be affected in a profound way, depending how alert and predisposed the organisation is towards such forces and how it will respond in terms of people management.

Internal influences are potentially more controllable as each factor is under the organisation's control – corporate values, leadership style and systems of governance, for example.

Finally, our framework is completed through the quality and effectiveness of internal and external business relationships. These would include customer, supplier and partner relationships – the 'extended enterprise'.

From this framework we propose to focus on those areas that current academic research and practitioner experience suggest are of fundamental importance to the effective management of people.

The book's structure is divided into three main parts:

1   Strategic human resource management agenda

2   The way people are managed

3   Management competencies for future success.

Figure 2 demonstrates the linkage of these three parts.

Figure 2 Strategic HRM, people management processes and managerial competencies

Part I commences with a provocative review of the 'state of the art' – where has people management come from, where it is now, and where is it heading? There are, of course, no definitive answers, but Chapter 2 identifies the major trends in HRM. Chapter 3 discusses what has come to be one of the key topics of corporate management – how we manage people as a true capital asset? Chapter 4 focuses on another strategic area – the way an organisation is perceived as a socially responsible business. Social responsibility is entirely in the hands of management and employees as it forms part of the value and behaviour sets embedded within the enterprise.

Part II focuses on transactional and functional aspects of people management. Performance management opens this stage of the book as this underpins the way in which people will be evaluated, developed and rewarded. Human talent acquisition and retention are viewed as essential elements of strong human resource management practice and a separate chapter is devoted to this topic within the section. We have selected the challenge of managing virtual teams as a unique future people management activity and this is addressed with discussion and analysis of future reward trends, systems and strategies.

Part III is devoted to future people management competencies. This integrates the previous two parts by pointing the way to successful people management implementation through appropriate levels of competency in critical areas. We have identified four key areas of competency – leadership, cultural fluency, learning and mentoring/coaching. Each of these has a chapter explaining the competencies required.

The book is completed with a short review of our work with an acknowledgement that future people management is a continuing process of experience, research and learning.

Strategic human resource management agenda

Managing people: back to the future?

David Rees

This chapter aims to stimulate thinking on the influences that have been significant on our understanding of how people are, or should be, managed. The question posed by the title is an invitation to the reader to reflect on where we may be going from here. Have we reached the end of the road in terms of ideas and approaches to people management, or are there imaginative routes ahead?

Since, the management of people was developed as a discipline worthy of formal study there have been many influences on how best to achieve this. Various texts (see, e.g. Torrington *et al.* 2002) suggest that the main strands of thinking can be categorised under 'personnel management' or 'human resource management'. This has become a somewhat tired – and unproductive – debate for many line and project managers who are more concerned with how to get things done, rather than align themselves with a particular school of management theory.

However, it should be clear to practising managers that the 'common-sense' argument of how best to manage people is not tenable. The problem here is that whilst the facts of a people management incident or activity are often not in dispute (i.e. they are 'common'), the interpretation of information and observations arising from such situations may be very different, provoking a range of different potential managerial responses. Most of us who have had experience of managing people know only too well how difficult it can be to convince others of what we perceive to be a 'common-sense' solution.

The 'one-way-fits-all' thinking simply does not hold in today's business environment. This may have been the case in previous times as entrepreneurs and political leaders attempted to rationalise management as a science (see Taylor *in* Torrington *et al.* 2002), but a number of strong forces have driven major changes in this approach. These are identified and discussed further in this chapter.

So, what people management capabilities are organisations looking for as they strive to build competitive businesses?

Literature (Holbeche 2001, for example) suggests that organisations are making great efforts to develop a strategic approach to the management of its human resources. Essentially, the basis of strategic human resource management is to see people as a unique resource, capable of creating competitive advantage for the commercial enterprise or delivering best value for the non-profit organisation. To achieve this, there has

to be clear alignment of HR strategies with business strategies – 'people performance' being the critical linkage.

Various models (Fombrun *et al.* 1984; Hendry and Pettigrew 1991; Wright
et al. 1994, as examples) propose approaches to the development of strategic
HRM. The success of an organisation's corporate strategy hinges significantly
on senior management capability to choose, design, plan and execute people
management strategies.

These strategies should aim to leverage the potential value of human assets in
pursuit of the achievement of performance goals. Many of the current contributors to this discussion describe this process as 'human capital management'.
Three key questions emerge:

1   How do we measure the value of our human assets?

2   How do we enhance the value of this capital?

3   How do we apply and manage these capital assets to achieve corporate
    success?

Managing people strategies

If we agree about the need for a strategic approach to human resource management, the next challenge is to decide what should shape our strategies – the
guiding principles. This provokes further questions.

● Are there discernible trends in people management that we can detect and
  confidently extrapolate into the future?

● Are we going down a one-way street – a constant search for 'new' ways in
  managing people?

● Do past management theories contain ideas, methods and concepts that are
  now considered museum pieces by the contemporary practitioner?

Later in this chapter we identify the major developments that are driving
changes in the way we manage people and propose key items to go on the future
HR agenda.

Before we look at these in detail it may be helpful to see what the past holds
for us. What can we learn from past people management experience? Does the
past, in fact, hold the future for HRM?

Some historical perspectives

As the origins of people management are traced, there is a somewhat curious
oddity amongst many academic writers to assume the origins of the topic lie

almost exclusively in nineteenth-century Britain. Torrington *et al.* (2002) suggest that personnel management was initially derived from social reformers such as Lord Shaftesbury and Robert Owen. Foot and Hook (2002) begin their historical background with a description of early personnel practitioners as 'welfare workers' born out of the industrial revolution. A similar theme is adopted by Holbeche (2001).

Whilst this is understandable as a comfortable reference point, such a heavy emphasis as the starting point for people management is rather misleading. At an extreme, it could imply that people management was/is only applicable to large-scale industrial organisations in the Western world.

How wrong it would be to draw such a conclusion. Anthropological studies show us how societies, communities and civilisations have grown and developed locally upon principles of people management that are embraced by managements around the world today.

Take, China, for instance. As Jacobs *et al.* (1995) indicate, Confucianism has performed an important philosophical role in China's business history. Indeed, this influence can be seen in the wider sphere of East Asia. On the one hand the strong sense of rigid hierarchy can be linked to a low level of worker participation and initiative, leading to business inefficiencies compared to competitors. On the other hand, from the roots of Confucianism, the Chinese work ethic is characterised by diligence, responsibility, co-operation and learning (Oh 1992) – features of corporate culture that are vigorously pursued by many Western companies, today.

It is not the purpose of this chapter to make value judgements or take sides on whether one system of people management is better than another. Rather, it is to stimulate an understanding that people management philosophies, principles, policies, strategies and practices have a far deeper historical source than the classic references suggest.

And, importantly, what can we learn from past and present experiences that could guide the way to effective people management in the future? Japan, Singapore and South Korea have succeeded in developing a management style based on a blending of Confucianism and Western scientific management (Jacobs *et al.* 1995). They have identified the 'best of both worlds'. However, these examples tend to be the exception rather than the rule.

Impact of culture on people management

In their analysis of managing people across Europe, Garrison and Rees (1994) alerted the reader to the trend of the 'virtual corporation' – a form of organisation contracting out value-chain activities that can be undertaken more productively by external providers. This organisational form has also been referred to as the 'extended enterprise' or 'clover-leaf' organisation (Handy 1985). Outsourced services could include logistics, information technology, training and even manufacturing. The key objective for the firm is to ensure it can sell the finished product in the markets of its choice. This business philosophy is based upon changing the organisational architecture in pursuit of profit and shareholder-value maximisation (Kotter and Heskett 1992). Such arrangements are not so readily found in continental Europe where their concept of partnership does not sit comfortably with treating the workforce as inanimate factors of production.

Reasons for this are, once again, historically deep and profound. Some are anthropological and sociological in foundation; for instance, the way in which power is gained, held and executed within an organisation. Social structures in the workplace in countries such as France, Spain and Italy have been greatly shaped by the influence of the Catholic Church – a historical time span of 2000 years. Are opportunities the same for men and women, and is there a differen-tiation made between workers on the basis of age? Answers to these questions will show us the extent of historical differences.

Other factors impacting on the development of people management systems will include economic doctrines (free market *versus* state intervention), geo-physical nature of location (manufacturing/agriculture/extractive/trading indus-tries) and stages of industrial development (human/machine balance).

Further, there is the psychological orientation. Do workers have a tradition of obedience, compliance, resistance or co-operation? Is there a powerful urge to indulge in risk-taking? Is entrepreneurialism part of the individual mindset? How do people react emotionally to workplace situations? What behaviours do people naturally exhibit?

An important conclusion to be drawn from a vast array of research studies is that the way people are managed is inextricably linked to the cultural environ-ment in which people work and live.

The analogy of the 'iceberg' (a popular concept in the field of behavioural training) is useful to illustrate this.

The Iceberg Model (from Garrison and Rees 1994) is reproduced below as Figure 1.1. This indicates the relationship between business culture superstruc-ture and business culture bedrock.

Rees (2003) modified this to propose an inductive approach to understand-ing the relationships between behaviours in the workplace, systems of people management and the bedrock values and beliefs in a business environment. This is portrayed as Figure 1.2.

The application of such an approach can be illustrated using the research of Laurent (1983). A particular question from Laurent's work was 'Should a superior have precise answers for the questions subordinates might ask?' This question was put to managers in the following countries: Belgium, Sweden, UK, Japan, Italy, USA, Holland, Germany, Denmark and France. The result pattern showed a vari-ance in terms of agreement to the above question ranging from 13 to 77 per cent.

Looking at the results, can the reader induct the reasoning to explain why managers working in different people management systems behaved so differently?[1]

This is where the 'art' and 'science' of people management merge. There are, indeed, logical reasons for the positions of these managers' responses but they require creative and lateral thinking to tease them out.

Figure 1.1 The business culture iceberg

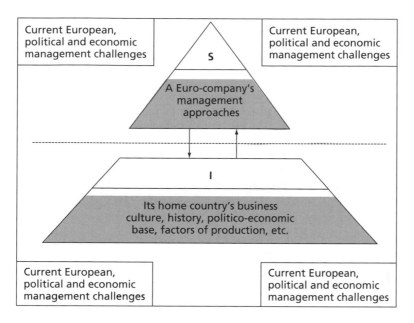

Source: Re-printed from *Managing People Across Europe*, Garrison and Rees, Page 10, Copyright 1994, with permission from Elsevier.

For example, why should Japanese managers be so convinced that they should be expected to know the answers to technical problems that confront employees as they do their jobs? The induction trail may go something like this.

Figure 1.2 Linkage between behaviours, management systems and cultural bedrock

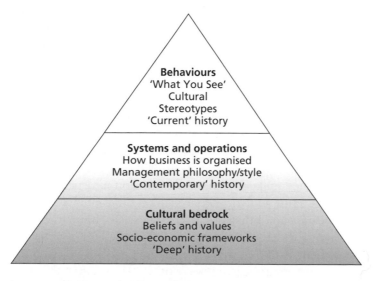

Source: © *People in Project Management*, Turner (2003), Gower Publishing Ltd.

Japanese management doctrine is based largely on Confucian principles of authoritarianism, technical expertise and positional power (Martinsons and Martinsons 1996). This maybe an accident of birthright, or 'fate'. As such, there are obligations on the part of people who are dominant over others (managers, for example) and those who are subservient to others (say, workers). The manager, or business owner, has a responsibility for providing protection and security for his/her workers (life-time employment) and in turn requires commitment and loyalty from these people (one employer for life). The relationship between the two groups is based on respect and trust where inequalities such as knowledge and education levels are openly acknowledged and accepted. This inequality supports social stability where everyone is aware of the expectations of the other party. Hence, if a worker on the production line of an automobile manufacturing company has a technical problem that he or she cannot solve, there is a high expectation on the part of both manager and worker that the manager will have to hand the correct technical answer. Not to do so would cause an unacceptable *loss of face*.

The resultant influence this 'roots finding' has on Japanese human resource management strategy clearly emerges. Managers are normally promoted to their positions on the basis of a long and sustained demonstration of technical excellence, often reaching their positions in middle age or later. How could a 22-year-old manager on a Japanese production line have the necessary experience and technical wisdom to handle such worker problems? Managers, therefore, are technical specialists rather than the generalists we see in the West – where 'face' is not an important issue. This is demonstrated emphatically when examining the composition of the Boards of Management of typical Japanese companies – they are largely specialists such as engineers, chemists and scientists.

Further, we can see how training and development strategies evolve. There is a parallel balance between the development of technical competencies and behavioural competencies in Asia. The training and education system is dominated by rote learning and acquiescence to the superior wisdom of the teacher, who is seen as the purveyor of absolute knowledge. A facilitated approach to management development does not fit so comfortably with Asian managers, and the learning style leans towards reflector/theorist rather than activist/pragmatist (Lessem and Neubauer 1994). It should come as no surprise, therefore, that Japan has not readily absorbed the concept of a general management education where managers are trained in a set of generic competencies to manage anything, anywhere, anyplace, anytime. For countries such as Japan, with very little ownership of natural resources and faced by uncontrollable external forces, people really do become the nation's (and organisations') most valuable asset. Hence the major investments they make in training, education and personal development.

Now perform the same analytical approach on the United States managers who scored at the opposite end of the scale. Here, we see a different management philosophy based upon a different set of bedrock drivers. This is a money-dominated business environment where everything else takes second place to making a pile of cash. Many commentators (e.g. Garrison 2001) suggest this is an outcome of the pioneer mentality, where adventurers set off for these distant shores to search for fortune. Equally, those persecuted for their religious affiliations or those seeking to preserve the purity of their beliefs sought refuge in the New World. Principally these were (initially) European Protestants who adhered to the word of the Bible. Weber (1930) in his masterful work *The Protestant Ethic and the Spirit of Capitalism* reminds us of the compelling need for Protestants to labour industriously whilst on Earth. What better way to demonstrate these endeavours than to show how much money one has earned from the fruits of one's labours.

Hence, a 'work hard, get things done' attitude prevails in the 'American way', that is action and pragmatism. Losing face is not such an issue as this is a generalist, egalitarian society, unencumbered by a dominating class structure, with a route to the top for anyone who has bravado and a risk-taking spirit.

Consequently, human resource management strategy is very different. The best people are hired with high reward retention strategies for the top performers, whilst the weakest need to exit from the organisation as soon as they can. Job security and a 'welfare' approach to the protection of workers is loose. Management development is highly generalist – witness the enormous growth of MBA programmes. Multi-skilling is a major feature of task accomplishment in this business context. Job titles are bewildering sometimes but this is a type of psychological recognition rather than a deep-rooted adherence to hierarchical status.

Theoretical development

The development of contemporary people management theory and practice has been spearheaded by the West, principally the United States. There are good reasons for this. Following the Second World War, the US economy became the strongest in the world fuelling the growth of huge organisations that required sophisticated systems of managerial control. Consequently, management grew as a discipline worthy of study at a formal academic level. This, of course, gave rise to a vast number of research initiatives conducted by the fast-growing business schools, later to be imitated in Europe. As Lessem and Neubauer (1994) commented 'one development influenced the other's progress'. They also observed that practitioners found pragmatic solutions for business problems for which the academics were providing the theoretical underpinnings. New tools and concepts were subsequently developed, extensively reported upon by business school professors who would be rewarded with career progression based upon their research publications. As English was the language in which most of these reports were written, this process of American influence was further aided by the growth of English as the common world business language. Management theory was broadcast around the world to audiences who could read and understand the language in which it was written.[2]

The classic studies, recalled by every student of people management, roll off the tongue – Taylorism, Scientific Management, Fordism, Elton Mayo, Hawthorne Experiments in the early part of the last century; Maslow, MacGregor, Herzberg and Chandler taking up the running after the Second World War.

The American view of people management was thus disseminated around the world as American companies expanded abroad and influence moved to a multi-national level. American executives naturally brought their management methods and systems into an ever-expanding sphere of global operation, passing them on to local managers. It was hard to resist. Here was a model of excellence that persuaded many to believe that the American approaches to people management were best, based upon the undeniable success of US firms at home and abroad.

Until, of course, the emergence of Asia-Pacific as a formidable competitive threat to western organisations, particularly those bearing the colours of Anglo-Saxon culture. Led by the remarkable success in the 1980s of Japanese companies breaking into markets hitherto dominated by local players, the academic community, human resource directors and people management consultants started to take a great interest in 'eastern' management philosophies in an attempt to understand (and later emulate) this new 'threat'. This spawned a plethora of books and articles that extolled the virtues of Asian management philosophy, backed by admirable case studies of organisations that had made these values and approaches work successfully around the world. Toyota, Nissan, Hyundai, Daewoo, Thai Airlines and Cathay Pacific captivated the attention of business school professors as examples of outstanding company successes based upon a different approach to the management of people.

However, a third major school of management thinking was to emerge in the 1990s – the European approach. Thurow (1992) argued that it would be Europe rather than America or Japan who would come to dominate the business world. Lessem and Neubauer (1994) suggested that there was little understanding of the constituent approaches of French, German, Dutch, British, Mediterranean and Nordic management philosophies. Yet these approaches potentially could combine in a rich mosaic to form dynamic organisational cultures, feeding off diversity and tensions to produce outstanding innovations. A good example of this 'European solution' is the recent Hoescht/RhonePoulenc merger to form the new life sciences company, Aventis. In his recent book, *20:21 Vision: The Lessons of the 20th Century for the 21st*, Bill Emmott (2003) suggests that Europe could champion the future direction of business management (although he still believes America is set to dominate in the foreseeable future).

Lessem and Neubauer have suggested that culture and psychology were considered peripheral to management until comparatively recently. To show the contrasts between people management philosophies around the world, these writers have mapped psychological types against national types and a simplified version of this is shown in Figure 1.3.

Their model shows how each of these business cultures has distinct influences on the way people are managed and the challenge is for organisations to decide what 'business sphere' they operate in and to design appropriate systems of people management in response.

So, what are the main driving forces that are likely to change the way in which we manage people in the future? What will be on the future HR agenda?

Figure 1.3 Global people management philosophies

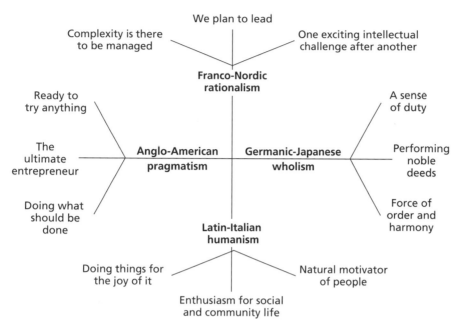

Source: Modelled on Lessem and Neubauer (1993).

LEEDS METROPOLITAN UNIVERSITY LIBRARY

The value of people to a business

In his recent book, *The Human Value of Enterprise* (2001), Andrew Mayo presents an inspiring vision of how we may be reviewing the transformation of the way people are managed and, in particular, the role of the HR profession. Reflecting back on today, from a 10-year future time horizon, he sees how HR directors are spearheading the intellectual capital movement, having won the argument that people alone drive value creation in business. Further, this value creation can be measured and managed systematically.

This drives the need for a paradigm shift where human resource professionals become powerful figures in the organisation and an executive's role is dominated by people management requirements. For most organisations this will become a difficult mindset change to make.

Human capital

If the proposition that people are the organisation's most valuable asset is sustainable, then we have to understand how these assets are acquired, retained and improved. Organisations will have to increase their attractiveness to the widest pool of talent, providing them with greater opportunities to recruit the best people. Becoming an 'employer of choice' rather than 'employer of necessity' could require revolutionary changes in many companies.

Retention strategies have to indicate what flows of human capital in and out of the organisation will provide the optimum balance of experience, knowledge and innovation.

Increasing human asset value no longer becomes an act of faith but is the result of defined programmes of investment in people's capabilities and future potential.

Performance management

A crucial aspect of managing human capital is to design and implement appropriate systems of performance management. These systems should provide clear linkages between the corporate objectives of the organisation and the management and people performance requirements needed to achieve such goals.

Performance management systems continually face the criticism of either being too simplistic or being too complex. There is pressure on human resource professionals to devise approaches that respond to these objections.

Political change

Government policies around the world share a common drive to develop an acceptable system of trading and business growth. Contrary to the principles of the free market doctrine, political leaders have recognised that government influence, participation and intervention is necessary to oversee acceptable trading between nations.

The dramatic expansion of the European Union and other trading blocs and the consolidation of world trade institutions such as the World Trade Organization (WTO) are evidence that those engaged in business will have to do so at an international level. This will require a greater understanding of how people are managed in different cultural environments and the development of appropriate skills to work effectively within and across cultures.

A large number of countries have signed up to conventions and protocols addressing issues such as human rights and the protection of minorities.

Social change

Political influences are both drivers and responses to social change. The term 'stakeholder society' has been brought into popular usage, particularly in Europe, by a range of groups – politicians, business leaders, pressure groups and so on. The idea that there is a wider range of interests in business activities rather than exclusive focus on shareholder interests has gained much ground over the past few years.

Hence, we have seen the appearance of various corporate social responsibility schemes, community involvement initiatives and affirmative action programmes over the past few years. A greater sense of environmental awareness has also become strongly apparent.

Legislation around the world has reinforced these social changes with more robust legal systems to enforce compliance.

Clearly, these dramatic social changes will impact extensively on how business is conducted, and attitudes in the workplace. Hence human resource policies need to be developed in response.

Technology

Technical change, too, impacts upon social norms. The development of technologies such as the Internet and mobile phone networks have started to change people's behaviours inside and outside the work environment.

People in knowledge-based industries are expected to have skills in information management. Systems of information have become an important element of competitiveness.

Technical advancements have opened up the expansion of world trade through the development of high-speed transport facilities and sophisticated communication platforms.

A key indicator of future corporate success is the extent and velocity at which individuals and the organisation learn. Information technologies have dramatically increased the appetite, capacity and quality of learning, a key aspect of human resource management strategy.

Lifestyle preferences

As a crystallisation of the changes above, many individuals have a greater range of choices over how they want to live and how they wish to work. For example, the portfolio career is a growing phenomenon amongst many people who value greater independence and control over their work preferences.

Prioritisation of a work-life balance in favour of family focus is a growing trend for those who can make this choice. Preferences for different ways of working has produced a growing number of people working from home, capitalising on the benefits of technology.

The selection of companies to work for is increasingly governed by intrinsically motivating factors – the corporate culture, the management style, interpersonal relationships. Indeed, it could be suggested that for whom you work defines who you are – are you a Gucci person, a Nokia person, a Mercedes person? Company and product brands are assuming great significance.

The future HR agenda

As a result of these change drivers, it is clear that a new agenda for the management of people needs to be identified.

The earlier part of this chapter has suggested that some of the influences for future people management may come from far and wide – not just the conventional wisdom developed in the West.

From the potentially vast array of agenda items, we have selected key areas that will shape the roles and responsibilities of human resource professionals, line and project managers.

Notes

1. This survey has been run countless times with a remarkably consistent pattern of results throughout the 1990s.
2. For a fascinating explanation on why this has occurred, Bill Bryson's *Mother Tongue* is highly recommended.

References

Emmott, B. (2003) *20:21 Vision: The Lessons of the 20th Century for the 21st*, London, Penguin.

Fombrun, C., Tichy, N.M. and Devanna, M.A. (1984) *Strategic Human Resource Management*, New York, Wiley.

Foot, M. and Hook, C. (2002) *Introducing Human Resource Management*, Harlow, Essex, Prentice-Hall.

Garrison, T. (2001) *International Business Culture*, Huntingdon, Elm Publications.

Garrison, T. and Rees, D. (1994) *Managing People Across Europe*, Oxford, Butterworth-Heinemann.

Handy, C. (1985) *Understanding Organisations*, London, Penguin.

Hendry and Pettigrew *in* Armstrong, M. (1997) *Strategies for Human Resource Management*, London, Kogan Page.

Holbeche, L. (2001) *Aligning Human Resources and Business Strategy*, Oxford, Butterworth-Heinemann.

Jacobs, L., Guopei, G. and Herbig, P. (1995) 'Confucian roots in China: a force for today's business', *Management Decision*, Vol. 33, No. 10.

Kotter, J. and Heskett, J. (1992) *Corporate Culture and Performance*, New York, Free Press.

Laurent, A. (1983) 'The cultural diversity of Western conceptions of management', *International Studies of Management and Organisation*, Vol. 8, No. i, pp. 75–96.

Lessem, R. and Neubauer, F. (1994) *European Management Systems: Towards Unity Out of Cultural Diversity*, Maidenhead, Berkshire McGraw-Hill.

Martinsons, M. and Martinsons, A. (1996) 'Conquering cultural constraints to cultivate Chinese management creativity and innovation', *Journal of Management Development*, Vol. 15, No. 9, 18–35.

Mayo, A. (2001) *The Human Value of the Enterprise*, London, Nicholas Brealey.

Oh, T.K. (1992) 'Inherent limitations of the Confucian tradition in contemporary East Asian business enterprises', *Journal of Chinese Philosophy*, Vol. 19, No. 2, 155–69.

Rees, D. (2003) *People in Project Management*, Aldershot, Gower Publishing.

Thurow, L. (1992) *Head to Head*, New York, William Morrow.

Torrington, D., Hall, L. and Taylor, S. (2002) *Human Resource Management*, Harlow, Essex, Prentice-Hall.

Turner, R. (2003) *People in Project Management*, England, Aldershot, Gower Publishing.

Weber, M. (1930) *The Protestant Ethic and the Spirit of Capitalism*, London, Macmillan.

Wright, P., McMahon, G. and McWilliams, A. (1994) 'Human Resources and sustained competitive advantage: a resource based perspective', *International Journal of Human Resource Management*, Vol. 5, No. 2, May, 301–26.

Future trends in HR

Malcolm Higgs

Having reflected upon the influences of the past on current human resource management practices, it is time to consider in more detail the emerging trends impacting upon the way people will be managed in the future.

Introduction

If we believe what we read, then organisations are increasingly seeing people as their most important asset and a key source of competitive advantage. However, in reality we must be tempted to ask whether this is idealised rhetoric or practical reality?

Where do these important resources appear in the financial reports? In accounting terms they are liabilities not assets. People appear as costs in our accounts, so the question arises as to whether the statement that "people are our most important asset" is rhetoric rather than reality.

What are the real business drivers which might move us from this rhetoric to a "people-focused" reality? Furthermore, how do we know that such a shift in business thinking is underpinned by something more than "alarmist" predictions. There is little doubt that the case for the importance of "people as a competitive asset" and the importance of effective people management has been underpinned by some dubious predictions of "doomsday" scenarios. For example, we have seen forecasts of major change in people management resulting from: changes in technology, the emergence of virtual working, increasing use of outsourcing, the impact of legislation (e.g. European Working Time Directive), the impact of dot-com models of business and the impact of the e-recruitment revolution.

The fundamental changes in practice and associated challenges arising from each of these have all been grossly over-estimated in the rhetoric.

This chapter is designed to drill below the rhetoric of people management and to explore a range of important questions:

- Has the impact of people management on the bottom line of a business been clearly demonstrated?

- Is the context of people management really changing?

- How are organisations responding to changes in terms of the HR agenda and priorities?

- Is HR really a strategic function?

- What changes are happening in practice?

- What skills and competencies will be required in a new HR environment?

- What will be the future role of HR?

- Where will we find people to fill the new role?

Of all these questions perhaps the most important one to begin with is "Do effective HR policies and practices make a difference to the 'bottom-line' of an organisation?"

Human resources and the bottom line

The move from the HR "rhetoric" to the business reality is seen as being conditional on the ability to demonstrate a "bottom-line" relationship. In exploring this it might be informative to begin by examining the broader question:

"Does the 'soft-stuff' make a difference to business performance?"

By the "soft-stuff" we generally tend to mean people-related policies and practices within an organisation rather than specific HR techniques and tools. If we explore relationships between the broader people-related policies, practices and behaviours, we encounter a growing body of evidence including:

- Work in the USA which shows a clear line of sight between interventions to change employee commitment, ensuing customer commitment and business performance (e.g. Dave Ulrich 1999).

- Studies which demonstrate that investors look now at "soft-issues" such as leadership behaviours and teamworking across functions as much as current earnings to inform their valuation of company stock (e.g. Dave Ulrich 1999).

- Consistent studies over 30 years which show that corporate culture impacts on business performance (e.g. Burke and Litwin 1989).

- Case studies which demonstrate that failure to consider "people issues" can damage business performance (e.g. Euro Disney).

- Studies which demonstrate the impact of corporate values on long-term business performance (e.g. Collins and Poras 1998).

In the past the HR community has failed to tap into these business-based arguments, preferring to rely on "moralistic" advocacy. However, in reality, the case for change in perceptions of the role of "people management" have been shaped in terms of sharper business imperatives. Organisations are becoming aware of the impact of skills shortages and the "war for talent". Leading and highly respected Chief Executives are publicly stating the importance of winning the "talent wars". Many have argued that those organisations which are successful in attracting *and retaining* more than their share of talent will have a sustainable competitive advantage. (The issue of "Talent Management" is the focus of Chapter 6.)

In moving from this broader "people management" argument to a more specific argument, there have been a range of studies which show the value-added of effective HR policies and practices.

In the UK, the Chartered Institute of Personnel and Development (CIPD) have commissioned and published research which has demonstrated clear linkages between good HR policies and practices and both productivity and product quality. Similar results have been found in other studies within the rest of Europe and in the USA.

The UK research findings are typified by the CIPD commissioned study conducted by David Guest and his colleagues which demonstrated clear performance relationships which are summarised in Figure 2.1.

Figure 2.1 Performance relationships: a study of 610 UK companies

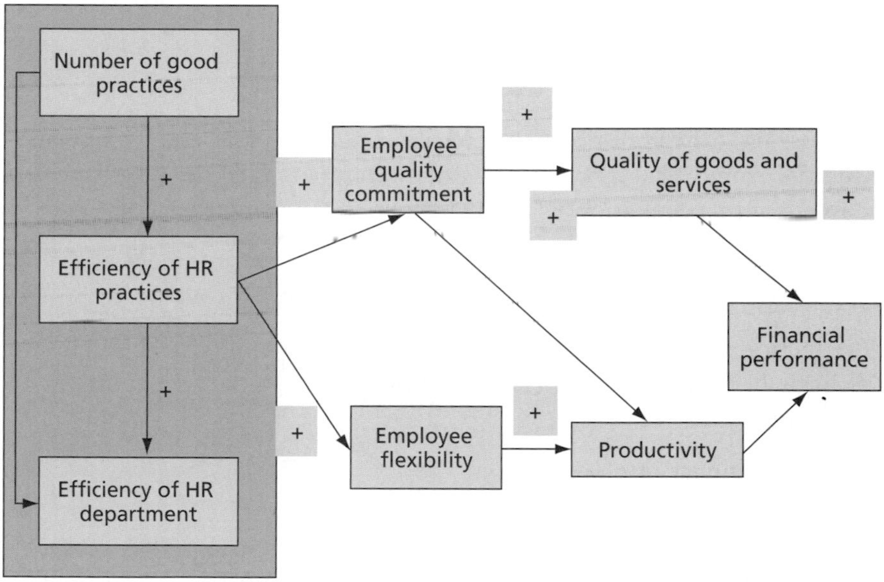

Source: Guest *et al.* (2000).

Pan-European studies have reinforced these findings demonstrating a clear relationship between effective HR practices and market value of companies. These studies are supported by results from the USA. Examples of the findings from these studies are shown in Figure 2.2 (overleaf).

Is HR operating in a "new world"?

It is quite clear that the world in which HR functions, and the specialists within these functions, are operating has changed significantly over the last 20 years. The key aspects of the contextual changes appear to be:

Figure 2.2 HR and corporate performance studies: Europe and USA

Studies in 16 European countries have shown that

- Improvement in HR practices   30% increase in market value
- Correlation between *quality* of HR practices and shareholder value

Studies in the USA have shown that

- In 1994–1999   Companies with good HR practices have delivered 103% total return to shareholders
- From January 1999 to June 1999   The best practice HR companies delivered 28% return to shareholders compared to the least effective 6%

Source: Watson Wyatt Survey (2000).

- Increasing complexity and volatility.

- A "blurring" or the distinction between consumers and employees (or potential employees). For example, many retailers face the need to recruit people from a population who have experienced using their services.

- A growth in the impact of a legislative/regulatory environment and a broadening of the range of important "stakeholder" groups.

- A reduction in new product life cycles (that is the ability to differentiate on the basis of product or service has a shorter-term impact on competitive advantage).

- Increasing impact of globalisation.

- Developments in technology.

- Significant changes in core values and expectations within societies and a move towards knowledge-based economies.

These changes are well-known and explored in books and research on strategy and economics. The purpose of this chapter is to explore the impact of contextual changes on HR policies and practices and, in consequence, changes in the role and requirements of the HR function. So how has the HR profession responded to these contextual changes? Some of the key issues and developments appear to be:

- Development of new selection criteria. Increasingly we are seeing a move from specific knowledge and skills (often technical) to attributes, potential and values in selection criteria (indeed one leading major UK retailer focuses on the values of potential employees and their ability to learn above their past experience and technical knowledge).

- Focusing on building employee commitment.

- Considering recruitment as a marketing activity (becoming an "Employer of Choice", developing an "Employer Brand") in order to attract and retain talent.

- Developing strategies to manage the organisation's reputation.

- Focusing on building effective leadership behaviours throughout the organisation.

At this stage it is worth focusing on the key challenge for the HR function. This may be summarised as building the "Employer Brand" in a way which will attract *and* retain the critical talent required to deliver the business strategy. This has to be done against a background of fundamental change in the underlying, "unstated" employment contract (known as the "psychological contract" or "deal"). This significant shift has had a fundamental impact on the "people management" issues in many organisations, beginning with the attraction and retention of key talent. The way in which this "deal" has changed is summarised in Figure 2.3.

Figure 2.3 The deal has changed

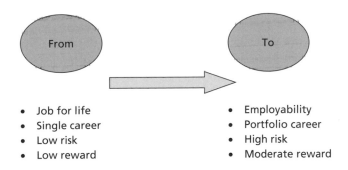

Prior to the 1970s the basic "deal" was that, in terms of employment, potential employees traded "loyalty" for a "job for life" and clear long-term career structure. The impact of business changes (e.g. business process re-engineering) and economic pressures (e.g. recessions) combined to shift this "deal". In particular the concept of "employability" and employer response to trading security for building transferable (and marketable) competence has led to the emergence of a talent pool with a distinctly different set of values. Indeed the change has meant that we are not so much facing a "talent war" as a "commitment war". The commitment emanating from a long-term deal needs to be replaced with a commitment from an "engaging deal" which can only be evidenced through effective "people management" policies and practices.

The importance of this shift is underpinned by research which shows significant links between employee commitment and organisational performance. At the same time, recent research in the UK has shown that 80 per cent of employees do *not* trust their organisation. Indeed this research is borne out by studies in both Canada and Australia. This represents a significant challenge for the HR function in many organisations and calls for a different view of the role of the function and the skills required by those working within this area.

How are organisations responding to these changes?

Against the above background we have seen a range of initiatives designed to reflect the new realities and address a significantly different employment environment. These include:

- *Applying marketing concepts and principles to build an "Employer Brand"* – The thinking here is that organisations can compete for talent in a similar way to competing for customers. A strong "Employer Brand", it is argued, leads an organisation to becoming an "Employer of Choice" thus enabling it to compete more effectively for new talent and to retain existing talent. Illustrative of this development is one major UK-based organisation which has recently recruited marketing professionals into its HR function.

- *Refocusing recruitment on potential rather than existing know-how* – Given the shortages of skills in a range of areas, some employers have begun to select new employees on the basis of tests, and other procedures, designed to identify potential talent which can be developed rapidly. This approach opens up a larger talent pool and at the same time offers potential employees skill development as part of the "deal" to attract and retain them.

- *Addressing the organisational culture* – Many organisations have recognised that employees come to the market with expectations and values which are different from those which may have been prevalent in earlier years of the organisation's history. It is often the historic models of success which are frequently, unintentionally, embedded in the culture of the organisation. Organisations which have recognised this have begun to review their current culture and implemented programmes designed to change the culture to one more appropriate to the current competitive environment.

- *Recruiting on the basis of values alignment* – Research has shown that in organisations with high levels of alignment between organisational values and individual values there are higher levels of employee commitment. In many organisations this realisation has translated into selection processes which attempt to capture (often through questionnaires) a profile of applicant values and to focus selection on individuals whose values most closely align with those of the organisation. At least one major UK organisation has developed a recruitment and selection process which is *exclusively* focused on values alignment. Only those whose individual values align with those of the organisation are considered for selection.

● *Building leadership capability* – Increasingly organisations are recognising that effective people management in today's environment requires effective leadership behaviours at all levels of leadership. This move is supported by research which has shown consistently over more than 30 years that individual's experience of, and commitment to, an organisation is strongly influenced by their experiences in the context of the behaviours of their immediate manager. Building on this an increasingly important item on the HR agenda of many organisations has become building leadership capability.

In reviewing the above responses an important question arises as to the extent to which the HR function is involved in the development of appropriate policies and their implementation. A core issue for HR is the extent to which it is seen as being a control function or a strategic one. Figure 2.4 provides a useful way of looking at this question.

Figure 2.4 HR position: control or strategic function

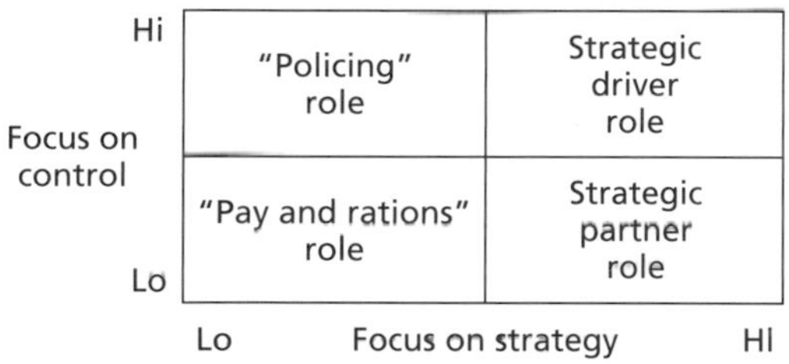

Many organisations (and often HR practitioners) have seen HR as occupying the left-hand side of the diagram in Figure 2.4. The "policy"-versus-"servant" relationship has traditionally been the focus of the power debate. However, the right-hand side appears to be the area in which the HR role needs to be debated in the current environment.

The nature of many of the above responses to the changing environment will, for many, rest uneasily with our practical experience of the reality of the role of the HR function in our organisations. The extent to which these changes are a reality are explored in the following sections of this chapter.

Can HR be a strategic function?

Many would question the extent to which HR can truly be a strategic function. However, this question, and the related debate may be rooted in historic perceptions of the nature of HR (and the people operating in the function) which only see it as relating to the left-hand side of the model shown in Figure 2.4. The real debate should be more focused on the extent to which people management (a more sensible term than either personnel or HR) is a strategic issue for an organisation. The preceding sections of this chapter do, hopefully, indicate that

Figure 2.5 Building a line of sight

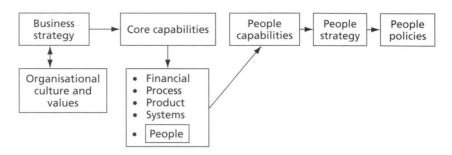

effective people management is a key strategic element for most organisations. If HR is to be strategic it is essential that there is a clear "line of sight" between an organisation's business strategy and its people management policies and practices. One way of establishing this "line of sight" is shown in Figure 2.5.

Within this model the strategic parameters for HR policies and practices are derived directly from the business strategy and should be designed to build the core people elements in the capabilities necessary to support the overall strategy. In broad terms the business strategy may require one or more of three types of HR strategy. These are:

1 *Cost strategy* – a strategy which focuses on delivery results and the lowest level of people costs.

2 *Capability strategy* – one which focuses on building current and future capability of employees.

3 *Commitment strategy* – a strategic focus on building employee commitment to the organisation's strategy and goals.

For example, an international fast food company may well have a need for an HR cost-based strategy. This requires the HR function to deliver high volumes of people who are rapidly trained to perform well-structured, low-skilled tasks with minimal requirements for commitment or initiative. The HR strategy for such an organisation would therefore focus on reducing acquisition and development costs whilst accepting high levels of attrition. On the other hand, a professional services firm may require an HR capability strategy which implies high selection and development costs with a strong focus on policies designed to optimise retention. In essence the business strategy provides parameters for HR to segment its employment market and determine a strategically competitive position. This positioning is summarised in Figure 2.6.

Thus the fast food firm described above may have a position of "Employer of Churn" whereas the professional services firm may need to position itself as "Employer of Choice".

In moving to a more strategic position there needs to be some significant shifts in the way in which the HR function operates in practice. One aspect of this shift is a change in where effort is focused. This is summarised in Table 2.1.

Figure 2.6 HR segmentation and positioning

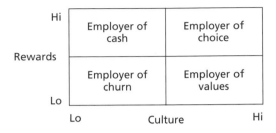

Table 2.1 Change in HR focus

Less of	More of
Concentration on operational matters	Participation in strategic matters
Responding to management's view of needed change	Proactively creating and managing chance
Assuming full responsibility for management of all human resources	Advise and counsel line management
Focus on individual employees	Focus on teams and groups of employees
Focus internally	Focus externally
Represent employees	Represent senior management

The move will also require a change in the relationship between the HR function and line managers. This change is summarised in Table 2.2 (overleaf).

A significant implication of the changes summarised in Table 2.2 is that HR becomes a part of line management rather than a "remote staff function".

Whilst the anchoring of HR in the business at all levels is welcomed in theory, such a move has significant implications for line managers. The move reinforces the line responsibility for managing people. HR has the role of equipping them to do this and providing support and guidance.

Where are the levers for change?

In practice there is little doubt that the most powerful HR lever for change in an organisation, in terms of employee behaviour and attitude, is reward policy and practice. In adopting a more business-based approach to HRM it is essential that any HR strategy encompasses a well-thought-through and integrated reward component. This need is well illustrated by the example of a US-based multinational which identified, for sound business reasons, a need to engender higher levels of teamwork throughout the organisation. They implemented a well-resourced team development process to shift the behaviours of managers and encourage greater teamwork between business units. However, the behaviours were not sustained. In exploring the problem it

Table 2.2 Change in the HR functional model

	Functional specialist	Business partner
Development of HR strategy and policy	HR management has full responsibility	HR and operating management share responsibility
Organisation of HR function	Functional structure reporting to staff	Flexible structure reporting to line
Profile of HR professionals	Career in HR as a specialist Limited financial skills focus on now Monolingual National perspective	Rotation & generalist Financial expertise Focus on future Multilingual Global perspective
Nature of HR programmes and function	Responsive Operational Internal Employee advocate	Proactive Strategic Societal Business partner

became apparent that the reward system, which contained a high level of bonus based on individual performance, was in fact reinforcing the previous "silo mentality". It was only when the reward system was changed to include team-based bonus elements that the investment in team development was realised.

In general it is essential that in building business partnership and alignment with business strategy that HR professionals recognise the power of the reward "lever". It is important to ensure that the behaviours required by the business are effectively reinforced through the reward system. For example, if the business requires that managers set stretching goals for performance, the reward strategy should reflect this in terms of what is recognised and not reward the wrong behaviours (i.e. rewarding managers for just making budget which would work against stretch goals and encourage unambitious goal setting). Reward strategies are discussed in more depth in Chapter 8.

How is the HR role changing?

Against the background outlined above it is useful to reflect on how the HR role needs to change to operate effectively in the new environment. We have already seen a range of issues being addressed within HR which reflect these changes. These are:

- working to build clearer linkage between HR policies and business realities;

- developing and articulating a new "employment deal" which reflects business needs and realities;

- building better relationships and real partnerships with line managers;

- demonstrating value for money in delivery of support services;

- focusing more on resource planning and development;

- focusing on building skill levels.

If HR is to contribute to business success, and become a genuine business partner, then it would seem that there are some critical changes necessary. These may be summarised as being:

- A shift from HR following on operational matters and issues to the adoption of a strategic approach to HR. This requires the HR function's participation in strategic discussions within the business and importantly demonstrating "added value" to these discussions. The demonstration of "added value" is a prerequisite for being seen as a true "business partner".

- A move from the HR function assuming full responsibility for, and control of, all HR matters and issues to becoming advisors to line management in relation to these issues. We are seeing in many of today's most effective organisations that line managers fully accept their accountability for people management. The HR function in these organisations tends to be focused on developing the capability of line managers to fulfil their people management accountabilities. This support contributes to building a business partnership.

- A shift in the focus of HR attention from being largely internally focused to becoming more external. In organisations in which this change is happening, there is a growing use of benchmarking against other organisations, and collection and analysis of data on competitor companies. However, the external focus has to go beyond analysis of HR practices. It is essential that HR keeps in touch with business trends and issues and considers their impact on the people management practices within their organisation.

- Becoming more anchored in the business involves moving from a view that HR is the representative of the employees to a view that HR is a central aspect of business and as such it contributes alongside all other functions in a way which builds commitment of employees to the business.

- A change in "mind-set" from being a reactive supporter of the line to a more strategic partner and advisor. The HR function needs to be in a position to anticipate changes required to people management policies and practices based on business trends, rather than responding to line management's requests for change. This does *not* mean ignoring the needs of line managers and their views and opinions. It does, however, mean keeping a trained eye on trends, issues and developments and considering the impact of these on business plans, strategies and performance. Such views need to be debated with line managers. HR practitioners need to be able to act as change managers through an ability to make a compelling business case for the changes which need to take place to support the business strategy.

The changes indicated above are not easy ones to make. They take time, effort and skill. Above all they need a significant shift in "mind-set". HR needs to move from being a specialist function, which is ancillary to the core business, to becoming an integral part of the business. To achieve this it is necessary for a real *business partnership* to be developed between line managers and the HR function. Realising this partnership needs a change in the mind-sets of line managers as well as HR professionals. This can be a difficult change to realise in practice. It not only entails developing a new relationship and understanding between HR and the line, it also entails line managers fully accepting their accountability for people management and devoting more time and effort to fulfilling this accountability. This change requires a clear articulation of the responsibilities of the line, together with investment in building the capabilities of line managers to fulfil these people management accountabilities more effectively.

What skills will it take to operate in the new world of HR?

There has been a considerable amount of research into the skills and competencies required of those in the HR role to enable them to operate effectively in this "new world". Dave Ulrich of Michigan University (1999), together with his colleagues, has been in the forefront of this research. In a major study he identified that the competencies associated with high performance in this environment are:

Knowledge of the business

The extent to which HR practitioners understand the activities, drivers and context of the business they are working within. These knowledge areas included:

● Common HR practices in the sector

● Organisational structures

● Customer relations

● Competitor business practices

● Financial drivers.

Delivery of HR practice

The capability to use HR practices to build business success. These capabilities include:

● Communicating consistent messages

● Effective performance appraisal

● Resource planning

- Effective promotion processes

- Organisation design

- Explaining purpose of business practices.

Management of change processes

A surprising area to emerge was that of competence in change management. Line managers highly valued HR professionals skilled in this area. They valued demonstrated abilities in managing change including:

- Being visionary

- The ability to establish trust and credibility

- Being proactive

- Able to "sell" concepts and ideas

- Effective face-to-face communication.

Within this capability framework it is notable that "technical" HR know-how is not surfaced. This is seen as a threshold or "needed to play" competency. It is the ability to relate these threshold competencies to the business context which is seen as being highly valuable to line managers.

Subsequent work by Dave Ulrich led to his development of a broader model which is summarised in Figure 2.7.

Figure 2.7 HR competence model

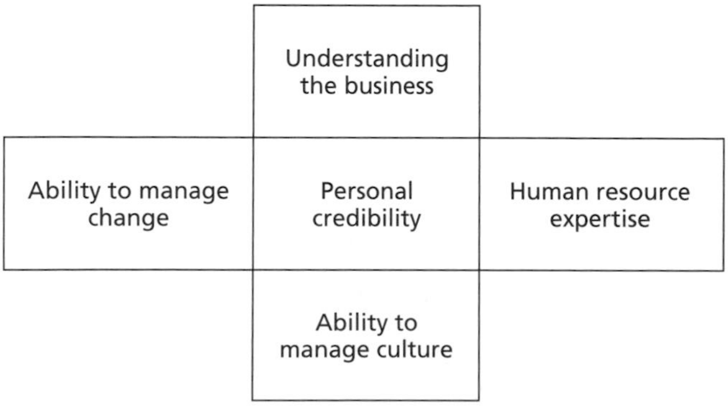

Source: Adapted from Ulrich (1999).

Within this model, Personal Credibility is at the centre as it was identified in the research as being the most important area of competency. It encompasses aspects such as: having a track record of success, instilling confidence, asking important questions, providing candid feedback and providing alternative insights on business issues.

The ability to manage change to place the change in a business context, and to help others to contribute effectively are core to success. Similarly the ability to manage culture again emphasised not only proactivity but also the ability to challenge the status quo and establish clear linkages between the business and the organisational culture. Business understanding is seen as critical, not only in its own right, but also in terms of how it is used within the other aspects of the role. Whilst the HR "expertise" cluster of competencies covered the normal scope of the function, there was a lot of emphasis, in this area, on being able to apply this expertise to the needs of the business.

Thus for an effective HR professional in today's context the detailed knowledge of HR policies and practices contributes a relatively small element of the overall competency profile.

What is the new role for HR?

Given the changing context, demands and competencies outlined above, the question arises as to what is the role for HR in this context? The answer is that there is not a single role. Rather there are a range of potential roles depending on the needs of the business and the broader resources and experience available. Whilst there is a wide range of potential roles it is feasible to group these into four main classifications which emerge from two main parameters:

1 the degree of focus on people;

2 the degree of focus on strategy.

This produces a model which is shown in Figure 2.8.

Figure 2.8 A possible range of HR roles

Source: Adapted from Ulrich (1999).

The potential roles within this model are summarised below:

- *Building change capability* – This role may be seen as one focusing on helping the organisation to lead and facilitate change within the organisation. This does not just encompass HR-related changes, but all change and transformation processes. A reason for this role being within the HR function is the growing realisation that a major cause of the very high level of failure of change initiatives is failure to take sufficient account of people-related issues. The role is most frequently implemented (in organisations adopting this model) through an internal facilitation and consultancy service. A number of major global organisations have, within the last few years, moved all of their change and transformation teams into the HR function.

- *HR advice and services* – This is primarily concerned with effective delivery of HR services to the organisation, and advice to both line managers and employees. Such services range from pay and benefits administration, through recruitment administration, to training and employee legislation. For many organisations this is the "typical" HR work. However, a number of organisations have seen this as work which needs to be done, but can detract from the potential of the HR function to add value to the business. Indeed a number of larger organisations have identified this as an area in which much of the service provision work may be appropriately outsourced. Large and diversified organisations which have not outsourced the service provision (including a number of global players) have recognised, and taken, the opportunities for cost reduction offered by providing this function on a Shared Services basis.

- *HR planning and measurement* – This role is focused on the efficiency of HR policy implementation and the development of metrics, which not only monitor HR's performance, but also provide important information for the business. In many organisations there has been a move to develop business metrics which go beyond financial measures. The balanced business scorecard is an increasingly used means for achieving this. In organisations using the balanced business scorecard approach it is common to find that the HR function is accountable for its implementation and ongoing use.

- *Strategic HRM policy development* – This role is primarily concerned with building a clear line of sight between the business strategy and the HR strategy. This is the arena in which business partnership is developed. Such partnership is focused on formulating people management strategies and policies, which add value to the business. It is not uncommon for this function to be accountable for the direct care of the businesses' strategic people resources. For example, senior level succession management and development sits within this role in many organisations.

This model is by no means universally applied. However an increasing number of organisations are looking at the role of HR within this framework and realising that the HR role required determines the competencies necessary for success.

Where will the effective HR practitioners be found?

Having developed an argument for a new role for HR and identified a range of competencies, the question arises as to where we will find individuals capable of fulfilling these roles.

Many of the competencies identified could equally be applied to other functional areas within a business. The main differentiator is the delivery of HR advice services. However, even here the emphasis is on delivery in a way which adds value to a specific business, and is aligned with the business needs. Perhaps, then, we should look to bring broadly based business managers into senior positions within the new HR function. Indeed a significant number of organisations are already pursuing this route.

If this becomes a more widely not only accepted way forward, then a question arises about the potential role for those who have an HR background, but also have developed the other required competencies? One answer is to move them into line roles, in the same way as line managers can move into an HR role. Such integration is happening in a number of organisations. For example, the current European head of a major oil company was formerly head of the HR function. This is a powerful signal of the value of people management for the organisation. However, there is another possible role. To date we have not considered how successful HR leaders often work in practice. The most skilful and effective HR leaders I have encountered have developed their ability to coach and support the top leadership of their organisation. Perhaps the combination of the personal competencies with a deep understanding of people issues and organisation behaviour enables the seasoned and successful HR practitioners to become the "people" coach and advisor for the businesses' top team. While this is a difficult role to fulfil, it may be the future "unique" role of the head of the HR function in an organisation.

Operating in such a way would lead to HR becoming more engaged in the formulation of business strategy and thus be in a better position to develop a clear "line of sight" between the business strategy and the day-to-day HR policies and practices. This line of sight, together with high levels of top team buy-in, would help to ensure that the "mantra" of "people are our major asset and competitive edge" becomes a business reality.

Conclusions: future implications for line managers and HR

This chapter has taken a relatively high-level view and has focused on the future. It has been evident that changes in the role of HR impact on the way in which line managers need to operate and behave. Perhaps, most importantly, the changes proposed result in line managers having to accept greater accountability for their "people decisions". The development of a more strategic approach to HR reduces operational limitations on the line. In turn this forces line managers to own their decisions. In practice this shift takes time to implement. For example in one US-based FMCG organisation the line managers had argued for a long time that they needed greater "freedom to manage their people". This organisation implemented a more strategic approach to HR and found that it took over 18 months to train, develop and support line managers to ensure that they were comfortable with their new role. A strategic approach to HR needs to be backed by good levels of skill amongst line managers and a willingness of the line to face the consequences of their "people decisions".

Key issues for HR in the organisation of the future are those of developing an employer brand and producing a clear linkage or line of sight between HR policies and practices and business realities. HR professionals will need to develop even greater levels of personal credibility and competence in order to enable the HR function to become a full business partner. If people management is to play as significant a role in the future success of businesses as many are suggesting, then we need to change our view of the nature of the role and contribution of HR functions in organisations. In this chapter I have outlined how thinking, and to a growing extent practice, has developed in the face of changes in the business environment. Making changes in the HR role, along the lines suggested, represents a challenge for both HR practitioners and line managers. However, if organisations commit to, and execute effectively, these changes there is a real possibility of their securing more viable and sustainable businesses in the long-term. Perhaps the point may be reached when mentioning that you work, or have worked, in HR may no longer be seen as an indication that your career is flawed or has peaked!

References

Burke, W.W. and Litwin, G.H. (1989) "A causal model of organizational performance", in J.W. Pfeiffer (ed.), *The 1989 Annual: Developing Human Resources*, University Associates, San Diego California.

Collins, J. and Poras, J. (1998) *Built to Last*, London, Random House.

Guest, D., Michie, J., Sheehan, M., Conway, N. and Metochi, M. (2000) *Effective People Management*, London, CIPD.

Ulrich, D. (1999) *Human Resource Champions*, New York, John Wiley & Sons.

Watson, W. (2000) Survey Report on HR Practices.

Managing human capital

David Rees

The previous chapter strongly emphasised the genuine desire for organisations to manage people as true assets. This contribution examines the development of human capital management.

Introduction

> Mma Ramotswe had a detective agency in Africa, at the foot of Kgale Hill. These were its assets: a tiny white van, two desks, two chairs, a telephone, and an old typewriter. Then there was a teapot, in which Mma Ramotswe – the only lady private detective in Botswana – brewed redbush tea. And three mugs – one for herself, one for her secretary, and one for the client. What else does a detective agency really need? Detective agencies rely on human intuition and intelligence, both of which Mma Ramotswe had in abundance. No inventory would ever include those, of course.
>
> *The No. 1 Ladies Detective Agency,* Alexander McCall Smith (2003)

As entrepreneurs, as managers, as designers, as engineers, as cleaners… people in business are the source of economic development, social advancement and wealth creation.

In business terms, 'wealth' can be described in many ways, depending on what purpose you are in business for. It may be expressed in financial terms such as profitability, asset values, or cash resources. For others 'wealth' could be measured as individual growth, job enrichment or simply 'experiences'.

A flurry of surveys and reports in the late 1990s and into the new millennium suggested that people were broadening their views on what was really important for them to achieve from their employment with an organisation. Most definitely this has been a period of reflection as people try to identify what they are really seeking from the world of work. Adherence to the doctrine of 'maximising shareholder value' – the war cry of many boardrooms around the globe – is now more balanced by the wider concept of 'stakeholder participation'.

How business can add value to a range of individual and collective interests has become a focal point for debate amongst governments around the world during the last decade. As a result new approaches concerning the relationships between business and various stakeholders have emerged. Europe, particularly the EC area, has witnessed the development of a new political philosophy – commonly referred to as the 'third way' – during the last few years. The manifestation of this is clear to see – massive privatisation, dramatic changes in employment legislation, public/private partnerships, participative business cultures, and so forth.

Whether this societal and political development represents a permanent mind-set shift remains speculative but it is certain that businesses will need new approaches to the measurement of their wealth. Specifically, they need to understand how this wealth is generated through people's efforts, capabilities and performance. Further, stakeholder communities – supported by government endorsement – are demanding better systems of reporting this wealth.

This chapter examines where we currently stand on these issues and identifies the forces driving change in the way we value people in a business. The literature refers to this as a debate on 'human capital management'. A deeper look at a contemporary model of human capital management is included with some proposals for further development and refinement. A recent research project on emergent best practice in this field is also reported. Finally, the implications for managers' roles in managing human capital are discussed.

Human capital management

'Capital' has many definitions and takes many different forms. When we talk about 'human capital' in business we are generally referring to the sum of people's capabilities, experiences, competencies, attitudes and behaviours that can be turned into 'output'. This 'output' (or 'achievement') could be valued and measured in different ways. Each stakeholder group has different expectations from their engagement with the activities of the organisation. An employee's perceptions of value-added for him or her may be quite different to those of a shareholder. Service in a fast food outlet is usually valued by customers in a markedly different way from the service a customer may expect in a Michelin Three Star restaurant. Measurement of value may be calibrated along different scales.

The key point here is to move away from the notion that capital is represented only in the form of tangible or financial assets. Human capital must be held at least on a par with other forms of capital. In fact, a case can be made for advocating the value of human capital will always be superior to, say, financial capital. Organisations do not begin their life through money and machines – they are the product of human endeavour, imagination, creativity and innovation. People design and implement technology. People are the ultimate decision makers.

There are two key dimensions to human capital measurement. One is the human capital brought into the business by the individual. Clearly, a person's education, qualifications and skills could be components of their individual human capital. The other dimension is the synergistic human capital created by people working together. A team of people building a car together on an automobile assembly line is an example of this. The way in which the team works together and interacts with other departments can influence the overall business performance of the company.

So, we need to measure both dimensions in order to arrive at a true worth of human capital in a business.

Easy? Of course not! As we continue to build business wealth on the basis of intangible assets such as knowledge and intellectual property, the valuation, reporting and management of human capital represents one of the greatest challenges to practitioners and theorists alike.

Valuing organisations

The marketplace – where investors, purchasers and providers meet – drives this need. Consider for a moment the chart below Figure 3.1, plotting the market valuation of companies on the Dutch stock market.

Figure 3.1 Market value of companies: example of the Dutch stock market

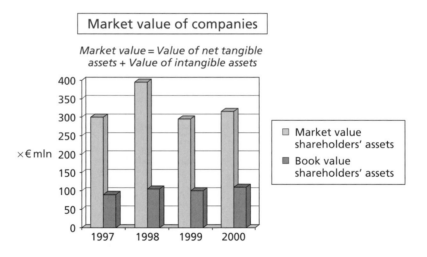

Source: Heijmans, N.V. Annual Report, 2000.

It can be seen that there is a huge gulf between market capitalisation and the 'tangible' assets in the organisation. How do we explain the difference? This is important if you are a stakeholder (say, an investor) in a company. You want to know how your stake is being managed and what returns you may expect on your stakeholding. Similarly, if a person is considering joining an enterprise they may well make their decision based upon potential future reward and career prospects. Again, this becomes a calculation of current and future added value.

Given the recent collapse of what appeared to be high-performing companies around the world the need for accurate assessment and reporting of organisational assets has been thrust into the public consciousness.

For most organisations there is no 'explanation' of their intangible assets – only 'speculation' or 'guesswork'. We can only suppose that other forms of capital or assets represent the huge gaps between company net book values and their market values. But if we do not know what they are or what their values are how can we effectively manage them?

Figure 3.2 Components of human capital

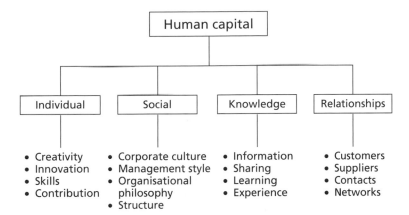

The term 'Human Capital' embraces potential areas where these assets may lie, as can be seen in Figure 3.2.

Often, intangible assets are accounted for under very general headings such as 'goodwill'. But what is 'goodwill' and how can this be effectively measured and valued?

If we do not have a system for measuring and reporting on our stock of human capital then people management becomes largely an act of faith. Stakeholders need something better than this. They want to be better informed about the potential for added value (profits, security, for example) and the risks of value-decline (losses, insecurity).

Tangible asset reporting is designed to ensure that investment decisions are made on the basis of truthful, complete and transparent financial information. The pressure is building for a similar level of reporting on intangible assets such as people.

So, where have we got to in the quest for an effective method of human capital management?

Approaches to human capital

In early societal development, tribal leaders would probably assess and forecast their human capital requirements very simply: 'how many men do we have, how many men do we need, and how strong are they'?

As economic and business systems evolved 'managing performance' became more significant when entrepreneurs were driven by output goals and financial gain. A major shift in human capital management occurred as societies developed from 'independency' to 'interdependency'. No longer did people live as self-sustaining families or community units. A number of factors changed work and social order. We began to trade our labour for a medium of exchange – money – that would enable us to purchase various goods and services. As capitalism, driven by the industrial revolution, emerged as a business philosophy, employee costs became more tangibly assessed. Factory bosses needed to know the cost of labour as they calculated the price at which a product could be sold for a profit. Labour was seen as one of the classic 'factors of production'.

For a long while we have understood the cost of employing people as this is not too difficult to calculate. And, whilst there was a sense of 'owning' human assets, this approach was easy to sustain as an accounting methodology. For long periods of time and across many societies of the globe, people have been implicitly or explicitly 'tied' to a boss or controlling authority. The vast extent of feudalism bears testament to this. Even in the aftermath of the abolition of slavery, many employees had little choice for whom they worked. The development of the trade unions was, in part, an attempt to exert human capital power on behalf of workers to counteract the control of business owners. It is only in very recent times that the shackles of a tied formal or informal employment relationship have been significantly weakened. This is a phenomenon we can witness all over the world. We seem to have entered a phase of providing business and employment opportunities that allow people to step away from the dominance of 'a boss' and thus have greater freedom of choice in what they do and who they choose to work for (Reeves 2000, offers useful evidence to support this). Legislation in many countries has provided guarantees concerning contracts of employment, human rights in the workplace and various forms of discrimination. Thus, in many respects, employees have emerged as a stronger stakeholder than previously under the old subservience regimes of the industrial age.

As the old confrontational approaches between managers and employees have given way to the 'psychological contract', our whole approach to human capital management has to change. But clearly human resource management has not caught up with this development yet. Still we are in the 'cost mode' of human capital management – as a glance at any company Annual Report and Accounts will confirm.

Even the contemporary employee/profit chain models make the assumption that the key goal is maximisation of shareholder value – rather than distributed value-added to all stakeholders (See, e.g. Rucci *et al.* 1998).

Some conceptualisation of the anthropological, economic and social changes that have been taking place is captured in Table 3.1.

Table 3.1 Phases of social, economic and cultural business development

Cultural arena	Dominant historical influences				Today
Social	Nomads	Communities	Economic groups	Networks	Mobile tribes
Business	Hunter/ gatherers	Agriculture/ crafts	Goods & services	Information & knowledge	Collaborative solutions
Workplace	Caves & forests	Villages	Factories & offices	Dispersed teams	Global roamers
Lifestyle	Survival	Security	Industries	Winning	Choices
Behavioural influence	Chiefs	Family heads	The state	Experts	Stakeholder relationships
Beliefs	Spirits	Religion	Political	Free market	Brand identity

Table 3.1 is not intended to depict in a formal academic sense the phases of transformation. It is more of an attempt to capture the essence of cultural development that impacts upon the way stakeholders behave in a business context.

It is argued that we are transforming into a new stage of society, now – the 'Mobile Tribes' society – a phrase coined by Hewlett Packard.[1] This would suggest that lifestyle identity is a significant influence on our behaviours regarding who we work for, what we buy, where we live, our relationships and so on. Marketing professionals have understood this well in their pursuit of 'brand leverage'. Brands are built on values – corporate and individual values – so once again we feel the impact of people on an organisation's worth.

The human capital concept advanced with the work of Flamholz (1999) and his 'human resource accounting' methods. Other researchers such as Lev (2001) have offered variants of this cost-based approach but generally there has not been widespread endorsement. This is likely to be because there are many technical and legal difficulties, it is not an exact science and, perhaps more tellingly, there has been little pressure to develop new methods.

Until, that is, some recent changes and events in the business world.

● The first of these has been the extraordinary rise during the 1990s, of differences between market capitalisation values of organisations and their accountable tangible assets.

● Secondly, many players in the 'new economy' feel intuitively that their true competitive advantage lies within their people in the form of intellectual capital.

● Thirdly, various studies in the 1990s (See, e.g. Purcell *et al.* 2002) consistently identified 'corporate culture' as a competitive differentiator in the marketplace.

● Finally, the Enron-type business fiascos of recent times have sent shock waves through the accounting and auditing professions.

With the change of political and social climate towards a more inclusive 'stakeholder' mentality being added to these factors, the time has arrived for a fresh look at human capital management.

New approaches

The basis for the development of contemporary human capital models really lies in the work of Kaplan and Norton's *The Balanced Scorecard* (1996). This does not focus on people alone but it argues that the four outcome measures are determined by people. Their work stimulated a number of further developments.

Ulrich produced his 'HR Scorecard' (See Becker, Huselid and Ulrich 2001) again with four elements that focussed on human resource management systems and deliverables.

Karl-Erik Sveiby created an 'Intangible assets Monitor' (1997) where a matrix is produced plotting indicators of growth, efficiency and stability against the external and internal structures of the organisation and competence levels.

Edvinsson (1997) adapted the balanced scorecard to design the 'Skandia Navigator' that links the original Kaplan and Norton scores through his own set of 'human focus' measures.

A more recent model has been proposed by Andrew Mayo, Professor of Human Capital Management at Middlesex University in the UK. This addresses many of his objections, gaps and weaknesses to existing human capital models that are detailed in his excellent book *The Human Value of the Enterprise* (2001). Building on a range of influences and experience, Mayo offers his 'Human Capital Monitor' as a framework for measuring and managing human capital. The model, reproduced in Figure 3.3, shifts the emphasis from a profitability focus on shareholders to adding value over a range of stakeholders.

Figure 3.3 The human capital monitor

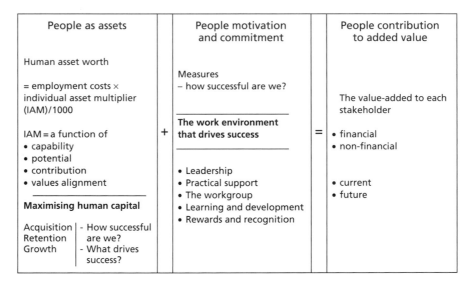

Source: Figure 3.7, page 65, *The Human Value of the Enterprise* by Andrew Mayo (2001) (published by Nicholas Brealey Publishing, www.nbrealey-books.com).

At a first glance, this seems a rather complex framework, but considering the scale and complexity of the topic, this is a tidy format to embrace the essential elements of a human capital management system.

There are three key components:

1 a formula for calculating the worth of human assets in the organisation;

2 the management of people and how they work with others; and

3 added value through people – now and in the future, to various stakeholders.

Individual 'Human Asset Worth' is derived from a formula whereby an employee is assessed via the performance management system to produce an 'Individual Asset Multiplier' (IAM). The IAM is then multiplied by the individual's employment costs to produce a 'worth' figure for a particular person. These figures can be summed for teams, departments, and so on and thus useful comparisons can be made between aggregate forms of human capital. (Having tested this out with a number of MBA groups at Henley Management College, the logic of the mechanics of this part of the model can be supported.)

'Motivation and Commitment' are really governed by the organisation's culture, particularly its management style and human resource management strategies. An assessment of the corporate culture is required with the options of using an established cultural change instrument or creating a customised template. The cultural measurement may be considered as a step improvement over many of the previous human capital frameworks.

Other measures that are essential to monitor will be how successfully the organisation recruits the right people, how well it does in retaining them, and how effectively people are developed so they can add even greater value in the future.

There are a number of reasoned measures for assessing aspects of HR strategies (such as rewards and training) picked up mainly through climate surveys.

Culture as a component of human capital

Culture in business revolves around people, and the way in which people get things done in the organisation defines this culture. Thus, 'culture' becomes an integral part of human capital and needs to be measured just as accurately as individual human asset worth. Corporate culture can become a powerful differentiator of organisational performance – thus unleashing a key weapon in the fight for competitive advantage.

There are further reasons why culture attains such a prominent role in human capital evaluation.

If an organisation has drawn up a strategy to be an effective participant in a chosen market, it needs to ensure that the way in which it will deliver its products and services supports the strategy. Essentially, the delivery of the strategy is achieved through processes, systems and practices that reflect how people are organised and managed.

So, 'organisational culture' cannot be assessed in isolation – it has to relate to the strategy determined by the organisation. If, for example, the company's strategy relies on achieving price leadership then attention to costs would be paramount in every decision taken by the organisation. Measures such as efficiency and productivity are likely to dominate over customer responsiveness, thereby partially defining the organisation's 'way of doing things'. On the other hand, if the company pursued a differentiation strategy based on providing the highest level of customer service, responsiveness would take precedence over how the organisation usually does things internally.

Indeed, the culture of the organisation can be a driver of future corporate strategy. A company initially may be in business to produce rubber tyres but transforms itself into a manufacturer of mobile phones because it has been able to capitalise on its people and management capabilities.

An obvious, but important, conclusion can be drawn from this discussion. To maximise both efficiency of human capital and its future potential, the organisational culture needs to be aligned with the business strategy. Let us consider one or two specific examples to demonstrate this.

Example 1:

A German telecommunications service provider develops a strategy to become a global competitor. It expands its business into new territories worldwide through acquisitions and strategic partnerships, retaining centralised control over its foreign operations. The Munich headquarters designs a standard format for processes, procedures and structures in each country.

Question

Will this top-down, centralised and administrative culture be the right one to win customers in these new areas of operation?

If you had more information at your disposal you may well find that the company's culture is out of alignment with its strategy. Critical success factors may include speed of response, local market knowledge and the development of 'appropriate relationships'. The corporate culture as it stands does not support this.

Example 2:

An Irish airline decides upon a customer-focused strategy to win a greater share of its full-service provider market on long-haul routes. It empowers staff who are encouraged to develop flexible responses to customer preferences. Younger people are recruited on the basis that they will bring a greater sense of dynamism to the business. A 'creative' atmosphere is cultivated through a relaxed management style.

Question

Will this energetic, youthful and informal culture be appropriate to serve a customer base that may place safety, security and discipline as high priorities when selecting an airline? Again, there may be misalignment between business strategy and corporate culture.

These misalignments may impede the effective deployment and use of human capital and it is imperative that a satisfactory method of assessing corporate cultures is needed.

Examining the limited availability of suitable tools and techniques, the author and a colleague at Henley Management College, Richard Lacey, have designed a new calibration instrument, the Strategic Culture Audit Tool (SCAT). The tool retains some of the influences of many cultural scholars and academics (e.g. Hall 1959; Trompernaars 1993; Hofstede 1994; Goffee and Jones 1998) but takes a strongly practitioner approach to ensure that the analysis and application of results are user-friendly to managers.

The areas of audit, with their focus of interrogation, are summarised in Table 3.2. Answers to these areas of investigation will be plotted along a dimensional line.

Table 3.2 Summary of the strategic culture audit probes

● **Corporate spirit – degree of formality**
'Employees feel the management style is "cold" rather than "warm".'

● **Organisational cohesiveness – strength of identity and belonging**
'People within this organisation display similar styles of behaviour, attitudes and values.'

● **Time horizons – orientation to past, present, future**
'Organisational planning and achievement for today and the immediate future takes priority over long-term aspirations.'

● **Organisational responsiveness – attitudes to stakeholders**
'Procedures and processes are designed to prioritise customer preferences over administrative needs.'

● **Management style – are people 'led' or 'managed'?**
'This organisation is characterised more by administrative managers than influential leaders.'

● **Managerial competencies – people or technical focus?**
'Managers in this organisation reach middle and senior positions more through general management competencies rather than technical specialist expertise.'

● **Structure – organisation of work, people, tasks**
'This organisation is structured more as a formal bureaucracy than an informal network.'

● **Investment in people – 'value of people': asset or liability?**
'Investing in people skills and personal development is a high priority for this organisation.'

● **Priorities: 'Me' or 'Us' – team orientation versus individual focus**
'In this organisation, the team comes before the individual.'

● **People performance – performance management as a strategic tool**
'The management of people's performance could be described as "weak" rather than "strong".'

● **Interpersonal behaviour – styles of communication**
'In this organisation feelings and emotions are concealed rather than openly expressed.'

● **Dynamism – level of activity**
'This organisation would be described as "highly dynamic" rather than "passive".'

In order to assess the fit between the organisational culture and the management's corporate strategies the cultural issues will be measured using the above twelve attributes, or dimensions, of the SCAT profile. That will result in a 'radar map' giving an overall profile of the perceived organisational culture.

The issue then is for the management of the organisation to determine what is the most appropriate position on each of the twelve SCAT dimensions for the chosen cultural profile to support or align with the business strategies.

Management should also determine the relative importance of each of the twelve SCAT factors as they may not all be considered as carrying equal weight for the particular strategy.

Logically, any variance from the desired position should be seen as counting against the successful implementation of the strategy. The variance figure will be calculated for each SCAT dimension and then multiplied by the relevant weighting factor. The average variance for the whole of the SCAT survey is then computed. The proposition is that 'cultural fit' is an influencer on the performance of the individuals working within the organisation. A perfect fit of organisational culture to the strategies being employed would increase the aggregated individual human asset value (we will now call this 'Collective Asset Value' – or CAV for short) to an extent greater than the simple sum of their individual component parts. Conversely, a total mismatch of the culture to the strategies would decrease the CAV. This variance analysis enables us to produce a 'Cultural Fit Modifier (CFM)' in our culture element of the human capital evaluation.

The CFM is derived empirically from the variance on an assumed basis that total congruence between preferred and actual culture doubles the asset value while total mismatch halves the asset value. This assumption mirrors the approach to individual performance assessment, that is, 1 = par performance, 0.5 = weak performance, 2 = excellent performance. It is readily acknowledged that these assumptions can be contested, but our early experiences suggest this is a reasonable position to take.

A radar map extracted from a live project is shown in Figure 3.4.

Figure 3.4 SCAT actual results plotted against preferred cultural profile

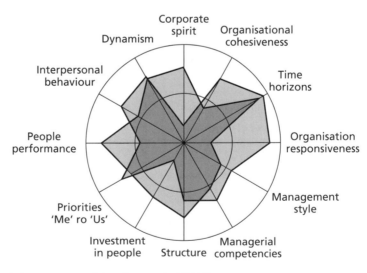

Source: Cultural Fluency Training & Development Ltd (2003).

Organisational climate

The third measure we need to complete our calculation of the organisation's human capital is based on calibrating how the individuals within the organisation *feel* about the various aspects that make-up the organisational culture. It is

LEEDS METROPOLITAN UNIVERSITY LIBRARY

important to distinguish between 'culture' and 'climate'. The former reflects *how things are done*; the latter *how people feel about the way things are done*. People may state that they work in, say, a bureaucratic structure (culture measurement) but they may feel happy or unhappy about it (climate measurement).

An opinion survey will be undertaken that assesses the extent to which people are satisfied with the organisational aspects probed in the SCAT survey. To those satisfaction measures the weighting factors ascribed by management for each attribute (as for the cultural measurements) are applied to determine their relative importance. Now we can measure the variance between the staff's feeling for the culture and the management's preferred culture.

As a consequence we will derive a total weighted average Satisfaction Index (SI) which we can use as an influencer on the CAV, in the same way as we did for the CFM.

The three human capital components – personal performance, working together and leadership influence – can be diagrammatically represented as Figure 3.5.

Figure 3.5 Human capital framework components

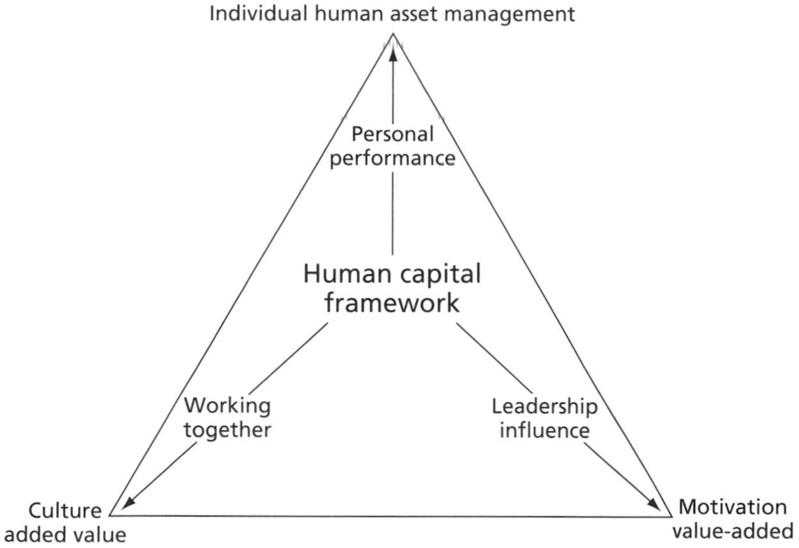

Source: Rees, Estonian Leadership Conference, Tartu, Sept. (2003).

New human capital formula

It is time to bring together these complicated calculations in a simplistic formula.

Our new human capital value (HCV) is the sum of the CAV and the added value we derive from the CFM plus the added value we derive from the satisfaction index (SI). As an equation:

$$HCV = \Sigma CAV \times (CFM \times SI)$$ From these calculations we are now in a position to construct a human capital balance sheet.

The human capital balance sheet

A human capital balance sheet may be built up as follows:

On the assets side we would put

- Collective human asset value (CAV)
- Added value of the organisational culture (CFM)
- Added value from satisfaction (SI).

On the liabilities side we would put

- Employment costs (Total costs of all employees)
- Replacement individual human assets[2]
- Cost of organisational effectiveness.[3]

A worked example

Let us assume we have four employees in our organisation as in Table 3.3.

Table 3.3 Example of aggregated human asset values

	Employment costs (in £)	Individual human asset value (in £)	Added value (in £)
Jenny	60,000	90,000	30,000
Giorgio	40,000	65,000	25,000
Sylvester	30,000	30,000	0
Imran	20,000	30,000	10,000
Total	**150,000**	**215,000**	**65,000**

Let us assume:

- the CFM is 1.5 (this is computed along a scale of 2.0 being a perfect fit, to 0.5 being a poor fit);
- the SI is 1.8 (calculated using the same scale above).

The total value of the CAV (as modified by the CFM) is:

CAV × CFM, where a CFM of 1 would represent no added value. Consequently, the *added value* of this positive cultural fit would be:

$$CAV \times (CFM - 1)$$

that is

$$= 215{,}000 \times (1.5 - 1) = £107{,}500$$

(This is also the cost of re-building the organisational culture.)

In the same way, the *added value* coming from a satisfied workforce is calculated as CAV × (SI − 1)

that is   = 215,000 × (1.8 − 1) = £172,000

On the liabilities side of the balance sheet, these two items would be added together for the line described as 'Cost to rebuild Organisational effectiveness'.

So, the balance sheet would look as shown in Table 3.4.

Table 3.4 Human capital balance sheet

Human assets		
Total individual asset value		215,000
Added value of organisational culture		107,500
Added value of satisfaction index		172,000
Total human capital value		**£494,500**
Employment liabilities		
Employment Costs		150,000
Costs to acquire knowledge, experience, training, etc.	65,000	
Cost to rebuild organisational effectiveness	279,500	
Total costs of replacing value-added human assets (i.e. net human capital value)	344,500	344,500
Total employment liabilities		**£494,500**

On their own, such calculations have little meaning – in the same way that absolute figures relating to the company's financial statements have little meaning. It is only when we compare data that these figures become meaningful.

It is outside the scope of this chapter to enter the arena of extensive technical discussion but it is not too difficult to see that we could interpret human capital value statements along the same principles of finance and accounting.

For example, we could compare one company against another competitor, against the market or against other suitable benchmarks. These comparisons could utilise some of the existing conventional techniques such as ratio analysis (e.g. market capitalisation to human asset value), capital efficiency analysis (e.g. use of human capital against alternatives) and risk analysis (e.g. impact of human capital loss).

We can proceed with more confidence to develop our methods and systems of human capital reporting.

Reporting on human capital

Many of the human capital model designers are keen to see the results reported. These reports can be confined to management and the HR function. They may be disseminated further within the organisation. Rarely, do we see any formal reporting outside the organisation, thus bringing us back to our starting point for the chapter.

There are some notable exceptions, particularly amongst Scandinavian organisations that have so far pioneered many of the recent approaches to human capital management.

In pursuit of seeing where we currently stand on human capital reporting, a research project was undertaken by cultural fluency – a UK training and consultancy organisation. The aim of the research was to identify examples of current best practice in the commercial sector within Europe.

The method was straightforward and the samples were self-selecting. Our premise (based upon the research alluded to earlier) was that although few companies were reporting systematically on their human capital there was an awareness of growing pressure to do so.

We posited that those companies who had started to tackle the issue of human capital valuation would wish to demonstrate this in their formal reporting systems. This seemed reasonable given the regular extent to which organisations like to publicly state their belief in people as their most valuable asset.

We concluded, therefore, that Annual Reports and Accounts would provide the best examples of good practice in reporting on human capital values and management. Further, we concluded that companies wishing to demonstrate their good practices in these aspects of managing their enterprise (and other aspects such as corporate governance, corporate social responsibility and environmental concern) would be more likely to engage in active investor relations.

Therefore, all the reports offered by the Financial Times Report Service and comparable bureaux in other European countries (excluding Investment Trusts) were obtained. Our research covered 912 companies from the reports we received during the time period April–Oct. 2002.

We accept that this research can be critiqued in terms of sampling and statistical analysis but the scope of this research effort was intended to start a preliminary trawl of company reports in search of best practice rather than attempting validity and correlation testing. Once we had identified 'interesting examples' we then engaged in correspondence with the organisations concerned to further probe their approaches to human capital reporting. Our initial findings have convinced us that a small number of companies in Europe are demonstrating an awareness of the need for reporting on human capital and some of these have developed a model for this.

However, the overwhelming impression left by these findings lead us to suggest that methodologies for reporting are extremely weak. Many companies agreed with the need for reporting but openly declared they did not have appropriate tools and techniques to achieve this effectively.

Many companies showed they could represent people as a cost/liability but almost none could demonstrate how they were represented as added value/asset. ('Goodwill' was ignored where this was shown as an intangible asset as the value of people could not be identified from these figures.)

Figure 3.6 Reporting on soft issues

Percentage of companies with formal reports on the following organisational activities:	
Social/community responsibility	5.6
Corporate culture	3.22
Environmental concern	21.79
People issues	23.87

Source: Rees, Primary Research.

A summary of key results from our research is identified in Figure 3.6.

Some qualitative responses given by the companies surveyed are documented below as a means of illustrating the thinking, attitudes and problems behind the challenge of human capital reporting (Table 3.5).

Table 3.5 Sample responses on human capital reporting

Company	Country	Question 1 – How do you account for the asset value of employees in your organisation?	Question 2 – Do you report on the 'culture' of your organisation in any formal way?
1	UK	We do not currently account for the asset value of our employees. It is however our intention to do that in the near future as part of our Value Based Management initiative. This entails the measurement of employee value, customer value, supplier value and shareholder value. We are currently working on a methodology that will assist us in identifying what creates employee value and measuring that for our employees vis-à-vis competitors. When exactly we will formally report on it is difficult to say at this stage.	We do not report on the culture of our organisation in any formal way. Again it is our intention to measure it against specific culture objectives we have set ourselves as part of our Value-based Management initiative. Our challenge is to change behaviour at all levels of the organisation so that daily activities of teams and individuals become progressively more aligned with the organisation's goal of value creation for shareholders, customers, employees and suppliers – a culture that keeps asking how do I create value and not to destroy value.

Table 3.5 (cont'd)

Company	Country	Question 1 – How do you account for the asset value of employees in your organisation?	Question 2 – Do you report on the 'culture' of your organisation in any formal way?
2	Germany	Our employees have an immense, you might as well say immeasurable, value to the company. However, accounting rules do not allow us to capitalise any amount for them, as it would be impossible to determine any cost of acquisition. Nevertheless we use a wide range of instruments to maintain and enhance the already high grade of employee identification. Measures to be named are: ● corporate wide HSE programmes ● social benefits and large scale corporate social responsibility activities ● education and training programmes offering a wide variety of improving personal qualifications and skills.	Reporting on values and quantitative analysis of our performance regarding corporate values have been forming an integral part of our communications policy for more than 25 years. In 1977 we were one of the first enterprises to publish a so-called 'social balance sheet' giving an overview of our contributions to society and environment. We also pride ourselves of having been a pioneer in environmental reporting. Our first fully fledged environmental report with large quantities of data and with the indication of targets to be achieved within the next two years was released in 1993. In 2001 we published our first sustainable development report. It contains qualitative assessment of our corporate social responsibility activities and qualitative and quantitative assessment of our environmental performance. Both areas are the most important elements of our corporate culture except for our strive for economic success.
3	UK	We report under UK accounting conventions which are based on historic cost. You are not allowed to represent the 'value' of any assets such as people, IPR and so on in the balance sheet except to the extent that they are acquired, in which case they are reflected in goodwill. As you say, they appear as a cost. I am not really sure how your idea would work in practice. You would have to assess the 'value' of each person individually and adjust the composite value dynamically as people leave and join? In a people business like ours, the value of the people are the revenue and earnings of the company, anyway.	'Culture' is incredibly important for our company, but it is a nebulous concept in terms of reporting. Of course there are many things we measure internally which are a reflection of the culture, such as: ● Success of recruitment ● Leaver debriefs ● Length of service ● Attrition ● Training days ● Special interest Group activity ● Attendance at staff meetings ● Results of regular employee opinion surveys ● Minutes of staff council meetings

				● Personal appraisals which are open to all staff ● Number of people introduced to the company by existing employees ● Employee shareholding activity, including take up of employee share schemes. At the end of the day, our success as a recruiter + the stats on staff retention are the only meaningful measure of how the culture is working for the business.
4	Belgium	You are absolutely right that employees are a very important asset to a company and it is not done to capitalise this asset on the balance sheet. It is therefore, also in the case of our company, a hidden value. Indeed in our branch the formation of a good worker takes a long time (for instance to form an employee in high quality printing, it takes a formation period of three years). As most of our workers are highly skilled and trained professional, the asset value to our company would be enormous.		We do not report on the culture of our organisation. However, we have been audited by Ethibel, which is the Belgian organisation that performs audits on ethical and social behaviour of Belgian companies. They provide a list of ethical shares and we are proud that our company was in the past one of the first companies that achieved the Ethibel quality mark. They have revised our company earlier this year and we maintain this quality label. Their audit is rather extensive and focuses not only on social behaviour but also on environmental and other general ethic issues.

Future implications for managers

The consequences of these developments in managing human capital effectively are far-reaching. They have only begun to dawn on senior managers and HR specialists in very recent times. Pressures are unstoppable and in the near future organisations will need to develop effective means for managing human capital and methods for reporting this to a wide group of stakeholders.

But, after all, this book is about the future HR agenda, the future role of managers and the future of people management.

Organisations will need to engage people from across the business in the design and implementation of systems for managing human capital. Managers will be expected to contribute to the formation of these approaches, both at strategic levels and operational levels.

The emerging role of 'Manager: as manager of human capital', spanning strategic, operational and transactional roles, is captured in Figure 3.7.

Figure 3.7 Manager: as manager of human capital

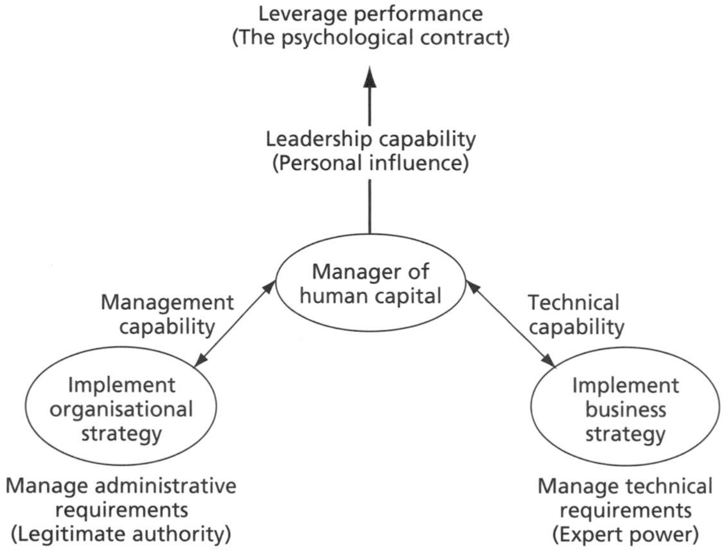

Source: Rees, Estonian Leadership Conference, Tartu, Sept. (2003).

It is clear that for many organisations this will demand new systems of performance management. Current 'soft' measures expressed in qualitative terms are more likely to be quantified in 'hard' measures. This will be underpinned by the need for quantifiable reporting to the public of capital management in the business.

In turn this demands new skills and competencies. These will be required to conduct performance management within new models of human capital management and to learn how to use results in people management decision-making.

This is a big agenda but one that will needed to be addressed with strong commitment.

Notes

1. Described as such at a Hewlett-Packard 'e-Bazaar' presentation, Espoo, Finland 2000.
2. This is the cost which we would assume would be incurred if the existing staff left and we had to bring new staff up to the same level of capability, networking, knowledge, and so on. It is taken to be the numerical result of subtracting the total employment costs from the collective asset value.
3. This is the cost of re-building the corporate culture and levels of motivation and commitment if we had to replace the existing staff.

References

Becker, B.E., Huselid, M.A. and Ulrich, D. (2001) *The HR Scorecard: Linking People, Strategy and Performance*, Boston, Harvard Business School Press.

Edvinsson, L. and Malone, M.S. (1997) *Intellectual Capital*, London, Piatlaus.

Flamholz, E.G. (1999) *Human Resource Accounting: Advances in Concepts, Methods and Applications*, Amsterdam, Kluwer.

Goffee, R. and Jones, G. (1998) *The Character of a Corporation*, London, HarperCollins.

Hall, E.T. (1959) *The Silent Language*, New York, Doubleday.

Heijmans, N.V. (2000) Heijmans, N.V. Annual Report, 2000.

Hofstede, G. (1994) *Cultures and Organisations*, London, HarperCollins.

Kaplan, R.S. and Norton, D.P. (1996) *The Balanced Scorecard*, Boston, MA, Harvard Business School press.

Lev, B. (2001) *Intangibles*, New York, Brookings Institution Press.

Mayo, A. (2001) *The Human Value of the Enterprise*, London, Nicholas Brealey.

McCall Smith, A. (2003) *The No. 1 Ladies' Detective Agency*, Abacus.

Purcell, J., Kinnie, N., Hutchinson, S. and Rayton, B. (2002) 'Inside the Box', *People Management*, Oct., pp. 30–38.

Rees, D. (2003) Estonian Annual Leadership Conference, 4 and 5 Sept., Tartu.

Reeves, R. (2000) 'All Change in the Workplace', *The Observer*, 30 Jan., p. 18.

Rucci, A.J., Kirn, S.P. and Quinn, R. (1998) 'The Employee-Customer-Profit Chain at Sears', *Harvard Business Review*, Vol. 76, Jan./Feb.

Sveiby, K.E. (1997) *The New Organisational Wealth*, San Francisco, Berrett-Koehler.

Trompernaars, F. (1993) *Riding the Waves of Culture*, London, Economist Books.

4

Socially responsible management

Jason Leonard

Earlier chapters have indicated the growing importance of organisations developing a socially responsible philosophy. Until recently, this aspect of corporate values and behaviour has taken a low priority, but indicators are that corporate social responsibility will emerge as a major area of professional concern for HR specialists in the future.

Introduction

The CEO of your company has just sent you, the Human Resources Director, an email asking what corporate social responsibility (CSR) and sustainable development (SD) policies are in place.

This is the first time you have been directly confronted by these two issues about which you have virtually no knowledge whatsoever. Time to do some research!

A starting point is to seek definitions. One definition of CSR is:

taking into account the social and environmental impact of corporate activity when making operating decisions, also known as "corporate citizenship". (Gilmour and Caplan 2002)

Why should such concepts be important to the company? Is this an HR issue? How will line and project managers be affected by CSR and SD initiatives?

This chapter outlines current approaches to CSR and SD, and discusses how organisations may respond in developing suitable policies.

CSR as a business strategy

A recent survey of 850 CEOs across Europe, Canada and the USA (Hill and Knowlton 2002) reported that many international CEOs saw CSR initiatives as a vehicle for increasing sales. American CEOs ranked recruitment and retention of employees as the most important business objective of CSR.

Seven hundred senior managers were surveyed for Ashridge Centre for Business and Society and showed that 77 per cent of managers saw responsible business practice as "very important" to the long-term commercial success of the company, with reputation, protection, recruitment and retention as key business drivers (Faruk 2002).

Competitors will be looking at how CSR and SD can add benefits to their business. In order to compete effectively the issues raised by such initiatives need to be carefully examined and understood.

CSR as a human resource strategy

With a tight supply of skilled labour, employees are looking for organisations that stand out as "decent to work for". CSR and SD demonstrates that they take a real interest in people and their communities. Employees like to tell their friends that they work for a responsible company (Marshall 2002), and the company's attitude towards CSR will influence their decision-making.

Social responsibility

Finding an agreed definition is difficult, as it is not a legal concept, but Cowe (2002) uses the legal analogy of "reasonable behaviour", where reference is made to a particular time. Attitudes change over time. So marketing campaigns from 40 years ago making exaggerated claims for products were considered reasonable practices at the time but modern audiences cringe. However "mud sticks" and in some situations (e.g. Nestlé's baby-milk), marketing and PR strategies employed by a previous generation of managers still have adverse impacts on an organisation's reputation today with certain sectors of the community.

Grimshaw *et al.* (1997) identify two aspects to social responsibility:

1 Understanding and taking into account not only the views and interests of people, organisations and other parties who are dealt with on a regular basis but also the wider environment in which the business operates;

2 Taking action to embrace the responsibilities that befall the corporate citizen and, where necessary, prioritising the areas where impact could be greatest.

Henderson (2001) suggests that CSR endorses the objectives of SD, of which there are three strands – economic, environmental, and social. Organisations often use the terms CSR and SD interchangeably, but CSR is seen as a broader concept focusing on risks and opportunities associated with economic, environmental and social issues (Ernst and Young 2002). It is about voluntarily contributing to a better society and environment (EU 2001).

This is not a new notion. Non-governmental organisations (NGOs) have been pressuring businesses for many years, and businesses have been advertising their interest in social and environmental issues.[1] There was a United Nations Conference on the Human Environment in 1972, and in 1987 the

World Commission on Environment and Development produced the Bruntland Report, which gave the well-used definition of SD as:

> development which meet the needs of the present without compromising the ability of future generation to meet their own needs.

The definition was expanded in the UK 1990 White Paper, "The Common Inheritance":

> Sustainable development means living on the earth's income rather than eroding its capital. It means keeping the consumption of renewable natural resources within the limits of their replenishment. It means handing down to successive generations not only man-made wealth, but also natural wealth, such as clean and adequate water supplies, good arable land, a wealth of wildlife, and ample forests.

Triple bottom line reporting – reporting on environmental and social indicators as well as traditional financial measures in order to assess the full impact of the organisation's activities – is a way in which an organisation tells the world how it is doing on these issues (Gilmour and Caplan 2002).

Customer, investor and political pressures

> If you make a promise as a company in today's increasingly transparent world, you will be held to account for that promise. Make no promise and you have no reputation. (Steadman 2002)

Technology has made information easily available on a global scale and bad news travels fast. For example, Shell's confrontation with Greenpeace over decommissioning the Brent Spar production platform in 1995 made headlines worldwide. Even when Greenpeace admitted mistakes in their analysis and apologised, the damage had already been done (Colegrave 2002). Mention "Bhopal", "Piper Alpha", "Exxon Valdez", "Herald of Free Enterprise" – and many people can recount the details of the organisations involved. The phrase, "the perpetrator of the world's worst industrial disaster" attributed to Union Carbide following Bhopal (McIntosh *et al.* 1998) is not the strapline an organisation really wants. MORI (Marketing and Opinion Research International) studies have revealed that three-quarters of people claim that reputation directly influences their buying behaviour (Steadman 2002). Rose (1998) describes how it is increasingly difficult for organisations to put these incidents behind them.

The public and investors are becoming increasingly aware of CSR issues. Children are being taught from an ever-earlier age about corporate social responsibility and environmental issues and pressure to take an interest is only likely to increase (Kraus 2002). Differentiating between organisations will be increasingly based on the way they operate and treat people. The emergence of global markets has meant that:

investors are becoming increasingly active and demanding higher standards of account-ability, behaviour and performance . . . their influence on the world's boardrooms is on the increase. (KPMG 2002)

Corporations are not all bad, of course, and economic growth has provided healthcare, improved living conditions, literacy, and increased life expectancy. But competition is more intense and organisations must look for ways to differentiate themselves.

At the "Earth Summit" (UN Conference on Environment and Development) in June 1992 nearly 180 states met in Rio de Janeiro. One of the agreements was an agenda for the 21st century to bring about SD, the so-called "Agenda 21".

This has been implemented in the United Kingdom through the publication of the *A Better Quality of Life*[2] which sets out the UK's strategy for sustainable development with four main aims:

1   Social progress which recognises the needs of everyone.

2   Effective protection of the environment.

3   Prudent use of natural resources.

4   Maintenance of high and stable levels of economic growth and employment.

It states that government policy will take account of ten guiding principles (reflecting the themes stated in the "Rio Declaration", Table 4.1).

The UK government measures progress on key issues relating to quality of life through the report mentioned above.

The UN also launched the "Global Compact Initiative" in July 2000 through which it is engaging with corporations. It sets out core values in the areas of:

● *Human rights* – respecting human rights as reflected in the Universal Declaration of Human Rights.

● *Labour standards* – upholding freedom of association and collective bargaining, not employing under-age labour, or forced labour, and not discriminating on grounds of race, creed, gender or ethnic origin.

● *Environment* – employing the precautionary principle, promoting environmental responsibility, and encouraging the development of environmentally friendly technologies.

Sustainable development is a global issue and all parties, including business, need to play their part. As Robinson (2001) stated:

"the United Nations does not ask or expect business to assume the responsibilities of government. It does ask businesses to act in a responsible way in their sphere of activities and join with governments, civil society and international organisations in promoting respect for the core values of the Global Compact."

Table 4.1 CSR/SD guiding principles

1 *Putting people at the centre*	As the Rio Declaration states "human beings are . . . entitled to a healthy and productive life in harmony with nature"
2 *Taking a long-term perspective*	Begin now to safeguard the interests of future generations
3 *Taking account of costs and benefits*	Not pursuing any single objective that imposes disproportionate costs elsewhere
4 *Creating an open and supportive economic system*	Conditions where trade can flourish and competitiveness can act as a stimulus for growth and greater resource efficiency
5 *Combating poverty and social exclusion*	Indispensable for SD. Everyone should have the opportunity to fulfil their potential
6 *Respecting environmental limits*	Severe and irreversible damage to some aspects of the environment and resources would pose severe threats to global society but often defining the limits is difficult, so precautionary action should be considered
7 *The precautionary principle*	This is directly from the Rio Declaration which defines the precautionary principle as "where there are threats of serious or irreversible damage, lack of full scientific certainty shall not be used as a reason for postponing cost-effective measures to prevent environmental degradation". This means that a cost benefit analysis should be used together with a transparency in decision-making
8 *Using scientific knowledge*	Means anticipating early where scientific advice or research is needed and identifying the source of high-calibre information
9 *Transparency, information, participation and access to justice*	
10 *Making the polluter pay*	This is reflected by the modern approach to environmental legislation, for example, organisations with significant pollution potential must finance the licensing, authorisation and consent processes

Source: Rio Declaration (1992).

The European Union have made it clear that it is no longer sufficient for business to merely pay taxes and comply with national legislation. They expect something in return for the "greater freedom and benefit conferred by globalisation" (Business Leaders' Input 2000).[3] The enactment of this directive in the UK has increased the number of organisations requiring authorisation to operate. There has been a move from looking at specific processes at a facility to include the whole installation and impacts on the environment. Authorisations are no longer limited to emissions controls, but now include energy efficiency, waste minimisation and noise and vibration.

Windsor (2001) discusses the idea of a "progressive responsibilities conception" that is, the unequal distributions of wealth and power in society implies that the more powerful and wealthy the firm, the greater has to be the firm's responsibilities to neighbours and community.

The focus on large corporations has been intensified with recent well-publicised failures in the US, provoking this response by US President George W. Bush:

There is a need for a renewed corporate responsibility in America. Those entrusted with shareholders money must, must, strive for the highest of high standards. (Speech 26, June 2002)

Competition and business relationships

The best organisations recognise that their public reports are as much about marketing as they are financial issues (Taylor 2000). Annual reports are essentially historical. The inclusion of data about non-financial and particularly cultural issues allows investors to make judgements about the future potential of the organisation.

The global business environment is continually changing and risk levels are rising (Bryan 2002). Product characteristics can be quickly copied, so differentiation comes with "process benefits" (making transactions more pleasant), and "relationship benefits" (Court et al. 1999).

We are seeing the rise of virtual organisations that are "centred around a key business with a high degree of integration of internal activities, with considerable blurring between functional business areas" (Stonehouse et al. 2000). As integration is the essence of the relationship, then organisations need to look closely at those they build relationships with, as these relationships lead to increased risk to brands and reputation.

Manufacturers are becoming more directly exposed to their customers, due to changing purchasing patterns. For example, if a consumer buys a substandard product from a retailer, it can be returned to the retailer. However if the same product is purchased from the manufacturer's website, then the manufacturer will be directly targeted (Dayal et al. 2000). This means that the manufacturers must look ever closer at the way they conduct their business. As Peter Brabeck (CEO of Nestlé SA) once said:

Brands today are very significant, and it will be even more so in the future. This is because the question of confidence and food safety will become more important. And in the final analysis, a brand represents the highest trust. (Lebensmittel 1999)

Financial institutes and insurance

A survey by PriceWaterhouse Consulting (Preston 2001) found that only eight per cent of investors thought companies maintained an open dialogue with them. They also reported that the benefits from more transparent information provision included:

● greater management credibility

● improved analyst following

● improved access to capital

● a lower cost of capital and higher share price for those who deserve it.

Research has shown that investors are willing to pay more for well-governed companies (Coombes and Watson 2000), and put corporate governance on a par with financial indicators when evaluating investment proposals (Watts and Copnell 2002). Investors are increasingly demanding that organisations meet internationally accepted standards of governance and disclosure.

Financial institutes and insurers want to reduce their exposure and need organisations to demonstrate that they are managing risk on a broad basis.[4] A demonstration of good proactive management of health and safety performance will be a defence when the insurance claims inspector comes knocking at the corporate door.

The Turnbull report guidance published in 1999 with regard to the implementation of internal control requirements of the Combined Code on Corporate Governance recommended the integration of a risk-based approach including "health, safety and environmental reputation and business propriety issues". It highlighted consideration of environmental and social impacts, the recognition of stakeholder relations and strategic value of corporate reputation (Miller 2002).

Legal trends

Miller's (2002) review identified a trend towards legal accountability particularly in the areas of human rights. He points to a variety of recent legislative changes that promote CSR including:

- Disclosure by pension fund trustees of "the extent to which social, environmental or ethical concerns are taken into account in the selection, retention and realisation of investments".

- Directors' responsibility for recognising the "importance of relations with employees, suppliers, customers and others, the need to maintain a reputation for high standards of business conduct and the impact of their actions on the community and environment".

- Anti-corruption legislation.

- Compulsory CSR reporting.

Advantage of effective CSR programmes

A review of the literature highlights many virtues of good CSR, but few primary research studies have been carried out to substantiate this. Some of the studies are detailed in Table 4.2.

In summary, the advantages of good CSR practice that can be taken back to the executive board are:

- Reputation is enhanced amongst customers and staff.

- Customer base is enhanced, cause related marketing can be added to the marketing strategy.

Table 4.2 Primary CSR research studies

The World Business Council for Sustainable Development business case shows that the Dow Jones Sustainability Index (DJSI) (15.8% annualised return) outperformed the Dow Jones Global Index (DJGI) (12.5% annualised return) in the Five years up to August 2001 (WBCSD 2001). This may reflect the fact that the better run organisations take an interest in SD and see it as a business opportunity

Research carried out at De Paul University in Chicago using the 2001 list of 100 "best corporate citizens" showed that these organisations performed significantly better than the rest of the top 500 companies (New Zealand Management 2002)

Marshall (2002) in his experience has found that reporting on CSR performance has allowed the organisation to see themselves as others do, important feedback which can be taken into consideration in decision-making. Also through the identification of investors and their motivations, CEO's can more accurately predict the direction of their share prices (Coyne and Witter 2002)

- Productivity is improved through increased innovation and efficiency.

- Recruitment of desirable people is enhanced.

- Motivation and commitment of staff is improved.

- Finance is increasingly available, and shareholder value may increase as socially aware investment is attracted.

An example of CSR in practice: "cause related marketing"

"Cause related marketing" is a phrase that has entered corporate language in recent years. This is about linking a company's brand and reputation with charitable activities, to leverage mutual benefits (Stubbs 2002).

British Gas: a case study

According to World Wildlife Fund figures the fastest growing component of the global ecological footprint is energy (WWF 2002), so organisations like Centrica (whose brands include British Gas and the AA) who have significant energy interests can expect to be under the CSR spotlight. Centrica have strategies in all CSR areas, developed through consultation with stakeholders. British Gas's stakeholders highlighted that with 30,000 deaths of older people in the UK directly attributed to cold-related illnesses, they thought the company should take an interest in keeping older people warm in winter (Waugh 2002a). In January 1999 British Gas formed a partnership with "Help the Aged" (a charity to assist elderly people) to address this. Through direct funding and in-kind support, British Gas has provided £4.3 million to Help the Aged. This partnership lobbied the government over winter fuel payments and these have risen from £20 in 1993 to £200 in 2003. The energy efficiency maximum grant has also risen from £700 to £2000. A recent MORI survey has shown that 57 per cent of people who are aware of this partnership feel better about British Gas. British Gas sees this approach as a responsible way of directly increasing sales. It has allowed them to focus on delivering wider business benefits including:

- consistent year-on-year positive impact on brand equity;
- positive development of the brand as socially responsible;
- substantial positive media coverage (the Partnership won the Cause Related Marketing Award at the Business in the Community Awards for Excellence in 2002);

- engagement and enthusiasm of employees, reflected in improved staff morale, motivation and teamwork;
- positive relationships with government, regulators and opinion formers, positioning British Gas as a company that far exceeds legislative and regulatory obligations (Waugh 2002b).

Implementing a CSR/SD strategy

Figure 4.1 represents one approach.

Figure 4.1 Representation of CSR strategy

Source: Ernst and Young (2002).

Stakeholder management

Understand and consult with your stakeholders. Use their responses as a basis for action. What is actually important to your stakeholders? Although communication is seen as the most influential factor in building and protecting a corporate reputation (Hill and Knowlton 2002), few companies actually put it into practice (Ernst and Young 2002). Stakeholders have conflicting ideas, and doing something right for one, may well go against the wishes of another.

Understand performance

Organisations also need to understand their current performance. A recent survey (Felton and Watson 2002) of 250 US corporate directors sitting on 500 boards together with interviews with corporate governance experts and investors found that:

- 44 per cent do not fully understand key value drivers.

- 23 per cent do not fully understand company performance against objectives.

- 23 per cent lack effective processes to monitor performance.

- 29 per cent lack sufficient processes to ensure management focus.

Ernst and Young (2002) have developed a "Common Path Forward" Figure 4.2, a series of steps in the development and implementation of a CSR strategy.

Figure 4.2 "Common path forward" CSR strategy

```
                                    9. Communication
                                8. Monitoring of performance
                            7. Organisational change (align to CSR agenda)
                        6. Develop supporting policies and procedures
                    5. Develop CSR strategy
                4. Identify and prioritise key risks
            3. Engage with stakeholders
        2. Build business case for CSR response
    1. Understand the relevance of CSR
```

Source: Ernst and Young (2002).

Table 4.3 (overleaf) gives practical examples of how this is translated into practice.

How far should you go?

Corporate social responsibility is voluntary (EU 2001), and activities should be backed by a business case. The extent to which an organisation invests in CSR is contingent on its business environment and stakeholder expectations. Each organisation must carry out its own cost-benefit analysis, taking the organisation's guiding principles into consideration. The organisation is trying to get a balance between what it says and what it does, as Figure 4.3 (overleaf) shows (Sillanpää 2002).

Focus on strategic benefits

Porter and Kramer (2002) warn that most strategies are aimed at boosting morale, positive publicity and goodwill, and not at improving the organisation's ability to compete. He states that the:

> acid test of good corporate philanthropy is whether the desired social change is so beneficial to the company that the organisation would pursue the change even if no-one ever knew about it.

Table 4.3 Ways in which companies can make a difference (on a local level)

Some of the ways that companies can make a sustainable investment in the community

People and skills	Money
● Board and management committee members ● Consultancy (public relations and media, finance, computing, premises, survey design, strategic planning, market research, office administration, personnel) ● Organiser of fun-raising events ● Trainers ● "Helping hands" ● Secondees ● Mentors	● Grants and charitable donations ● Fund raising ● Matched employee fund-raising ● Loans: interest free or below market rate ● Awards ● Sponsorships ● Matched payroll giving ● Project funding ● Membership fees ● Joint initiatives ● Charity of the year

Services and facilities	Other
● Graphics and design help ● Copywriting and printing ● Computing assistance ● Surplus office equipment ● Load of meeting rooms ● Tools and supplies ● Product donations ● Free or discounted services ● Long-term load of office space ● Use of vehicles	● Work experience places ● Re-training and ready for work schemes ● Business start-up programmes ● Organising collections (e.g. of materials, food, toys, clothes) ● Publicity for causes or organisations ● Places on training courses ● Hosting and organising special events ● Team events ● Sitting on local partnership boards

Source: Davies (2002), published from Guide to *Business Sustainability* with kind permission of Caspian Publishing.

They quote an example of Cisco Systems' Networking Academy to train computer network administrators to alleviate potential constraints on its growth through the lack of trained staff. Organisations do not function in isolation from the society around them, and the education level of the local workforce can substantially affect the organisation's competitiveness.

The organisation can operate at different levels and the influencing tactics are contingent on the situation, as shown in Figure 4.4 (overleaf).

Sources of guidance

Various legal requirements, international protocols, global agreements and initiatives that have been mentioned previously will be good sources for developing CSR and SD.

The EU Commission has set up a Multi-Stakeholder Forum on CSR with a timetable to adopt the Forum's report in Spring 2004 (Toomer 2002). Their recommendations are likely to include:

● No detailed legislation until CSR has "matured" and good practice elements are identified.

Figure 4.3 Balance in CSR management and reporting

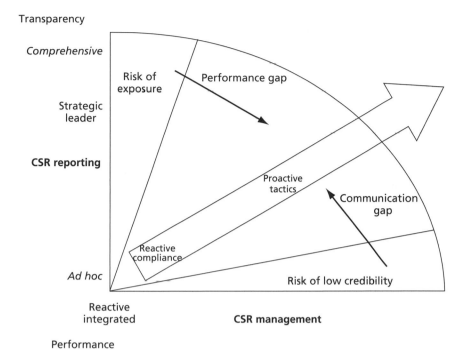

Source: Sillanpää (2002), published from Guide to Business Sustainability with kind permission of Caspian Publishing.

Figure 4.4 Spheres of influence

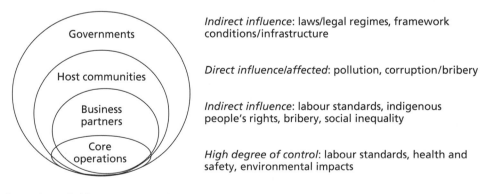

Source: Amended from WBCSD (2002).

- CSR initiatives should have the approval, endorsement, and commitment of the board of directors.

- A CSR champion is appointed.

- Staff should understand their roles in CSR.

● CSR should be part of existing business processes.

● To avoid duplication, then the relationship between risk management, CSR and corporate governance needs to be established.

● CSR advice and verification should be independently sought.

Reporting

Why do some organisations report on non-financial issues in great depth devoting significant resources, when it is not required? The answer is to strengthen or regain trust of customers, communities, investors, employees, business partners, and others who influence the success of the organisation (White 2002). Sceptics of the reporting process, suggest that the focus on reporting is avoiding the real questions like how to make the transition to sustainability (Ballard 2002), and could be seen as a public relations exercise (Seppala 2002).

> Social accounting and reporting are increasingly important processes that will allow direct comparisons between professing the importance of certain values and codes and actually acting on them. (Bush 2002)

Stakeholders want to know (Gonella 2002):

● What are the significant CSR issues for the organisation and the rationale for identifying them.

● The attitude of the organisation towards these issues and its performance.

● The quality of management in place to manage and make improvements in the identified areas.

● Achievements relative to previously set improvement targets.

● What the organisation intends to do and targets achieved.

Reporting standards

In order that comparisons can be made between organisations, standard reporting systems have been developed to fill this need.

The Organisation for Economic Co-operation and Development (OECD) has compared the different standards in detail in their Guidelines for Multinational Enterprises (OECD 2001). The Global Reporting Initiative (GRI) differs from the others with recommendations of performance indicators, rather than giving specific standards of performance and is in the process of developing sector indicators to support the general guidelines. SA8000 contains an auditable code of practice and is accompanied by an accreditation process. The Table 4.4 shows the range of topics covered in the different reporting standards.

Table 4.4 Topics included in sustainable development reporting

Area of reporting	Topics included
Accountability	Transparency, reporting, monitoring and verification
Business conduct	Compliance with law, competitive conduct, political activities, corruption & bribery, proprietary information/intellectual property rights, whistle-blowers, and conflicts of interest
Community involvement	Employment of local workers, community economic development, and philanthropy
Corporate governance	Rights of shareholders
Environment	Precautionary principle, product life cycle, stakeholder engagement, public policy on environmental issues, and established environmental management system
Human rights	Health and safety, child & forced labour, freedom of association/collective bargaining, wages and benefits, working time, discipline
Marketplace/consumers	Marketing/advertising, product quality/safety, consumer privacy
Workplace/employees	Non-discrimination, harassment/abuse, training, child/elder care, maternity/paternity leave

The following case studies illustrate the way in which CSR and SD initiatives have been developed and implemented in different parts of the world.

Case study: local involvement – Komi Arctic Oil

The Komi Artic Oil joint venture started in the 1990s between Gulf Canada, British Gas, and Luc Oil. An agreement was made at governmental level for the exploration and production of oil in Usinsk, a town approximately 1000 miles north of Moscow, Russia. It was recognised that organisations work within communities, and their ability to compete depends a lot on the local circumstances in which they operate (Porter and Kramer 2002). With this in mind a significant social fund was identified for the project to provide the town with, amongst other things, a swimming pool, hospital, skating rink, and improved road system. The community gained tremendously from this project, but so did the joint venture. Employees were provided with recreational and medical facilities. Local people were given medical and dental training, which was of value to the town and company. Local business people, as primary suppliers to the project, were educated on running businesses profitably and were supported financially. Preferential cash-flow arrangements were put in place to ensure that local workers were guaranteed payment until the businesses found their feet. The project supported a community of 8000 local people. It provided an avenue for communication, building personal relations between the organisation and local government – ensuring that problems were sorted out at a local level before they escalated.

At a practical level it ensured there was a swift response by the emergency services when needed, and bureaucracy at the airport was reduced.

Case study: the Karachaganak community project

A similar set up was put in place for the Karachaganak project, an oil exploration and production project in Kazakstan (a joint venture including British Gas, Texaco, Agip, and Luc oil), again in the 1990s. Apartments were built to house workers, to be transferred to local people when the project was finished, and domestic water supplies were improved. A railway was built from the airport to the town, routed through the local villages to improve transport of material to the project. A hospital was upgraded, fire engines purchased, dental and medical training given to local people, all to improve emergency services to the joint venture and local community. The cost of building this support system for the project (about $10 million per annum) was small in the context of the total budget nearing $6 billion for the life of the project, but was a major regeneration project for the area. With such a wide range of issues being addressed it was important to keep a tight focus on ensuring activities brought direct benefits to the project, as well as the local community. For example, local politicians tried to divert funds to other projects outside of the immediate geographical area. This would not have benefited the project at all. This work also allowed the negotiation of tax benefits for the import of equipment for the project.

Implementing CSR/SD: a cultural change with implications for managers

Any manager trying to implement a CSR/SD culture within their organisation will need to consider the following steps:

1   *Commitment from the top* – This needs to be thought through carefully to add real value to the organisation. This is the key to getting those managers focused on their bottom line to take an interest in the SD approach. Communicate this to employees with proper explanation of business benefits. SD needs to be part of the values of the organisation. It is about pragmatic leadership. So, when the CEO or members of the executive board visit a facility, have those expensive chauffeur-driven cars they arrive in been converted to run on a fuel that reduces their impact on the environment? Do they ask key questions in relation to SD objectives, such as how the facility is reducing accident rates or energy usage?

2   *Objectives and targets* – SD objectives and targets need to be fed down through business units to individuals. Their objectives and targets need to be pragmatic, demonstrating how individuals can make a difference. An SD approach must be seen as good management, and therefore reviewed and rewarded through the performance management systems.

3   *Communication* – Use the systems that work for your organisation. You need to explain the global picture, and how an SD approach by the organisation and its employees can contribute to improving the organisation and the environment in which individuals live and work.

Champions are needed at different sites to push the message on a daily basis, trained so they deliver a consistent message, with a network forum for support and sharing of best practice to make a difference. Providing channels for two-way communication to learn from employees is essential to ensure continuous improvement in driving the process forward.

Recruitment, induction material, and other company publications, such as the annual report need to reflect the SD philosophy.

4 *Measurement* – Make it relevant, and use existing systems. A range of relevant SD questions in employee satisfaction surveys. Employees like to feel they are working for responsible organisations, and word of mouth is an important advertising channel. Communicate progress, for example by putting league tables on the company website.

Processes need to be changed in order to make the SD approach the "way we do things around here", not just a one-off campaign which fades away. So, for example, purchasing may change their tender documents, challenging potential suppliers on how they can contribute to the organisation's SD way of doing business. It could range from continuous research by suppliers to reduce energy usage of their machinery, to providing a range of different computer equipment for the same cost to encourage employee diversity.

Future implications for managers

There is strong evidence to suggest that socially responsible management will occupy a central role in the future reporting of an organisation's performance and activities. It is likely that social responsibility will be integrated into the corporate governance systems of most organisations in the near future.

Clear policies will need to be developed as stakeholders recognise their influence on corporate attitudes towards social and community behaviour. Strategies are likely to be developed that can exploit the potential advantage of such policies. With a strengthening legislative framework starting to gather momentum, strategies will also have to be developed so that businesses do not fall foul of existing and future legal requirements.

Strategies will need to engage managers at all levels, both in the formation of policies and their implementation. Managers will have to genuinely understand the power of modern systems of communication that can quickly enhance or destroy an organisation's reputation.

For many organisations and many individual managers this is new – and unfamiliar – territory. This will not be a "passing fad" – corporate social responsibility is here to stay and we are likely to witness many leading edge developments over the next few years.

Research and practitioner observation suggest that many individual managers do not appreciate how unprepared they are to carry out such responsibilities.

Most managers remain untrained or poorly briefed on issues of social responsibility. Training and development programmes will be needed not only to explain the technicalities of social responsibility in business but also to facilitate a mind-set change amongst managers that this issue will be inextricably linked to organisational and individual manager performance. An important part of this is ensuring that resources are committed wisely on ventures that clearly benefit the organisation, rather than just satisfying external stakeholders.

Notes

1. For example, with Johnson & Johnson's Credo which has been guiding the company since 1943.
2. Available online at www.sustainable-development.gov.uk.
3. This is shown, for example, with the European Integrated Pollution Prevention and Control Directive which demands proactive prevention of pollution, rather than merely end-of-pipe pollution control for the most polluting industries.
4. For example, with the recent increase in insurance claims comes a significant increase in the cost of public and employer liability insurance (Essen 2002).

References

Ballard, D. (2002) The Danger Lies in Obscuring the Real Issues, in *Sustainable Development* series edited by the European Business Forum in *International Herald Tribune*, Monday, Sept. 2.

Bryan, L.L. (2002) "Just-in-time strategy for a turbulent World", *The McKinsey Quarterly*, No. 2 from website www.mckinseyquarterly.com accessed 10/6/02.

Bush, G. (2002) "Time well invested", in *Business Sustainability – Business Guide 2002*, Caspian Publishing Ltd, pp. 48–53.

Colegrave, S. (2002) The Brent Spar Story, p. 12, in *Cause Related Marketing, Critical Marketing Knowledge from Chartered Institute of Marketing*, CIM.

Coombes, P. and Watson, M. (2000) "Three surveys on corporate governance", *The McKinsey Quarterly*, No. 4, pp. 74–77.

Coyne, K.P. and Witter, J.W. (2002) "What makes your stock price go up and down", *The McKinsey Quarterly*, No. 2, pp. 29–39.

Court, D., French, T.D., McGuire, T.I. and Partington, M. (1999) "Marketing in 3D", *The McKinsey Quarterly*, No. 4, pp. 6–17.

Cowe, R. (2002) "Winning board games", *Business Sustainability: Business Guide 2002*, Caspian Publishing Ltd, pp. 6–11.

Davies, P. (2002) "Investing in local communities", *Business Sustainability: Business Guide 2002*, Caspian Publishing Ltd, pp. 41–47.

Dayal, S., Landesberg, H. and Zeisser, M. (2000) "Building digital brands", *The McKinsey Quarterly*, No. 2, pp. 42–51.

Essen, Y. (2002) Souring Public Liability Costs Stun Industry from www.telegraph.co.uk. Filed 16/8/02.

Ernst and Young (2002) "Corporate social responsibility: a survey of global companies", *Environment and Sustainability Services* accessed from website www.ey.com on 16/11/02.

EU (2001) European Union Green Paper on Promoting a European Framework for Corporate Social Responsibility, presented by the Commission of the European Communities, Brussels, 18/7/01 COM (2001) 366 final website icsca.org.au accessed 23/11/02.

Faruk, A. (2002) "Corporate responsibility: beyond niceness", *The Ashridge Journal*, Summer 2002, pp. 28–31 from www.asridge.com\directions accessed 7/12/02.

Felton, R.F. and Watson, M. (2002) "Change across the Board", *The McKinsey Quarterly*, No. 4, pp. 31–45.

Gilmour, G. and Caplan, A. (2002) *The Future of Corporate Reporting: Corporate Social Reporting – Who Cares?* PricewaterhouseCoopers website www.pwcglobal.com accessed 16/11/02.

Gonella, C. (2002) "How to measure it", *Business Sustainability: Business Guide*, Caspian Publishing Ltd, pp. 65–71.

Grimshaw, C., Howard, M. and Willmott, M. (1997) *The Responsible Organisation*, The Future Foundation.

Henderson, D. (2001) "Misguided virtue: false notion of corporate social responsibility", *New Zealand Business Roundtable*, June 2001, from website www.nzbr.org.nz accessed 16/11/02.

Hill and Knowlton (2002) *Scandals Turn Spotlight on Company Reputation*. Press release 12/9/02 on Corporate Reputation Watch 2002 survey of 800 CEO in Europe & North America, from www.euractive.org, accessed 30/10/02.

KPMG (2002) Corporate Governance in Europe KPMG Survey 2001/02, from website www.kpmg.co.uk accessed 24/5/02.

Kraus, B. (2002) Personal Communication from the CEO of ERM Certification Verification Services (ERM CVS) at *ERM CVS ISO 14001 Lead Auditors Training Course*, 8–12 April 2002.

Lebensmittel, Z. (1999) *Working on the "Something Better" Trend – The Future of Nutrition*. Interview with Peter Brabeck CEO of Nestlé SA by Renate Sulzmann, 8 Oct. 1999. English Translation from Nestlé SA intranet pages accessed 2000.

Marshall, A. (2002) "The road less travelled", *Business Sustainability: Business Guide*, Caspian Publishing Ltd, pp. 25–29.

McIntosh, M., Leipziger, D., Jones, K. and Coleman, G. (1998) *Successful Strategies for Responsible Companies: Corporate Citizenship*, Financial Times Pitman Publishing.

Miller, A. (2002) "Developing legal trends", *Business Sustainability: Business Guide*, Caspian Publishing Ltd, pp. 78–24.

New Zealand Management (2002) "'Do-good' Companies do Well", *New Zealand Management*, Vol. 49, No. 8, p. 8, Sept. 2002 (Proquest).

OECD (2001) The OECD guidelines for multinational enterprises and global instruments for corporate responsibility. Background and Issues Paper, 16 May 2001 accessed from www.oecd.org on 16/11/02.

Porter, M.E. and Kramer, M.R. (2002) "The competitive advantage of corporate philanthropy", *Harvard Business Review*, December, pp. 57–68.

Preston, A. (2001) Rewards Likely to Come from Greater Openness: Transparency by Adrian Preston: Companies may fee burdened by legislation and other pressures requiring that they have a more transparent information strategy, but they may ultimately benefit from it. *Financial Times*: London, Nov. 15 (Proquest).

Robinson, M. (2001) Human Rights and Global Civilisation, 2nd Annual BP Lecture by Mary Robinson, United Nations High Commissioner for Human Rights. The British Museum, London 29/11/01. Speech transcript from www.business-humanrights.org/UN-High-Commissioner-Human-rights.htm accessed 23/12/02.

Rose, C. (1998) *The Turning of the 'Spar'*, Greenpeace.

Seppala, N. (2002) Is Environmental Reporting just Public Relations? in *Sustainable Development* series edited by the European Business Forum in *International Herald Tribune*, Monday, Sept. 2.

Sillanpää, M. (2002) "Get the balance right", *Business Sustainability: Business Guide*, Caspian Publishing Ltd.

Steadman, D. (2002) "Keeping your good name can provide the key to success", *Sunday Business*, 15 Sept. (Proquest).

Stonehouse, G., Hamill, J., Campbell, D. and Purdie, T. (2000) *Global and Transnational Business: Strategy and Management*, Chichester, John Wiley & Sons Ltd.

Stubbs, J. (2002) "Entering the Mainstream", *Cause Related Marketing, Critical Marketing Knowledge from Chartered Institute of Marketing*, CIM, p. 4.

Taylor, C. (2000) New Twist for Old News in *BC Business*, April 28, i4, p. 11 (Infotrac).

Toomer, C. (2002) "The buck stops where?" *Business Sustainability: Business Guide*, Caspian Publishing Ltd, pp. 54–57.

Watts, D. and Copnell, T. (2002) "Directors and durability", *Business Sustainability: Business Guide*, Caspain Publishing Ltd, pp. 12–17.

Waugh, S. (2002a) "More than company conscience", *Cause Related Marketing, Critical Marketing Knowledge from Chartered Institute of Marketing*, CIM, p. 5.

Waugh, S. (2002b) "Older and warmer", *Cause Related Marketing, Critical Marketing Knowledge from Chartered Institute of Marketing*, CIM, p. 18.

WBCSD (2001) The Business Case for Sustainable Development. Making a Difference Towards the Johannesburg Summit 2002. World Business Council for Sustainable Development, Sept. accessed from www.wbcsd.ch on 7/12/02.

WBCSD (2002) Corporate Social Responsibility. The WBCSD's Journey. World Business Council for Sustainable Development, Jan. 2002 accessed from www.wbcsd.ch on 7/12/02.

White, A.L. (2002) Company Reporting Comes of Age, in *Sustainable Development* series edited by the European Business Forum in *International Herald Tribune*, Monday, Sept. 2.

Windsor, D. (2001) "The future of corporate social responsibility", *International Journal of Organizational Analysis*, Vol. 9, No. 3, pp. 225–26 (Proquest).

WWF (2002) World Wildlife Fund Living Planet Report 2002. www.wwf-uk.org.

The way people are managed

Managing performance

Elizabeth Houldsworth

Part II opens with the key area of managing people performance. This is an over-arching theme of how people are managed – in order to deliver high levels of performance.

Introduction

Teachers, police, City 'high-flyers' along with the majority of the work-force have in common the fact that their performance is increasingly being managed, monitored and measured. This chapter explores performance management from a multi-disciplinary perspective in the first instance before adopting an HR perspective in keeping with the rest of the book. It begins by describing the high-profile positioning of performance management within organisations from both the public and the private sector and the emphasis on efficiency, best value and performance targets which has created a multitude of practitioner books and articles, consultants and HR professionals seeking to deliver heightened organisational performance.

Before dealing with performance management and how organisations manage performance, the first section initially questions what is 'performance' anyway? 'Performance' seems to mean different things within different organisations and to different individuals. Therefore, for the line or project manager, who is essentially a 'performance manager' it is important that he or she be aware of the variety of different meanings and ways of explaining, describing or accounting for performance.

Having looked at these fundamentals, the next section examines in more detail the myriad of ways in which performance initiatives are being interpreted, designed and implemented within organisations. In so doing we will chart the development of performance management, from its origins in performance appraisal, through management by objectives and ultimately to its positioning as a key business process. Particular developments along the way, such as European Model for Business Excellence (EFQM) and balanced scorecard will also be referred to. In considering performance management and its evolution the chapter will make reference to appropriate theories from the field of HRM.

The third section of this chapter prompts the reader to question whether performance management is about measuring or motivating employees. It considers the linkages between performance management and motivational theory. The fourth and final section seeks to ground these theories by use of real examples to illustrate the differing guises which attempts to manage performance may take.

Defining performance and how performance may be managed

To move straight to a description of the evolution of performance management could be judged to be putting the cart before the horse. How can performance *management* be properly be addressed before looking at performance?

Performance and its importance have become all pervasive in all aspects of modern life. We have all become susceptible to falling under the influence of performance in our ways of looking at things and people, as well as our ways of behaving. The notion of performance has become of central importance for our perception of our activities, our self-perception and self-worth and our understanding of the world.

Corvellec (1997, 2001) tells us that

> In organisational life performance touches on every aspect of business administration. Any review of the management literature would confirm this. Browsing through management journals, one can find articles that relate an organisation's performance to a firm's ownership or location, culture, organisational learning, top management compensation, labour force quality, team building, management control systems, balanced scorecards, information technology, even diet and exercise programmes!

Performance is, therefore, the ultimate life or death criterion of business, yet surprisingly a uniform definition of organisational performance has not emerged. Definitions of performance vary, in part as a reflection of the author or 'measurer' of performance. Gomez-Mejia *et al.* (1987) declare that performance is 'a composite of (the firms) financial success and the extent to which it maximises the welfare of its stockholders'. Others do not share this commitment to a solely financial approach. Among them, Meyer and Zucker (1989) claim that organisational performance is a function of the attainment of objectives or goals.

For most management practitioners and academics it is probably true to say that performance is concerned with measuring some kind of output. As a result practitioners and particularly consultants have spent many years developing a range of performance measures. However, this is not to say that for corporate managers it is enough to simply 'hit your numbers'. As Corvellec (2001) suggests, 'increasingly it is about "performing right on the organisation's scene". This includes fitting the social rules that govern dress or vocabulary, being perceived as a reliable team member, or endorsing the official organisational reality as the only one'.

So, performance is about both achieving hard targets as well as the ways in which this measurable performance is delivered. What emerges is a two-category framework to capture both the 'what' (of performance) and the 'how'. The former is usually seen to include the hard targets by which the organisation will be judged externally whereas the latter is concerned with achieving the values and behaviours which the organisation has declared are important for itself. Figure 5.1 illustrates this.

Figure 5.1 Understanding performance

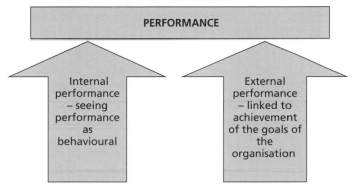

- A two-category model emerges:

PERFORMANCE

Internal performance – seeing performance as behavioural

External performance – linked to achievement of the goals of the organisation

The link between people management and business performance

A 'Captains of Industry'[1] survey at the end of 1999 reported that around half of those surveyed anticipated purchasing consultancy services in the area of pay and performance 'in the near future'. Although commissioned by a management consultancy organisation as a part of ongoing market research, the results are not surprising when one considers how common the terms 'performance management' and 'performance improvement' have become within organisations.

For a number of reasons, therefore, the management of performance has become a quest akin to the Holy Grail. These reasons include within the public sector, the 'Modernising Government' agenda that has raised the emphasis on outcomes and measures of success. Within the private sector concern with 'shareholder value' has similarly put pressure on organisations to predict and deliver business improvements. Not surprisingly against such a backdrop, consultancy firms of both large and small size are offering support to organisations in the design and implementation of all aspects of 'performance management' with the promise of heightening organisational performance as a result.

People are increasingly now exalted as the most important asset of any firm, see for example Ulrich's (1997) book which concludes: 'Ultimately a firm's human resource community holds crucial responsibility for adding value and delivering results'. Hendry and Pettigrew (1990) explain that this emphasis on human resources as an organisational asset goes back at least to Drucker in the 1950s. Part of the reason for such interest in recent years has been driven by a belief that effective people management will lead to tangible business benefits. Much has been written about new approaches to HR, strategic HR and the link to business performance, for example see Huselid *et al.* (1997), Richardson and Thompson (1999) and Guest *et al.* (2000), and of course, earlier chapters of this book.

A CIPD research report in 2000 (Guest *et al.* 2000) considers exactly the sort of questions we have already looked at in the previous section – if we are looking at performance how exactly should this performance be defined? Most research to date has focused on measures such as productivity or financial results. Researchers in the US, particularly Huselid *et al.* (1997), are currently working on the refinement of such measures, but differences in accounting practices between the UK and the US make comparisons difficult. If we want to understand why HRM contributes to performance, surely we also need to measure the HRM outcomes of employee attitudes and behaviour, internal indicators such as productivity and quality of goods and services and external indicators such as sales and financial performance?

An IPD study by Richardson and Thompson (1999) reports that there are in the region of 30 empirical studies that have sought to address the relationship between HR practices and business performance. This fieldwork has been pioneered in the USA and the bulk of the articles do report studies there. However, there are now a growing number in the UK. Pfeffer (1998) cites evidence that HR practices can raise shareholder value by between $20,000 and $40,0000 per employee. A study by Huselid (1997) suggested that the 'market value per employee' was strongly correlated with the sophistication of the HR practices adopted. Similarly in the UK, although they did not put a sum to it, Patterson *et al.* (1997) found changes in profitability among a panel of over 60 small to medium size manufacturing businesses correlated with the adoption of certain HR practices.

Further on in this section we will seek to categorise performance initiatives into two broad types – those which demand a quantifiable return on investment (see later description of the Michigan School) and those which concentrate instead on the less tangible motivational benefits (see later description of the Harvard School).

Before moving on to discuss the evolution of performance management it is worthwhile taking a few moments to reflect upon the following questions:

● How is 'performance' defined and measured in your organisation?

● Is this similar or different to other organisations/industries with which you are familiar?

● How is your own performance managed?

Defining performance management

This section will seek to define performance management and to provide an account of its evolution. To set the scene, a practitioner definition as to what is meant by performance management from an HR perspective is provided below:

> A process for establishing a shared understanding about what is to be achieved, and how it is to be achieved; an approach to managing people which increases the probability of achieving job-related success. (Weiss and Hartle 1997)

The definition captures the fact that performance management is about an ongoing process of managing people with the aim of increasing job-related success. Within any organisation professing to have a performance management system, it is usually possible to discern the three stages. These are depicted in Figure 5.2 planning; managing and reviewing. The stages may be emphasised to greater or lesser degree, depending on the design of the process and the organisation's culture. An account of what is typically contained within each stage may be found after the Figure 5.2.

Figure 5.2 Performance management cycle

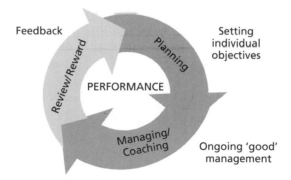

Stage 1: planning

This stage typically embraces:

- definition of job responsibilities;
- setting performance expectations;
- goal or objective setting at the beginning of the period.

Historically, in many organisations this stage occurred on the 'anniversary date' of an individual joining the company. However, more recently, the trend has been towards a convergence around the business planning cycle of the organisation. Although this places a heavy workload burden on managers – particularly those with a number of direct reports, it does support the notion of using performance planning to cascade the strategy. In order for this cascade to be effective, the business plan for the year and a set of objectives need to be communicated prior to the objective setting period. Wherever possible more senior managers should set their objectives before they discuss objectives with their direct reports and so on. The objective setting and planning discussion may include reference to development planning or this may be carried over to a formal development review discussion.

Stage 2: managing

This stage typically embraces:

- monitoring performance and achievement towards objectives;
- feedback and coaching;
- competency review;
- development planning.

At its most simple this 'phase' of performance management is difficult to discern within the organisation. It may not involve any 'formal reviews' but be about good management practice, regular informal updates and effective coaching and mentoring. In organisations where this cannot be assumed to be happening, or where more formal processes are thought to be required, it is common to have mid-year, quarterly and even monthly reviews of progress. One or more of these discussions may be set aside specifically to discuss development plans.

Stage 3: reviewing

This stage typically embraces:

- formal performance appraisal, resulting in a rating if used;
- links to reward, if deployed within the organisation;
- possible 360 degree feedback around competencies or other feedback tools.

It is around reviewing performance that managers and staff often have the most vivid recollections about performance management. We are told that practice has come someway since the days of the old-style 'annual reprisal' interview. However, ask any group of managers to rate their own last appraisal against a scale of 1–5 and you will find few scores higher than 3, with the majority being

1s and 2s. It can be quite sobering for managers if they are asked to reflect on the probability of their own appraisal skills producing a more positive response from direct reports. What gets assessed in the annual review differs depending on the design of the process. Achievement against objectives will invariably be assessed. Some organisations also include a full competency review (i.e. looking at the individual's fit with the competency requirements of the role, as specified in the job description); others review the achievement of development objectives.

Ratings become problematical when managers describe the performance of all their team as being 'above average'. 'Ratings creep' can occur in organisations as a result, with good performance becoming the 'new average'. For organisations applying a pay matrix to the outcomes from the ratings exercise this not only impacts on the paybill but also erodes the 'differentiation' element so that high performers are no longer really rewarded above and beyond those whose performance is average or below. In such instances the high performers are likely to be demotivated as a result. A recent survey (Houldsworth 2003) of 400 line managers reported that 69 per cent saw a link between the performance management process within their organisation and salary or bonus. However, only 46 per cent felt that reward was effectively differentiated based on performance outcomes.

One way around such problems is to apply 'forced distribution' which has gained popularity in some organisations. An example is the 'vitality curve' from GE, which Welch (2003) expounded during his time as CEO. Under this approach managers were forced to rank all their direct reports in terms of the top 20 per cent, the core 70 per cent and the bottom 10 per cent. The underlying intention being that each year the bottom 10 per cent are removed from the business, thus raising the 'performance bar'.

The evolution of performance management

In practitioner terms it is possible to trace the development of performance management from its initial origins as 'management by objectives' a personnel driven appraisal process, through to the performance management or performance improvement processes of the 21st century. In rhetoric at least, these are very different. During the 1980s many organisations became more 'performance-oriented'. There was an increased focus on defining the outputs of jobs, and on linking job performance to the objectives of the organisation. This was the era of 'management by objectives'. During the 1990s performance management began to be seen as more of a core management process – capable of delivering the business vision by developing and reinforcing the key behaviours/ values.

The continuum captured in Figure 5.3 reflects a study by Armstrong and Baron (1998) who suggested the following trends in the development of performance management from the early to late 1990s.

Figure 5.3 Performance management continuum of evolution

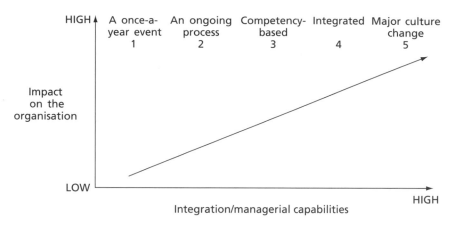

Source: Model produced by Hay Group (1995).

1991 **FROM**	1998 **TO**
SYSTEM	*PROCESS*
APPRAISAL	*JOINT REVIEW*
OUTPUTS	*INPUTS*
PRP driven	*DEVELOPMENT driven*
RATINGS COMMON	*RATINGS LESS COMMON*
TOP DOWN	*360 DEGREE FEEDBACK*
DIRECTIVE	*SUPPORTIVE*
MONOLITHIC	*FLEXIBLE*
OWNED BY HR	*OWNED BY USERS*

Source: Adapted from Armstrong and Baron (1998).

Both the Hay Group continuum and the work of Armstrong and Baron suggest that performance management may be seen to have grown out of its 'appraisal' box (point 1 of the continuum). At point 2 the continuum suggests that an ongoing process of some type is in place, likely to be linked to the business planning cycle. Here one would expect to see management by objective type approaches, with an emphasis on the 'what' of performance. From the late 1980s however, the trend has been to include not just the 'what' of performance but also the 'how'.

Point 3 of the continuum therefore reflects a key milestone for many organisations in performance management development. It includes the 'what' of performance, expressed through objectives and targets, and the 'how' of performance, invariably expressed through behavioural competencies. For more information on the inclusion of competencies in performance management (see Guile and Fonda 1988).

> **Example – BT**
>
> An example already written up in the public domain is the case of British Telecom (BT) (IDS 1999). This presents a fairly typical description of the kind of performance management intervention rolled out in mid-1990s. It states that the performance review at BT aims to place individual achievement and competencies in the context of its business values and direction. The company has structured an appraisal mechanism as a continuous process with employees receiving regular feedback on performance with formal meetings taking place at least quarterly, supplemented with an annual performance review. Individual objectives are linked to the company's scorecard, with a competency review being incorporated. In the case of BT, seven core management competencies have been defined and in 2002/2003, a reviewed approach to performance management was implemented to strengthen the 'competency-based' element of the review, supporting this via a computer-based system.

Beyond level 3, performance management interventions are typified by their fully integrated nature – they are 'how' people are managed and are a key aspect of business management. At the highest level, performance management is being used as a vehicle either to introduce or reinforce a major change programme. Performance management can achieve this in that it typically includes:

- visioning/top team workshop and resultant strategy clarification;

- statement around key priorities and organisational values in their pursuit (i.e. the essence of what and how);

- communication internally and externally;

- management training/briefings;

- cascade to all managers and all employees as to what is important around here.

Full-blown performance management may therefore be seen to be related to the appraisals of old, but is very much the strategic, 'grown-up cousin'. 'State-of-the-art' performance management is now typically described as an ongoing process of good management practice throughout the year. According to the changes in practice reported by Armstrong and Baron (1998), manager and individual are now increasingly involved in a joint review which places emphasis on both the objectives ('what' of performance) and also the behaviours associated with success ('how' of performance). A development plan will usually be produced and although ratings still occur at most annual review meetings, they are not given the emphasis of old and the link to pay is usually less direct. If it is done well, performance management is espoused as motivational and developmental, capable of supporting and reinforcing a culture change.

Against such a description it is easy to see why performance management has developed to occupy a key people management role, as depicted in Figure 5.4.

Figure 5.4 Performance management as a fundamental of people management

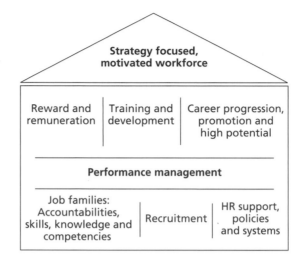

The model suggests that core aspects of HR exist as the building blocks of a people management process. Performance management exists as a key element of the integrated structure once individuals have been recruited and roles defined. It then serves to drive reward, training and development, promotion and career progression. The result should be motivated employees aware of and committed to the mission and strategy of the organisation. Although the 'house' image in the figure might serve to capture the main elements of a specialised HR role or department, this chapter assumes that all the 'building blocks' will be relevant to all people managers within an organisation, recognising that they might call on specialist HR support for a number of aspects. In particular, the management of performance is likely to be key; not only as it integrates and coordinates with the whole gamut of people management processes within an organisation, but also because it is one area where the manager can make a real difference to team culture and hence its performance through leadership style and the application of motivational techniques.

Using the theories of motivation to underpin performance management

Motivation is a key issue for those involved in designing, implementing and operating a performance management process. Earlier authors have suggested that an individual's performance is a product of their ability level and their motivation level (Vroom 1964):

$$\text{Performance} = \text{Function (ability} \times \text{motivation)}$$

Because of the complexity of motivation, there is no single answer to the question of 'what motivates people to perform well'? It is not the intention to rehearse or to critique all the earlier literature on motivation. However, a short overview of some of the main theories which *may* be used in relation to performance management are included below.

- *Extrinsic motivation* – This is related to the 'tangible' rewards such as salary and fringe benefits, security and promotion. Such tangible rewards are often determined at the organisational level.

- *Intrinsic motivation* – This is related to 'psychological' rewards such as the opportunity to use one's ability, a sense of challenge, achievement and recognition. The strength of this type of motivation is usually influenced by the actions and behaviours of other people in the organisation.

Content theories – These place emphasis on what motivates an individual – the non-conscious aspects of people's needs; their strengths; and the goals they pursue in order to satisfy these needs. The theories suggest that individuals behave as they do in order to meet their needs. Examples of these would include:

- *Hierarchy of needs* (Maslow 1943) with the five level hierarchy of needs.

- *Three motives theory* (McClelland 1987) who describes need for achievement, affiliation and power as the three key social motives at work.

Process theories – These place emphasis on the actual process of motivation that is how an individual is motivated. They are concerned with the conscious aspects of motivation: how behaviour is initiated, directed and sustained. Major theories include:

- *Expectancy theory* (Vroom 1964) – The strength of an intention to act upon a goal depends on the degree of conviction that an act will be followed by a given outcome, and the attraction of that outcome to the individual.

- *Equity theory* (Adams 1965) – Based on the belief that people want to be treated fairly, this theory proposes that people compare themselves with others to see if their treatment is equitable.

- *Goal setting theory* (Locke 1968) – This theory describes how people strive to achieve goals in order to satisfy their emotions and desires, which guides individual behaviour, and therefore performance.

- *Reinforcement theory* – With its origins in behaviourism there is a large amount of research evidence to suggest that people will exert higher levels of motivation in performing tasks which are reinforced. (See Luthans and Kreitner 1985 for a description in the organisational behaviour area.)

Managing the performance of others would appear to involve both intrinsic and extrinsic motivation. The actual process of performance management relates to intrinsically motivating people through performance reviews, training and development and objective setting whereas the actual outcomes of performance management, the 'tangible' rewards, relate to extrinsic motivation. The motivational theories have implications for practitioners at each of the three stages of performance management: planning, managing, reviewing, and these are described below.

Stage 1: planning

To maximise motivation at this stage, it makes sense for the goals set to be clear, specific, challenging and accepted by the individual. In addition, an individual's performance 'contract' must be clarified and managed in terms of targets and development objectives as well as behaviours. Problems further down the line might be prevented if at this stage the likelihood of possible rewards can be effectively communicated.

The motives of an individual can also be considered in this stage. For example, setting too challenging goals is not likely to maximise motivation, particularly for those with a high achievement drive.

Goal setting and associated processes and techniques play a key role here with most workshops and training programmes emphasising research around the increased probability of achieving an objective if a goal is set. For example, an individual who wishes to lose weight is more likely to achieve this goal if they set a SMART target such as:

I will have lost 3 kilos by the time I go on holiday in June.

SMART is taken in this instance to mean SPECIFIC, MEASURABLE, ACHIE-VEABLE, RELEVANT and TIME-BOUND. Once a SMART objective has been defined it is possible to work out the steps and possible milestones which will be required in order to achieve the overarching goal.

Stage 2: managing

Feedback and coaching can play an important role as reinforcers and shapers of previous behaviour. Team members are likely to continue delivering high performance for the team leader who notes this performance and takes the time to thank them for their efforts. Regular feedback is important to all high achievers and the skill required to provide honest and constructive feedback should not be under-estimated. For those with a high need for power or affiliation, the method of delivery of feedback will be particularly important as they will be anxious to avoid confrontation.

Providing coaching for ongoing performance improvement is another key aspect of managing performance. Although many managers self-report that they are involved in considerable coaching activities (particularly given the current fashion around it), it is likely (and consultancy experiences confirm) that direct reports do not always recognise or acknowledge this to be happening. For a high-performing manager it may often be easier and quicker to correct poor performance by saying 'do it like this' than by really coaching the individual so that he or she works through the problem and is able to respond to it in the future.

Stage 3: reviewing

Reinforcement and equity are extremely important to motivation at this stage. Consequently recognising appropriate behaviours and rewarding them is paramount. Inequities in pay awards or promotion can result in either improved or reduced performance, due to changed motivation levels. The problem, which will always arise at this stage, is that one person's equity is another's inequity. This highlights the importance of setting the expectations of the individual at the beginning of the performance management process in the planning stage.

This stage also includes rewarding performance. In some organisations there is a conscious link to pay and in others it is more subtle. According to Armstrong and Baron (1998) there was a trend during the 1990s away from 'hard' performance related pay (PRP). They reported reasons for this to include the problem of managing expectations, having sufficient money in the pot, equity and fairness and management capability to take and communicate decisions. However, a recent survey (Houldsworth 2003) found that 69 per cent of managers surveyed did report a link between performance management and base pay or bonus.

So far this section has looked at the stages of the performance management cycle and considered how they might be impacted by motivational approaches. Now it is time to consider managers' experiences of performance management and a framework for understanding its implementation.

Managers experiences of the two faces of performance management

This section moves on to look at some of organisational realities around managers' experiences of performance management. It suggests a possible framework of performance initiatives, based on hard or soft manifestations of HRM and explains some of the tools which have developed to support such approaches. It then provides two short organisational case studies to illustrate the different approaches.

An article in the *British Journal of Management* by Fletcher and Williams (1996) suggests that there are potentially many beneficial elements to a performance management system. These include:

- the development of a mission statement and business plan and the enhancement of communication so that employees are aware not only of the objectives and business plan, but can also contribute to their formulation;

- the clarification of individual responsibilities and accountabilities (through job descriptions, clear role definitions and so on), leading to the defining and measurement of individual performance;

- the implementation of appropriate reward strategies (which may include an element of performance-related pay).

In addition the same authors report that performance management approaches deliver benefits including ownership by line management (rather than by the personnel or HR department) and increased emphasis on shared corporate goals and values. At the same time it is claimed (IPM 1992) that performance management should result not only in profitability or in the improved delivery of services, but also in an enhancement of employee motivation, satisfaction and identification with the organisation.

Although the rhetoric about performance management may be all about its positive influences, the organisational reality, as experienced by line managers is not always so. See, for example, Houldsworth (2000) for a description of interviews with line managers involved in performance management. Line managers' views about managing performance seem to include:

- assessment

- judgement

- getting more out of people

- control

- raising false expectations

- managing the paybill.

It would appear therefore that there are 'two faces' to performance management, one around development, motivation and two-way communication, with another around assessment and monitoring. In part, we can understand this dichotomy by reference to the HR literature which has already described approaches to managing people that may be described as 'hard' or 'soft'. Guest (1987) and Storey (1992) view the distinction as being whether the emphasis is placed on the *human* or on the *resource*. Soft HRM therefore is associated with the human relations movement, the utilisation of individual talents and McGregor's Theory Y (1960) perspective on individuals (with a belief that individuals are essentially self-motivated and desire to work hard to achieve good results). Soft HRM is also associated with the goals of flexibility and adaptability and implies that communication plays a central role in management.

Beer *et al.* (1985) are commonly cited in relation to this view on HRM, and have become known as the 'Harvard school' of thinking on this issue. They place most emphasis on 'people' focus, seeing the impact of managers on organisational climate as being at the heart of HRM, along with the relationship between management and other employees. They recognise the existence of a range of HR levers and the context of stakeholder interests as well as situational factors. The policy areas, which they identified within HRM, are employee influence, human resource flow and reward systems and work systems. The rationale behind this may be found in the assumption that committed employees will be more satisfied, more productive and more adaptable. Beer *et al.* (1985) see this as a key dimension, resulting not only in more loyalty and better performance, but also in self-worth, dignity, psychological involvement and identity for the individual. Other authors, including Legge (1995a,b) have noted that employees working under such an HRM system will positively commit and give added value through labour, as a result of feeling trusted, developed and having control over their own work.

Hard HRM on the other hand stresses the quantitative and business-strategic aspects of management – the 'headcount resource' – as 'rational a way as for any other factor of production' (Storey 1992). It has been referred to as utilitarian instrumentalism and focuses on the importance of 'strategic fit' where human resource policies and practices are closely linked to the strategic objectives of the organisation with the aim of heightening competitive advantage. In terms of its view of human nature it has been seen to have an emphasis on McGregor's Theory X (i.e. people dislike and will try to avoid work) leading to tight managerial control through close direction. This approach has been described by Fombrun *et al.* (1984) (known as the Michigan school). They describe the critical managerial tasks as being 'to align the formal structure and the HR systems so that they drive the strategic objectives of the organisation'. The key HR systems and processes they had in mind were: selection, appraisal, training and development and rewards, and they sought the alignment of these in specific ways to channel behaviour and create an appropriate organisational culture. For a fuller discussion of hard and soft HRM (see Truss *et al.* 1997).

Although the types as described may be seen as 'extremes' it is perhaps possible to discern elements of them in the design of HR policies and practices within your own organisation. In particular, it may be possible to identify the philosophy underpinning each approach in the design and implementation of performance management initiatives. The big distinction appears to revolve around whether the organisation is seeking to 'manage' performance through leadership and motivational managerial styles or if it is seeking to 'improve' performance through its careful measurement and monitoring. More detail on these two manifestations of performance initiatives is discussed below.

Performance management

This may be described as being more aligned with softer approaches to HRM than with harder. Its emphasis is upon 'employee commitment', the focus is therefore organisational climate initiatives, managerial style feedback, personal development and employee involvement in the objective-setting and review processes.

Such approaches take as their starting point the premise that an essential element of the role of a manager is to 'manage' the performance of others in order to ensure they have clarity around what is expected of them. Good management it is espoused, results in greater motivation and commitment from employees who are hence more inclined to deliver 'discretionary effort'. This approach is typified by management development, leadership and coaching interventions. Although its end goal is still around improved business performance, this approach is still associated more with 'soft' HR than with hard (or strategic) HR. Business benefits are delivered by virtue of the fact that it equates with good management practice.

Performance improvement

Increased emphasis on the business benefits of HRM and growth of HR accounting has led to a greater demand within organisations to see a tangible 'return' from performance management. In many instances it is no longer enough to accept in good faith the assertion that good management leads to greater employee commitment and effort and hence to improved performance. This has contributed to an approach to managing performance that has more in common with harder HRM approach than with softer ones.

Such approaches take as their starting point the goal of business benefits. This may be couched directly in financial terms (e.g. economic value-added approaches) or a collection of measures, such as a balanced scorecard to combine both 'hard' and 'soft' measures. Employee motivation, commitment and development are still considered, but within the context of driving up overall business performance. There may well be attempts to quantify these 'softer' aspects of performance, for example, through competency coverage. The approach rests on the premise that organisations struggle to clearly define, articulate and cascade their strategy. By clearly articulating what needs to be done by a series of a set of metrics, it is believed that quantifiable business benefits will result, that is 'what gets measured gets done'. The two manifestations of performance initiatives are summarised in Figure 5.5.

Experience in research and consultancy within the area of performance management between 1995 and 2003 suggests that within the past five years there has been a trend towards harder performance improvement approaches. This is perhaps not surprising given the rise of management accountability in Britain and other parts of the world. As a result, HRM and personnel professionals have increasingly been asked to 'justify personnel work in accounting terms'. One of the most common means of working towards this end has been the popularisation of the balanced scorecard methodology.

The balanced scorecard

Originally conceptualised (Eccles 1991; Kaplan and Norton 1996) as a means of overcoming the short termist tendencies of management accountancy, the

Figure 5.5 Summary of different styles of performance initiatives

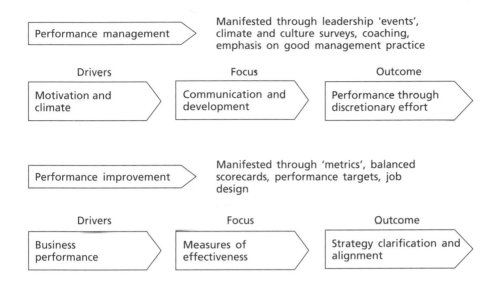

balanced scorecard should in theory allow for a full range of measures, hard and soft, long and short term. The balanced scorecard is premised on the notion that measurement motivates and aims to move away from the problems that a short-term reliance on financial measures alone creates. The scorecard outlines four different perspectives under which to identify performance measures and track organisational performance. These are summarised in Figure 5.6.

The first step for an organisation in term of deploying the balanced scorecard is to produce a 'driver model' as a means to clarify and cascade strategy – as illustrated in Figure 5.7.

Having produced a driver model, the organisation seeks to identify key measures of success which in a causal fashion drive success. The intention being that measures associated with learning and growth (e.g. a measure of the fit between employees and role requirements), has an impact on the efficiency of internal processes and hence of what is delivered to the customer. These in turn impact on financial measures via a causal flow.

In theory because of its inclusion of both 'hard' financial measures and 'softer' measures associated with training and development (e.g. the number of managers having personal development plans) the balanced scorecard can be seen to combine elements of both the hard and soft approaches. However, in practice this is difficult to achieve. Although organisations may seek to produce 'balanced measures' the default tends to be to revert to those which are 'easy' to measure. Things that are easy to measure are not necessarily the most useful, and are often primarily financial. Even where a good mix of measures is achieved, their implementation – for example, via a link to

Figure 5.6 The balanced scorecard categorisations

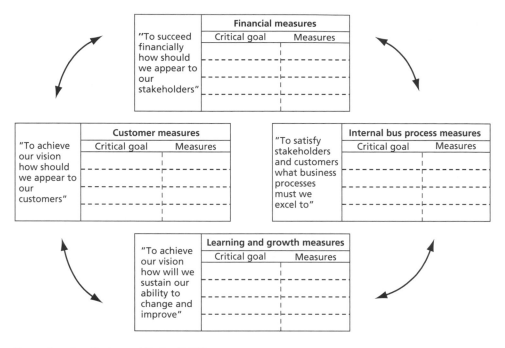

Source: Based on Kaplan and Norton (1996).

executive remuneration is often to highlight those which have a short-term financial impact.

Having described a framework for understanding different types of perform-ance initiative, this section provides two examples of different organisational practice.

Figure 5.7 An illustrative driver model

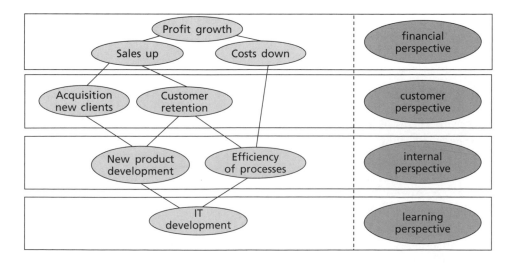

An example of a performance management approach: linked to soft HRM

Our first example (which we will refer to as 'Company A') is a former Government Agency, now working more closely with the private sector and increasingly being charged with profitability targets. The organisation was established six years ago under an enthusiastic and entrepreneurial Chief Executive. From its small-scale origins (with 10 staff initially) it has now grown in size to 200 employees. This has meant that a range of more professional 'support services' have been implemented. The Management Services Director has recently appointed a full-time HR manager and one of his priorities for the year for this new individual is to work on both motivation and morale and performance management. Many of the staff within the organisation are young, and for many this is their first job. They report informally that the culture is one of 'blame' and 'name and shame'. Staff turnover is surprisingly high for the local area and exit interviews suggest lack of development and support from managers as key reasons for leaving.

Against this backdrop the organisation decided to review its approach to performance management, moving away from the older style Civil Service approach which had been used before. This allowed for a re-design of the whole process and Company A (via a Steering Group of the most senior managers apart from the CEO) determined that it would focus on both objectives and development plans. There would be no overall 'rating of performance' although managers were all to be asked every six months for their current assessment of potential amongst all their direct reports. The organisation did not have a highly geared PRP system, but a link did exist at a subtle level between the performance discussions and resultant salary increases.

In order to emphasise development they decided to include a 'compulsory objective' for all people managers around conducting timely performance reviews, quarterly reviews and the production of development plans. At the same time, the HR Manager persuaded the Board to look at culture within the organisation – where are they looking to get to in the light of their increasingly commercial imperatives? This work led to the creation of an eight-strong-competencies model, linked to the new values of 'Succeeding Together'; 'Serving the Locality'; 'Honesty and Integrity'; and 'Delivery Focus'. Not only were these competencies incorporated in the development and performance review sessions, but at the same time a 360-degree feedback tool was piloted with the Executive. It produced interesting results. Most of the Executives received feedback which did not surprise them – with the exception of the CEO. His feedback pointed to a strongly autocratic and 'controlling style', one likely to engender a climate of fear. The new HR Manager feared for his life, but upon reflection the CEO began to recognise elements of this behaviour and to discuss ways of better managing and masking these. He took the surprising decision of finding a personal 'coach' and worked with her to complete a further range of diagnostics and (for the first time ever) a development plan.

Eighteen months later, the HR Manager was happy to still be in post and was able to report on progress. Staff turnover had reduced considerably, staff feedback suggested this was a motivating place to work. Objectives in an increasingly commercial and competitive market place were tough, but development went hand in hand with this trend.

An example of a performance improvement approach: linked to hard HRM

Christian Salvesen is a European logistics organisation based in the middle of the UK and employing 15,000 staff and operating in nine countries across 200 sites in the UK, Belgium, France, Germany, Ireland, the Netherlands, Italy, Portugal and Spain.

In 1999 business results were poor and despite an excellent year in 2000 the downward trend re-emerged in 2001 and looked set to continue in 2002. At the end of January 2002 thirty members of the Senior Management Team met to discuss and work on developing ideas for urgently improving the organisational performance of the company. A nine-person strong cross-disciplinary group was established to look at ways of improving organisational performance. They represented the main divisions, general managers, finance and HR.

The core principles for the project were defined as in Figure 5.8.

Figure 5.8 Core principles

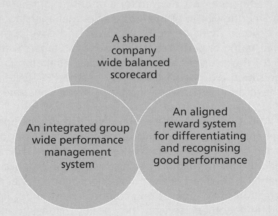

The group were influenced by Jack Welch's ideas of the vitality curve and as a result it was decided to seek to implement more effective performance measures around a balanced scorecard to allow for accurate differentiation between staff. The intention was to 'raise the performance bar' by eliminating the bottom 10 per cent of performers each year.

What emerged from the design meetings of the core performance improvement team?

Essentially a fairly 'hard' approach to performance management emerged, with a primary focus on the 'what' of performance. The 'how' was also included via a new leadership competency model which was to form a 10 per cent element of the final review.

The core business imperatives were captured as being:

Finance – Improve group return on capital (ROACE) by improving profit and using less capital.

People – Improve employee effectiveness and contribution through reduced turnover, absenteeism, accidents and improved management capability.

Customer – Improve customer sales and margin growth.
Improve customer satisfaction through the achievement of agreed terms of service delivery, with reduced claims, credit notes and queries.

Operations – Improve the cost of operations and transactions against the revenue achieved.

Beneath these 'headline' measures, eight KPI's or key measures were translated across the 4 scorecard categories. These key measures became the improvement numbers and targets for every part of the business from group to division and regions through to site levels. As a result everyone within the business knew the targets and what was being expected from them for this year.

Implementation details

The balanced scorecard was 'rolled-out' initially to 250 managers in the higher managerial grades. It was supported by a new performance management process, underpinned by a revised reward architecture aiming to:

- link individual performance contribution to overall company performance contribution;
- assess individual manager performance contribution across all four scorecard categories;
- differentiate between performance in terms of three types across the peer groups (the top 20 per cent, middle 70 per cent and bottom 10 per cent).

The new reward system was designed for introduction one year into the new balanced scorecard performance approach. This was in order to give the business one year to become familiar with the process before any hard monetary rewards were associated with it. The new bonus system was underpinned by weightings which stressed the importance of the achievement of financial measures shown in Figure 5.9.

Figure 5.9 Bonus system

Category	% bonus weighting
Finance	45
People/Employee	25
Customer	15
Operations	15

In addition, the new reward system was designed so that it would only pay out if overall company performance reached a pre-defined percentage of the target levels. This percentage could be set at the beginning of each year.

The flow diagram (Figure 5.10) summarises the process which was rolled out at Christian Salvesen.

Implementation support

The impetus behind this performance initiative at Christian Salvesen came from the Chief Executive himself. As a result there was never any doubt as to the degree of

Figure 5.10 Performance appraisal implementation process

1. Business scorecard objectives/targets set.
2. Objective setting exercise Individual sets personal objectives against the scorecard targets.
3. Individual requests and identifies 6 feedback respondents.
4. Individual organises the anonymous feedback gathering process from their 6 feedback respondents.
5. Individuals has 1:1 feedback sharing interview with an external coach/consultant.
6. Appraisal meetings with line managers take place and overall performance agreed.
7. Business scorecard targets set for 2003/2004.

support from the top. Even with such a high degree of commitment, the implementation of such a different approach to people management within a fairly 'traditional' organisation required considerable planning and resources. It was decided to support the objective setting, balanced scorecard and the roll-out of the leadership element via automated software (Figure 5.11).

Figure 5.11 Example of software package

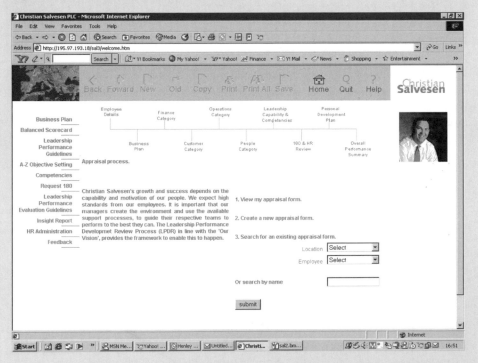

In the first instance an e-learning approach was deployed, supported by HR, around objective setting. This equipped managers to set personal scorecard objectives against their business unit's overall scorecard objectives – an illustrative example of this is provided below:

Illustrative objective

Divisional scorecard – People KPI: Staff turnover
Improve staff retention throughout the division by 15 per cent by March 2003.

Personal scorecard

Target objective: Develop and action a plan to measurably improve employee morale in the Logistics Project Team by end of March 2003.

Performance objective milestones:

- Conduct structured focus groups with team members in order to identify morale issues and suggestions for improvement – *Quarter 1*
- Review turnover data and reason for leaving for 2000–2001 so that the top 5 reasons are clearly identified – *Quarter 1*
- Develop an action plan with actions, timings and costs and obtain sign off from Logistics Director and HR Manager so that improvement takes plan – *Quarter 1*
- Work with HR Training Manager in order to produce individual training plan for each team member and present to team – *Quarter 1*
- Schedule monthly team meetings, set up agenda and actions file in order to ensure importance and regularity of communications – *Quarter 1*
- Design and run a team building event and produce action plan in order to address issues raised during event – *Quarter 2*
- Conduct mid-year review of training plan and turnover stats and conduct mini employee survey within team in order to identify degree of improvement – *Quarter 3*
- Review T & D plan In order to identify areas to be carried over to 2004 – *Quarter 3*
- Conduct attitude survey in team in order to review end of year t/o stats – *Quarter 4*
- Present results of 'morale improvement' project to Senior Management Team at December management meeting so that they can evaluate progress – *Quarter 4*

Once produced, the objectives were entered into the automated system which supported the whole performance management process, linking together the scorecard, business unit objectives and leadership capability element. The 'how' or behavioural element has been captured via a 180 degree feedback process, with each manager receiving feedback from 5 direct reports and their line manager.

Interestingly, although the 180 degree feedback element accounts for only 10 per cent of the total performance evaluation, it was one of the aspects that caused most disquiet. Managers appeared to be concerned about its apparent 'subjectivity' and worried how they might fare in the giving and receiving of 'personal style' feedback. As a result the feedback process was designed to be as objective as possible. Composite feedback collating the views of all the nominated reviewers was prepared by HR. In addition a follow-on discussion to review the feedback was available for each manager with an external consultant.

In summary, Christian Salvesen are pleased with their innovative and technologically supported solution, though they acknowledge that it is a 'top-down' approach in place of a bottom-up paper approach. Although they needed to 'outsource' the technology-supported element, they feel they have succeeded in the first part of their performance project – determining the business objectives and scorecard through top management buy-in rather than via consultancy intervention.

Reflections on practice and a review of the 'improvement' and 'management' approaches to people performance

Applying to your own practice

Having read the two short examples above reflect on what you believe to be the likely advantages and disadvantages of a performance management or a performance improvement approach.

A review of performance management approaches

Possible disadvantages of 'softer' performance management approaches.

- Lack 'edge' or a sense of urgency – making it perhaps inappropriate for situations where short-term results really matter!
- Difficult to establish a causal link and can feel like an act of faith.
- Focuses on the 'hows' of performance, particularly for the business leaders, puts them in the spotlight.
- Can work unless leaders are all committed.
- Behaviours are harder to measure objectively.

A review of performance improvement approaches

Possible disadvantages of 'harder' performance improvement approaches.

- It's a hard approach, be mindful of what it feels like and what it might do to motivation.
- Consider how skilled are managers at giving firm but fair feedback.
- Do not skimp on processes/resources.
- Be wary of the risk of favouritism if processes are not transparent and perceived fair.

Chapter summary and future directions

This chapter has sought to pull together a number of different themes relevant to performance and its management within organisations. It has sought to make this discussion relevant to all people managers not HR specialists, although it does present some of the key HR literature debates by way of context.

The chapter began with a reflection on what is performance anyway. This seems an obvious question, but for any manager it is helpful to question for his or her own context:

- what is performance within my organisation, how is it construed, judged and rewarded?

- as a result of the above, how is my own performance likely to be monitored and rewarded.

Some of the literature around the link between people and organisational performance were discussed. Following this contextual piece, the main elements of performance management in terms of its three key elements, its evolution and its linkages to motivational theories were presented. The chapter has sought to describe management experiences with performance management and presents a model of two different manifestations: performance management and improvement. These two are illustrated by case studies and the advantages and disadvantages of each approach were outlined.

In the future there is likely to be an even greater emphasis upon measurement within approaches to managing performance. At the same time, and as a result of having learned from previous experience with performance management, organisations will need to strike a balance between the need to measure performance and the need to motivate its people. This brings will inevitably require a greater focus on the importance of developing managerial capability and leadership in order to unlock the full potential of performance management processes and practices.

In conclusion, the chapter suggests that performance management has come a long way since its original appearance on the organisational scene. Done well there is no doubt that performance management is about good management practice and a common-sense linking of leadership and motivational qualities with key HR processes such as reward and high potential recognition. However, in many organisations this 'holy grail' is some way off and the challenge for its delivery lies not only with top management in terms of strategy clarification and leadership but all with people managers at all levels in terms of securing its safe delivery.

Note

1. Directors of Britain's leading companies covering: Top 500 by turnover; FTSE 500; Top 100 by capital employed. Seventy-six percentage of respondents are Chairman, CEO, MD; 204 face-to-face interviews lasting up to an hour (versioned) – a response rate of 31 per cent.

References

Adams, J.S. (1965) 'Inequity in social exchange', *Advances in Experimental Social Psychology*, Vol. 2 (edited by Leonard Berkowitz), New York, Academic Press.

Armstrong, M. and Baron, A. (1998) *A Performance Management: The New Realities*, IPD.

Beer, M., Mills, D.Q. and Walton, R.E. (1985) *Human Resources Management: A General Manager's Perspective*, New York, Free press.

Captains of Industry Survey (1999) Internal Consultancy Report commissioned by Hay Group.

Corvellec, H. (1997) *Stories of Achievements-Narrative Features of Organisational Performance*, New Brunswick, NJ Transaction Publishers.

Corvellec, H. (2001) 'For a Narrative Criticism of Organisational Performance', Conference Paper for New Directions in Organisational Performance, Newcastle, UK, 28–29 March.

Eccles, Robert G. (1991) 'The performance measurement manifesto', *Harvard Business Review*, Vol. 69, No. 1, Jan.–Feb. 1991, pp. 131–37.

Fletcher, C. and Williams, R. (1996) 'Performance management, job satisfaction and organisational commitment', *British Journal of Management*, Vol. 7, pp. 169–79.

Fombrun, C., Tichy, N. and Devanna, M. (1984) *Strategic Human Resource Management*, New York, John Wiley & Sons.

Gomez-Mejia, L.R., Tosi, H. and Hinkin, T. (1987) 'Management control, performance, and executive compensation', *Academy of Management Journal*, Vol. 30, No. 1, pp. 51–70.

Guest, D. (1987) 'Human resource management and industrial relations', *Journal of Management Studies*, Vol. 24, No. 5.

Guest, D., Michie, J., Sheehan, M., Conway, N. and Metochi, M. (2000) *Effective People Management: Initial Findings of the Future of Work Study*, CIPD.

Guile, D. and Fonda, N. (1988) *Performance Management Through Capability*, IPD.

Hendry, C. and Pettigrew, A. (1990) 'Human resource management: an agenda for the 1990s', *International Journal of Human Resource Management*, Vol. 1, No. 1, pp. 17–44.

Houldsworth, E. (2000) 'Understanding Performance Management Through Partnership-Based Research'. Paper Presented at British Academy of Management Conference.

Houldsworth, E. (2003) 'Trying to Motivate and Measure Through Performance Management – Can the Hard and Soft Approaches be Reconciled?' Presentation at CIPD Conference Harrogate, Oct.

Huselid, M., Jackson, S. and Schuler, R. (1997) 'Technical and strategic human resource management effectiveness as determinants of firm performance', *Academy of Management Journal*, Vol. 40, No. 1.

IDS Study 667, April 1999 – BT as an example of Company Practice in Performance Management.

IPM (1992) Performance Management in the UK: An Analysis of the Issues.

Kaplan, R.S. and Norton, D.P. (1996) 'Using the balanced scorecard as a strategic management system', *Harvard Business Review*, Boston, Jan./Feb. 1996.

Legge, K. (1995a) *Human Resource Management: Rhetorics and Realities*, Macmillan Business.

Legge, K. (1995b) 'Human resource management: a critical analysis', in J. Storey (ed.), *New Perspectives on Human Resource Management*, London, Routledge.

Locke, E.A. (1968) 'Towards a theory of task performance and incentives', *Organisational Behaviour and Human Performance*, Vol. 3, No. 2, pp. 157–189. .

Luthans, F. and Kreitner, R. (1985) *Organisational Behaviour Modification and Beyond*, Glenview.

Maslow, A.H. (1943) 'A theory of human motivation', *Psychological Review*, Vol. 50, pp. 370–96.

McClelland, D. (1987) *Human Motivation*, New York, Cambridge University Press.

McGregor, D. (1960) 'Theory X and Y', in D.S. Pugh (ed.), *Organisation Theory: Selected Readings*, London, Penguin.

Meyer, M.W. and Zucker, L.G. (1989) *Permanently Failing Organisations*, Newbury Park, California, Sage.

Patterson, M., West, M., Lawthorn, R. and Nickell, S. (1997) *The Impact of People Management Practices on Business Performance*, London, IPD.

Pfeffer, J. (1998) *The Human Equation*, Boston, HBS Press.

Richardson, R. and Thompson, M. (1999) *The Impact of People Management Practices on Business Performance: A Literature Review*, IPD.

Storey, J. (1992) *Developments in the Management of Human Resources*, Oxford, Blackwell.

Truss, C., Gratton, L., Hope-Hailey, V., McGovern, P. and Stiles, P. (1997) *Soft and hard models of HRM: a reappraisal*, in L. Graton, V. Hope-Hailey, P. Stiles and C. Truss (eds) (1999) *Strategic HRM*, Oxford, Oxford University press.

Ulrich, D. (1997) *Human Resource Champions: The Next Agenda for Adding Value and Delivering Results*, Boston, Harvard.

Vroom, V.J. (1964) *Work and Motivation*, New York, Wiley.

Weiss, T. and Hartle, F. (1997) *Re-engineering Performance Management*, Eastbourne, St Lucie Press

Welch, J. and Byrne, J. (2003) *Jack: Straight from the Gut*, Boston, Warner Business.

Managing human talent

Tim Osborn-Jones

Part I identified the attraction and retention of people as a strategic human resource issue and management task. Chapter 5 has described the significance of managing the performance of people in the quest to develop a high-performance culture. This chapter continues our examination of how people are managed, with special reference to attracting and retaining managerial talent.

Introduction

The global competition to attract and retain talent is a key corporate challenge. It takes place in a world where technological development and global competition are driving widespread change in organisational structure and patterns of employment; a world where, whilst it is often asserted that employees are a company's most valuable asset, few companies now offer employment security or regular promotions, let alone a 'job for life'. This chapter explores the new context for employment relationships and identifies key issues relating to managerial talent. The traditional 'psychological contract', an exchange of employment security for loyalty and commitment, has been widely undermined. Quantitative solutions, big salaries, golden handcuffs and golden hellos, do not of their own secure loyalty and commitment. They are too easily matched and topped by competitors leading to an endless round of poaching. A typology of psychological contract terms and types is used to identify and map emergent theories of career. It is presented, with an assessment of contemporary interpretations of the psychological contract, as a framework to assist individuals and organisations to manage their relationships more effectively in a turbulent world.

In a subject widely debated in terms of theory and conjecture, the chapter provides empirical data on some aspects of one key sector of talent, *managerial talent*. It draws on the findings of a research project undertaken in collaboration with Henley Management College to provide a snapshot of managerial attitudes to work, employment and careers amongst 476 managers from around the world. In offering action checklists for individuals and organisations the chapter indicates how qualitative (non-financial) interests and values may be key features in psychological contracts for today's talented executives. It introduces typologies and exercises that can assist an individual to understand and act, in the light of their own attitudes, values and interests, in relation to work, employment and careers.

Conclusions emphasise the importance of linking corporate strategy, HR policy and practice, and individual contracts. Responsive organisations will be prepared to negotiate and sustain hybrid psychological contracts to meet diverse individual needs and wants in order to attract and retain talent.

Context

Downsizing, delayering and decentralisation

There is extensive literature, popular and academic, on both sides of the Atlantic which describes how external environmental forces are driving widespread changes in organisational structure and patterns of employment (Handy 1989; Kanter 1989b; Scase and Goffee 1989; Sparrow 1998; Rubery *et al.* 2002). The impact of information technology, deregulation, commoditisation and global competition, has reached most corners of the labour market. In an age of downsizing, delayering, decentralisation, outsourcing and global mobility, few employers can afford to offer job security, let alone a job for life. If lean organisations need effort and commitment to get the work done and a willingness to take risks in pursuit of innovation (Herriot *et al.* 1997), why should managers commit without the incentive of steadily rising pay and status (Cappelli 1999).

This contribution considers whether predominate practice in organisations around the world, facing similar competitive pressures, leads mainly to the compliance of reluctant managers. Corporate leaders seeking to establish through 'strong cultures' the all-embracing commitment of managers to 'excellent cultures' will '...depend critically upon the retention of high achieving managers and the conversion of what have elsewhere been called "reluctant managers"' (Goffee and Scase 1992: 383). 'To compete effectively in the global economy business must attract, retain, motivate and utilise most effectively the most talented people they can find' (Kanter 1993: 323). In sum, our attention here is focused on how, in the early years of the 21st century, talented managers view work, employment and career and how organisations win the 'War for Talent' (Chambers *et al.* 1998).

Employment relationships

The relationship between individual and organisation is our key focus (Schein 1978). It is a relationship widely regarded as involving a 'psychological contract'. The idea of the 'psychological contract' was established in the 1960s to describe the employer–employee relationship. It has become the focus of attention again as a perspective for viewing the fundamental changes in the employment relationship. It is a set of implicitly agreed expectations between two parties, operating over and above the formal contract of employment, incorporating the parties' beliefs, values and aspirations.

One model of the psychological contract is based on a Continuum of Contract Terms (Rousseau 1995) anchored at one end by a *relational* form of contract and at the other by a *transactional* form. The relational form, associated with the traditional employment relationship, is characterised as an exchange of loyalty and commitment for security of employment (social exchange), the transactional form as a fair day's work for a fair day's pay (economic exchange). Sullivan (1999) offers a broadly based model of factors influencing choice of employment relationship and individual and organisational outcomes. It is adapted to provide a framework for exploring the changes in the patterns of employment. Managerial attitudes to work, employment and career are conceptualised as the *form* (relational-transactional) of psychological contract and represented as Sullivan's 'Types of Employment Relationship'. The adapted model is set out in Figure 6.1.

Figure 6.1 Types of employment relationship

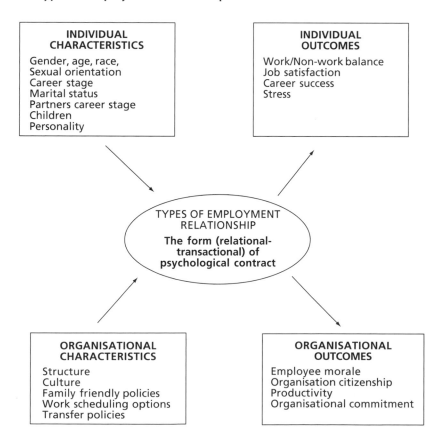

Source: Adapted from Sullivan's (1999), Model of factors influencing choice of employment relationships and individual and organisational outcomes.

Before considering types and terms of psychological contract and emergent theories of career, it will be helpful to identify some of the other key issues that arise from the changing pattern of employment relationships.

Key issues

Organisational commitment

> Motivation and morale are fundamental since lean organisations need effort and commitment to get the work done, and at the same time a willingness to take risks in pursuit of innovation. (Herriot *et al.* 1997: 152)

Many commentators agree that motivation and morale are fundamental. However, despite the fact that many HR programmes are designed to boost commitment 'employee attachment and binding to an organisation is complex, multifaceted and paradoxical' (Iles *et al.* 1990: 155). Counselling or developmental activities can create new clarity of thought, or higher levels of self-esteem leading to greater criticism of, and less attachment to the current employer, and/or stronger intentions about leaving the current career field. In attempting to foster commitment through HRM practices '...*perception* is more important than reality' (Meyer and Allen 1997: 88).

Psychological success

The focus has shifted to the individual; 'psychological success' and personal fulfilment rather than organisational rewards.

Many prescriptions for careers in the 21st century shift the focus to the individual. 'Psychological success' (Mirvis and Hall 1996), personal fulfilment rather than organisational rewards, the path with a heart rather than the path to the top, become the key drivers. Portfolio careers (Handy 1989), balancing professional paid work, with unpaid community work, self development, investment in second career and family, will beckon at an earlier age as the period of core full-time employment with peak earnings is reduced and IT facilitates work at any time, in any place.

These notions are no longer extraordinary, but increasingly real choices. Writing in the *Harvard Business Review* (2000) under the title 'Goodbye Career, Hello Success' Randy Komisar a Harvard law graduate, describes how after many false starts he successfully established a 'non-career career' as a 'virtual CEO', working with a variety of Silicon Valley start-ups: 'Don't let a career drive you, let passion drive your life' (Komisar 2000: 174). Speaking in more measured tones but with no less impact, Peter Drucker also in the HBR, focused on the theme of independence. Under the title 'Managing Oneself: Success in the knowledge economy comes to those who know themselves – their strengths, their values, and how they best perform', Drucker concludes that existing society has taken it for granted 'if only subconsciously' that organisa-tions outlive workers and that most people stay put. 'But today the opposite is true. Knowledge workers outlive organisations, and they are mobile' (Drucker 1999: 74).

Employability

It is long since Charles Handy urged all to 'invest in themselves' (Handy 1989: 57), rather than rely on HR departments and employers. This theme has been widely developed in popular phrases such as the prescription to own and man-age your own career, sometimes caricatured as Me PLC and associated with the end of corporate careers (Bridges 1996). Just how can employers realistic-ally portray attractive opportunities for a career in the organisational context of the 21st century? What can they offer in place of the traditional psycho-logical contract which will compete with the apparent passion of the self-employed? Some organisations aspire to offer what has been termed 'employability security' (Kanter 1989b: 321), a package of measures which will help individuals develop and maintain 'employability', across depart-ments and units within their current employment, and outside. This approach focuses on a joint commitment to continuous learning and personal develop-ment but also, critically within the gift of an organisation, exposure to relevant and up-to-date experience and contacts.

'Bundles' of HRM policies and practices

To win individual commitment in a competitive situation, HR managers face a complex task in devising appropriate HR policy and practice to accommodate employee expectations within corporate strategy. 'Bundles' of HRM policies and practices (Guest 1998a: 40), especially those relating to recruitment, reten-tion and training, must be integrated to provide not only acceptable written terms of employment but also often in an implicit understanding between the parties, a new psychological contract.

Market realities

In recognising market realities, retention strategies must target particular employees or groups of employees. Poaching talent is as old as the hills. In an article entitled 'A Market-Driven Approach to Retaining Talent', Peter Cappelli, Professor of Management Studies and Director of the Centre for Human Resources at the Wharton School, summarises the problems bluntly. Suggesting that most executives are inveterate poachers of each others talent, he argues that the focus must shift from broad retention programmes to highly targeted efforts aimed at particular employees or groups of employees. The new goal is '...to influence who leaves and when' (Cappelli 2000: 104).

Work-life balance

If money, share options and other quantitative elements of the remuneration package are too easy for competitive poachers to 'top', what are the qualitative interests and values of today's talented executive? Many reports have urged that work-life balance is a key concern (Scase 2002). Referring to the UK's first Work-Life Balance Week, Cooper (2000) reports that some corporates are beginning to react to the hidden costs of the excessive working hours culture '…prompted by growing competition for talent…', and that the government has set up a Challenge Fund to pay consultants to advise organisations on how to introduce flexibility and lifestyle-friendly employment policies.

The psychological contract

Terms and types: the contract continuum

The psychological contract has become the subject of much debate and various definitions. For some the focus is on the 'content' of the contract (Guest 1998b). For others the emphasis is on the process (Herriot 1992: 6): 'The individual's objective external career is the sequence of positions she or he holds in the organisation, but their subjective, internal career is the process of psychological contracting.' Rousseau and Schalk (2000: 284) overcome the technical difficulty concerning the representation of the organisation in the relationship, by emphasising that the psychological contract is '…the individual's interpretation of an exchange of promises, mutually agreed and voluntarily made between two or more parties'. In this chapter the focus is on the transactional–relational *form* of contract derived from Rousseau's (1995) Contract Continuum.

Rousseau (1995: 92) specifies seven typical contract terms with a corresponding *transactional–relational* continuum, that is:

Contract term	Contract continuum	
	Transactional	Relational
focus	economic/emotional	emotional
inclusion	partial	whole person
time-frame	close-ended, specific	open-ended, indefinite
formalisation	written	written, unwritten
stability	static	dynamic
scope	narrow	pervasive
tangibility	public, observable	subjective, understood

Transactional and relational terms are basic elements in most employment contracts. However, to describe modern employment contracts adequately, we must take into account two key contract features closely intertwined with transactional and relational terms, time frame and performance requirements. *Time-frame* refers to the duration of the employment relationship (limited/short term, or open ended/long term), but *performance requirements* involve the specification of performance as a condition of employment (well specified or weakly specified). When these features are arranged in a matrix, four model *types of contract* emerge (ibid.: 98) with distinct behavioural implications for workers:

1   **Short term/specified**

- *transactional contracts*: of limited duration with well-specified performance terms

2   **Short term/not specified**

- *transitional contracts*: essentially a breakdown in contracts, reflecting the absence of commitments regarding future employment, as well as little or no explicit performance demands or contingent incentives

3   **Long term/specified**

- *balanced contracts*: open-ended and relationship-orientated employment with well-specified performance terms subject to change over time

4   **Long term/not specified**

- *relational contracts*: open-ended membership but with incomplete or ambiguous performance requirements attached to continued membership

Whilst two forms of contract, relational and transactional, anchor the ends of the psychological contract continuum, more recent research has demonstrated that the continuum is not bi-polar (Millward and Brewerton 2000). Transactional and relational terms are not necessarily mutually exclusive. As Rousseau (1995) points out, for example, 'balanced contracts' occur when relationships are desired and the organisation is able to specify the performance demands as a condition of membership. In effect a *hybrid* mixture of transactional and relational terms may best meet the wants and needs of an individual. Rousseau's scheme of contract types, adapted to incorporate the notion of hybrid contracts is set out in Figure 6.2.

Despite extensive research '...we are still some way from fully understanding the relationship between trust, loyalty, motivation and commitment and their impact on business performance' (Guest 1997: v). Drawing on the principles of Maslow's hierarchy, it is suggested that basic needs such as money are dealt with by the formal contract of employment or transactional elements in the psychological contract, whereas higher order wants such as self-actualisation and self-esteem, which are the source of people's greatest satisfaction and motivation, are

Figure 6.2 Types of psychological contract

| | Performance terms | |
	Specified	Not specified
Duration Short term	**Transactional** (e.g.: retail clerks hired during Christmas shopping season) ● Low ambiguity ● Easy exit/high turnover ● Low member commitment ● Freedom to enter new contracts ● Little learning ● Weak integration/identification	**Transitional** (e.g.: employee experiences during organisational retrenchment or following merger or acquisition) ● Ambiguity/uncertainty ● High turnover/termination ● Instability
Long term	**Balanced/hybrid** (e.g.: high involvement team) ● High member commitment ● High integration/identification ● Ongoing development ● Mutual support ● Dynamic	**Relational** (e.g.: family business members) ● High member commitment ● High affective commitment ● High integration/identification ● Stability

Source: Adapted from Rousseau (1995).

met in relational terms (Makin *et al*. 1996). Old values such as success at the workplace are being replaced by new values such as self-fulfilment, which relates closely to the higher order needs (Furnham 1997).

Emergent theories of career

The issues relating to work, employment and career form a complex web drawing from many disciplines which has led to an abundance of overlapping theories arising from the current state of change. Some clear views on new forms of career have been established. These may be described as emergent theories of career and are often associated with particular authors. Many reflect the increasing interest in the relationship between work and non-work activities, 'lifestyle', and particularly feature the interests and values of the individual. Four emergent theories have been identified and mapped (Osborn-Jones 2000) against Rousseau's continuum of contract terms and model of contract types. It is suggested that the four theories of career may be approximated to Rousseau's model contract types as follows:

1 'Boundaryless' careers – tend towards a *relational* contract

2 'Protean' careers – tend towards a *transactional* contract

3 'Instrumental/calculative' careers – tend towards a *transitional* contract

4 'New deal' careers – tend towards a *balanced/hybrid* contract

Boundaryless careers

The notion of a 'boundaryless career' (Arthur and Rousseau 1996) as a new perspective for organisational inquiry has become one of the most influential viewpoints. It makes the critical break from the world of viewing career as happening in a single, steady state organisation – the 'bounded' or organisational career. The logic of vertical co-ordination, job grades, promotions, demotions, plateauing and fast tracking – orderly levels – has gone.

The boundaryless career encompasses six specific meanings:

1   when a career moves across the boundaries of separate employers;

2   when a career draws validation – marketability – from outside the present employer;

3   when a career is sustained by external networks or information;

4   when traditional organisational career boundaries, notably those involving hierarchical reporting and advancement principles, are broken;

5   when a person rejects existing career opportunities for personal or family reasons;

6   when a career actor perceives a boundaryless future regardless of structural constraints.

Protean careers

From an early point in the history of careers, Hall (1976) identified the individual as the driver of career rather than the organisation:

> The protean career is a process which the person, not the organisation is managing. It consists of all the person's varied experiences in education, training, work in several organisations, changes in occupational field etc.

Hall *et al.* (1996) summarise the position with the enigmatic comment that 'the organisational career is dead, while the Protean career is alive and flourishing'. The term protean is taken from the Greek god, Proteus, who could change shape at will. A protean career will be re-invented by the person from time to time as the person and the environment change. The ultimate goal of career is psychological success: the feeling of pride and personal accomplishment that comes from achieving one's most important goals in life, be they business, family happiness, inner peace, or something else. This is in contrast to vertical success under the old career contract where the goal was climbing the corporate pyramid and making a lot of money.

In summary, the features of new Protean career contract are:

● It is managed by the person, not the organisation;

● It is a lifelong series of experiences;

- where development involves continuous learning, it is self directed, relational and found in work challenges;

- where development is not (necessarily) formal training, there is retraining or upward mobility;

- the ingredients for success change from know-how to learn-how, from job-security to employability, from organisational careers to protean careers and from work self to whole self;

- the organisation provides challenging assignments, developmental relationships and information and other developmental resources;

- the goal is psychological success (Hall and Moss 1998).

New deals, new dealing

Most theories treat the psychological contract as essentially a content based concept. Herriot and Pemberton (1997) draw attention to the process implications of psychological contracting. A process model for facilitating new deals should emphasise that a psychological contract differs between individuals. It is a two-way exchange process rather than a unilaterally imposed one, and should stress the importance of business and social contexts, of information exchange, of equity and of monitoring and honouring the deal. An imposed deal is no deal. Only if the reality of the employment relationship is contractual rather than coercive will the conditions for motivation be present:

> The four basic elements of the process – inform, negotiate, monitor, renegotiate or exit – each allow individuals to achieve agency and autonomy in their relationship with the organisation…to take risks, and engage in innovative teamworking projects. (ibid.: 48)

Appropriate process, it is argued, can secure a new psychological contract to the satisfaction of all parties which may be relational or transactional or some mixture of both. This emphasises the reciprocal nature of the employment relationship which permits a pluralism of interests, rather than assuming that all employees did or would want to contract loyalty for security.

Instrumental/calculative careers

Managers have traditionally been highly rewarded, in terms not only of their salaries and fringe benefits, but also in their status and working conditions. However, organisations are reviewing their operating practices, redesigning jobs and reassessing the effectiveness of their structures in response to rapidly changing external and internal circumstances and 'managers may now be developing more *instrumental* and *calculative* attitudes towards their employing organisations' (Goffee and Scase 1992). More are calculating the emotional and psychological costs of career success. As such, managers are more inclined to define jobs in almost solely instrumental, non-affective terms – as sources of income for achieving self-fulfilment outside employment.

Contemporary interpretations

The psychological contract has continued to be adopted by many commentators as a vehicle for mapping and commenting on changes in contemporary employment relations. Definition and interpretation has become complex and contentious. Particular interpretations are associated with particular views about employment relations. Further attempts to identify a new employment orthodoxy have been made by various academics and researchers (Kanter 1989b, 1993; Herriot 1992; Sparrow 1998; Hendry 1999). Sparrow (1998: 133), for example, outlines three possibilities. In substantive terms he suggests that the majority of employees may 'self-correct', re-invent themselves making a new, more instrumental deal to accommodate the changed circumstances, a more transactional psychological contract. The alternatives follow respectively from whether the traditional motivational drivers are seen to be temporarily or permanently changed.

There is a diversity of opinion as to whether empirical evidence supports the widespread assumption and commonly made proposition that there has been or will be substantive change (ibid.). Four interpretations of the psychological contract are identified, substantive change, status quo, new dealing and hybrid contracts, as representative of the key perspectives on contemporary employment relations. The four interpretations are summarized as follows:

1 *Substantive change* – There is a substantive change in psychological contracts. Most, if not all, employees have shifted or will shift from a relational to a transactional form of psychological contract.

2 *Status quo* – There is no material change in the psychological contract. Analysis of the content of psychological contracts shows that the extent of change in employment patterns and career aspirations has been exaggerated.

3 *New dealing* – Methods of new dealing and renegotiating, psychological contracts, based on a more transparent process, facilitates more individual, equitable and sustainable contracts.

4 *Hybrid contracts* – Most psychological contracts are hybrid, containing relational and transactional elements, reflecting the diversity of individual needs and wants.

The substantive change and status quo interpretations reflect at one level a subjective, politicised debate about the state of contemporary employment relations, in terms of relative prosperity, security and quality of life. At another more objective level they relate to different things, form and content, which cannot be directly compared. The new dealing interpretation is of a different nature, driven by a principled conviction in the importance of the individual and the need for a transparent process. It is not clear whether this laudable approach will have any great impact in resolving the contemporary challenges. The notion of hybrid contracts has emerged in part as a response to theoretical prescriptions for a radically changed new order. It represents a more pragmatic approach, reflecting the complexity of the reality, and addresses the increasing importance of individual aspirations.

The next section will report the outcomes of the study designed in part to test the validity of the first interpretation, the extent to which the attitudes of talented managers, represented by the form of psychological contract, are now more closely related to a transactional rather than a relational contract.

Researching managerial talent: a case study

The data

The data is drawn from a questionnaire survey conducted amongst participants of Henley Management College programmes. At a time when job roles and titles are undergoing wide-ranging change, a pragmatic definition of 'manager' was adopted in the form of people attending programmes at a 'management college'. Henley presented an attractive source for obtaining a cross-sectional view of international managerial talent, offering a wide range of qualification and non-qualification programmes, on face-to-face and a distance-taught basis.

Methodology

The questionnaire was posted, with an international reply paid envelope in hard copy format together with a personalised covering letter as an enclosure with the Autumn 2000 edition of the College alumni magazine, the *Henley Manager*. Distribution was limited to alumni who had completed their programme within the last five years. In addition, copies were distributed to participants of programmes at the College over the three months October to December. In total just under 2000 copies were distributed, 476 completed questionnaires were returned giving an excellent response rate in excess of 20 per cent.

Findings

Biodata

There is a normal, bell-shape distribution of age across the sample, reflecting Henley's emphasis on post-experience education; 50 per cent of the sample lies in the age range 36–45. The population splits female: 21 per cent, male: 79 per cent. An analysis of *age groups by gender*, shows a tendency for more females (39 per cent) than men

(23 per cent) to participate in programmes at an earlier age (21–35-years-old). The global nature of the market place for managerial talent is demonstrated in the mix of *nationalities*: UK: 60 per cent, Europe 25 per cent, New World (Americas, Australia and South Africa) 6 per cent and Asia 5 per cent. Related data on *current location* shows a similar distribution. A traditional pattern of *employment status* is indicated, with a substantial majority (93 per cent) remaining in full-time employment, 2 per cent in part-time employment, 5 per cent self-employed. In terms of *programme type*, participants in qualification programmes (MBA/Diploma) represent 74 per cent, participants in non-qualification programmes (Open Executive and Short Courses) represent 26 per cent.

Figure 6.3 shows *Years in current location, employment status, and job*. A minority are mobile in all respects: 17 per cent have changed location and 25 per cent have changed employment status in the last two years, but in both categories many (location = 54 per cent; employment status = 39 per cent) have been static for more than 10 years.

Figure 6.3 Mobility

Conversely there is a universally high degree of job mobility; 56 per cent have changed in the last two years, only 7 per cent have been static for more than 10 years.

Members of the sample rate their *self-esteem* in very positive terms. Based on a 10-item scale, each item measuring responses from 1 = Strongly agree (indicating high self-esteem) to 7 = Strongly disagree (low self-esteem), Figure 6.4 shows that, summed for all items, 47 per cent of the sample rated their self-esteem at level 1, 41 per cent at level 2 (agree), 10 per cent at level 3 (partly agree), 2 per cent at level 4 (neutral) and nil per cent at levels 5, 6 and 7.

Further analysis shows that in this context perceptions of self-esteem are not significantly related to gender or age group.

Figure 6.5 reports what respondents see as *The most important thing that people look for, or want out of life*. From a list of nine values the top three

Figure 6.4 Self-esteem

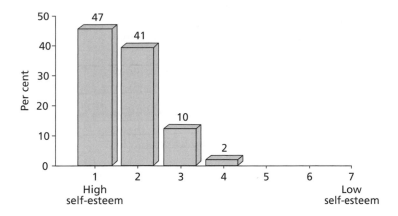

Figure 6.5 Values

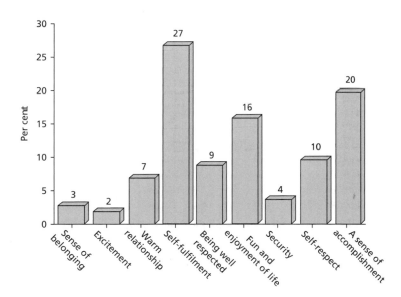

choices were: self-fulfilment – 27 per cent, sense of accomplishment – 20 per cent, fun and enjoyment of life – 16 per cent. The bottom three choices were: excitement – 2 per cent, sense of belonging – 3 per cent and security – 4 per cent.

The priorities expressed were broadly endorsed in a related exercise where respondents were asked to rate *each* of the nine items on a scale from 1 = very important to 7 = very unimportant. The top three (cumulative per cent choosing Levels 1 and 2) were: sense of accomplishment – 84 per cent, self-fulfilment – 83 per cent and self-respect – 76 per cent. The bottom three (cumulative per cent choosing Levels 5, 6 and 7) were: security – 10 per cent, sense of belonging – 5 per cent and excitement – 4 per cent.

Further analysis again showed that in this context choice of values is not significantly related to gender or age group.

Figure 6.6 represents *plans for continuing in the current work situation*. A minority at one pole intending to 'Continue until retirement' (8 per cent) is closely matched by that at the other pole intending to 'Change as soon as possible' (10 per cent). The substantial majority in the middle ground is evenly divided between those inclined to 'Change if something better turns up' (40 per cent) and those who will 'Change only if something exceptional' turns up (42 per cent).

Figure 6.6 Continuity: views about the current work situation

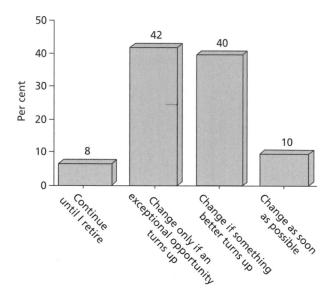

Analysis of age group shows a relatively greater proportion of 46–55-year-olds intending to stay until retirement; conversely the three age groups are equally represented amongst those seeking change as soon as possible. Analysis of gender shows a relatively greater proportion of women (52 per cent) in the 'something better' category than men (37 per cent).

Figure 6.7 summarises data from a 19-item multi-dimensional scale measuring organisational commitment as a sum scale and, separately, four components of commitment, as follows:

1 *Organisational commitment* (OC) – a psychological state which characterises the employee's relationship with the organisation; employees with high levels of OC are more likely to stay with an organisation than those with low OC.

2 *Affective commitment* (AC) – refers to emotional attachment to, identification with and involvement in an organisation; employees with high AC *want* to stay.

Figure 6.7 Views about the organisation: organisational commitment

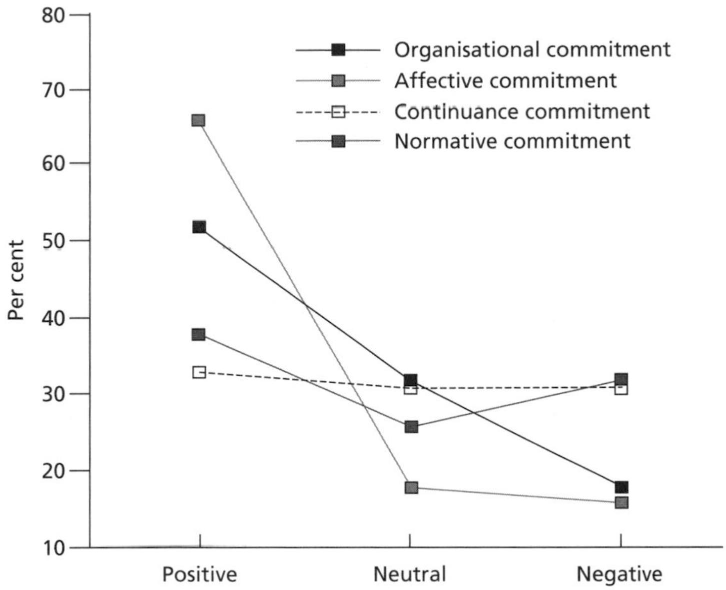

3 *Continuance commitment* (CC) – refers to an awareness of the costs of leaving an organisation; employees with high CC remain because they *need* to.

4 *Normative commitment* (NC) – refers to a feeling of obligation to stay with an organisation; employees with high NC remain because they feel that they *ought* to.

The data demonstrates some important general points and makes some significant distinctions. At a general level, measured in terms of organisational commitment, a bare majority (52 per cent) indicate positive levels of commitment to their organisations and significant minorities indicate neutral (32 per cent) and negative (18 per cent) levels. In relation to affective commitment there is a substantially more positive pattern: 66 per cent positive, 18 per cent neutral and 16 per cent negative. Only a minority relate positively to their organisation in terms of continuance (33 per cent) and normative commitment (38 per cent).

Figure 6.8 summarises data from an 18-item multi-dimensional scale describing the perceived character of the employment relationship in terms of three separate components and a sum scale, using the relational/transactional typology as follows:

1 *Contract focus (transactional orientation)*: working to the letter of the employment contract; limited level of involvement and investment in the job; focus on remunerative and personal benefit.

2 *Equity of the employment deal (relational orientation)*: perceived organisational reciprocation for employee's efforts at work – fairness/justice.

Figure 6.8 Views about the perceived character of the employment relationship: the form (relational/transactional) of psychological contract

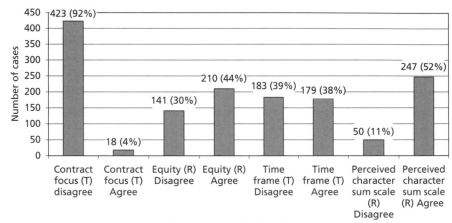

The form of psychological contract

Notes
1. 'Agree' represents an aggregation of points 1–3 and 'Disagree' represents an aggregation of points 5–7 from a 7-point Likert Scale; point 4, Neutral/No opinion, excluded.
2. Maximum number of cases was 476; actual number for each dimension varies.
3. T = transactional orientation; R = relational orientation.

3 *Time-frame (transactional orientation)*: perceived, likely length of time to stay with the organisation.

4 *The perceived character of the employment relationship (sum scale: relational orientation)*: a summation of the three components to represent the perceived character (form) of the employment relationship. Values for the transactional components are reversed such that the sum scale is presented in a relational orientation.

The data suggests that contrary to much conjecture in the literature there has been limited movement in terms of this sample from traditional relational perceptions to transactional perceptions of the employment relationship. Only 4 per cent (Contract focus) and 30 per cent (Time frame) express positive agreement with the components addressing transactional perceptions, whereas 44 per cent express positive agreement with the relational component (Equity) and the aggregation of the components for the sum scale shows 52 per cent expressing positive agreement with the relational orientation as their perception of their employment relationship.

Key points from the research

● The report draws on empirical evidence from a new *database of 476 managers*, 79 per cent men, 21 per cent women, aged 21–55, who were in the period October–December 2000 engaged in, or who had in the period

1995–2000 completed, a significant management development programme at a leading business school. The participants represented a global spread of nationalities (60 per cent UK, 40 per cent Europe, New world and Asia) and location.

- Patterns of mobility in terms of *location and employment status* vary considerably but there is universally high degree of *job mobility*: 56 per cent have changed jobs in the last two years.

- Members of the sample rate their *self-esteem* in very positive terms: on a scale 1 (high) to 7 (low) 47 per cent register at level 1 and a further 41 per cent at Level 2.

- From a list of nine *values* the top three choices were: self-fulfilment (27 per cent), sense of accomplishment (20 per cent) and fun and enjoyment (16 per cent). The bottom three choices were security (4 per cent), sense of belonging (3 per cent) and excitement (2 per cent). Values which may be associated with a traditional relationship between individual and organisation are rated as significantly less important than values which are representative of a more independent orientation.

- A substantial majority take pragmatic views about the *current work situation* expressing an intent to move only if 'something better' (40 per cent) or 'exceptional' (42 per cent) turns up.

- *Organisational commitment* is critically segmented by type; 66 per cent view their organisation positively in terms of *affective commitment* (*want* to stay), but positive levels of *continuance commitment* (*need* to stay) and *normative commitment* (*ought* to stay) are substantially less at 33 per cent and 38 per cent respectively.

- *A majority (52 per cent) continue to view their employment relationship as a whole in relational terms.* Only 3 per cent and 32 per cent respectively express positive agreement with a transactional orientation, in terms of working to the letter of their employment contract and expecting to stay with their current employer on anything other than a short-term basis.

Conclusions

- The participants in this survey view themselves, and/or are viewed by their organisation, as being worth substantial investment in their management and personal development. They may be regarded as 'high potentials', key targets in a 'war for talent'.

- The majority of the sample are mature, experienced managers. They rate their self-esteem in very positive terms and attach great importance to achieving self-fulfilment and a sense of accomplishment, with fun and enjoyment. They view their work situation in balanced terms, but are ready to move when appropriate.

● Commitment to an organisation is a conditional state, chiefly driven by the extent to which an emotional attachment, a sense of *wanting* to stay, is engendered.

● The importance of values such as *security* and *sense of belonging*, which may be regarded as characteristic of the traditional *relational* psychological contract, have been down rated in favour of more individually orientated values such as *self-fulfilment* and *sense of accomplishment*. Yet a majority (52 per cent) of managers continue to perceive their employment relationship as a whole in primarily *relational* terms. Any historical consensus on employment relationships is replaced by a more enigmatic mix. Talented executives may want to negotiate transactional and relational elements, *hybrid* psychological contracts, to meet their diverse needs and wants.

● *Where the right mix of terms, benefits, values and attitudes can be established managers will commit to and apply their talents in the interests of the organisation and their aspirations for a sense of accomplishment and self-fulfilment.*

Actions for organisations

● *Check corporate values* – Build a sense of belonging; be flexible; recognise and respond to values. Ask: would you (and your friends) *want* to work for this company?

● *Get the basics right* – Manage the mix! Focus on 'bundles' of integrated HRM policies and practice; joined-up thinking about how an employer relates to, manages, inspires, motivates, develops and rewards employees.

● *Develop, develop, develop*! – Appoint mentors to support Personal Development Plans; regard high self-esteem as a resource to be harnessed; look for fit between ambitions for self-fulfilment and corporate needs; engender education and training, expect and plan for personal growth; keep in touch: communicate!

● *Foster communities* – Communities matter as much or more than the reputation of the firm. Talented people join organisations, but leave individuals.

● *Have fun*! – Don't substitute pay for attention.

Actions for individuals

There is an extensive academic and 'self-help' literature in relation to the changing patterns of career and personal development. Many feature typologies, exercises and questionnaires (self-perception instruments) which can assist an individual in understanding their attitude to work and employment and securing the development they wish in their chosen style of career.

Career anchors

This exercise is designed to help individuals make difficult decisions about work-life and home-life, that is 'career' in the wider sense. It is based on an individual's growing self-knowledge, drawing on three components: self-perceived talents and abilities, motives and needs, and attitudes and values. The exercise is clearly explained in a self-help style booklet (Schein 1990) and involves a self-perception questionnaire and an interview process structured in accordance with a prescribed framework. The outcome identifies a growing area of stability, a 'career anchor' for each individual from eight options as follows: technical functional competence, general managerial competence, autonomy/independence, security/stability, entrepreneurial creativity, service/dedication to a cause, pure challenge, and lifestyle.

Career grid

Sullivan *et al.* (1998: 168) propose a career grid typology, based on a simple, self-assessment procedure designed to integrate career theories and evolving organisational structures. It assumes that evolving organisational forms are moving workers away from traditional career patterns and seeks to provide a framework by which all parties can examine new career types. It may help managers consider and describe in a measurable format, their future in work, employment or career terms.

The typology is based on 'two continua':

1 *Transferability of competences* (portable/organisation specific knowledge, skills and abilities);

2 *internal work values* (intrinsic job satisfaction).

The grid is used to demonstrate four model career types:

1 *Provisional*: focus on extrinsic rewards; have portable skills and may be long-term temporary employees.

2 *Traditional*: focus on extrinsic rewards; have limited marketability and strong identification to firm.

3 *Self-designing*: focus on self-fulfilment; have portable skills and strong identification to profession.

4 *Self-directed*: focus on self-fulfilment; have firm specific skills and strong identification to profession.

Sullivan (1999: 458) extends the conceptualisation providing a useful comparison of traditional and boundaryless careers based on seven criteria: the employment relationship, boundaries, skills, measurements of success, responsibility for career management, training and milestones.

The future manager profile

Hiltrop (1998) describes a future manager profile in a model highlighting four key themes: self-reliant, expert, resilient and networker. The themes and associated characteristics are set out below:

'Self-reliant'	'Expert'
● initiative	● enthusiasm
● vision	● professionalism
● creativity	● up-to-date knowledge
● risk taking	● intellectual curiosity
● self-motivation	● life-long learning
'Networker'	**'Resilient'**
● communication skills	● stress tolerance
● negotiation skills	● flexibility
● problem solving skills	● team working
● project management	● adaptability
● open minded	● determination

Source: Adapted from Hiltrop (1998).

Career meta-skills: self-knowledge and adaptability

In a world of relentless competition and organisational change, the shelf-life of talent becomes shorter and shorter. The response as discussed above in relation to employability, must be '…a joint commitment to continuous learning and personal development…'. Development is the basis on which employer and employee interests can be successfully brought together in traditional or new style careers. Individuals must learn how to develop self-knowledge and adaptability, 'meta skills', skills of a higher order than basic skills or knowledge, since they are the skills required for learning how to learn (Hall 1996).

Linking strategy, HR practices and contracts

Fit

It is suggested that where the right mix of terms, benefits, values and attitudes can be established talented individuals will commit to the organisation, but there is no one 'right mix'. Talent, like strategy, comes in all shapes and sizes.

There is a growing body of literature tackling the questions of linkage between strategy formulation and implementation; between content and process; between hard and soft approaches and ultimately 'fit' between individual and organisation in the context of rapid and continuous change. Reviewing the 'soft' and 'hard' models of HRM, Truss *et al.* (1997) focus on strategic integration and commitment; the '...fit of human resource policies with business strategy'. The key issue is the strength of 'clusters of people processes' to create linkage between business strategy and individual performance. 'Business strategies are translated through human resource strategies and human processes into individual and organisational performance' (Gratton *et al.* 1999). Ultimately the performance benefits of organisational innovations '...depend on clustering,...patterns of coherent, interlinked changes...'; there must be 'interdependencies' between the three main dimensions of organisational change '...structures, processes and boundaries...' (Whittington *et al.* 1999).

Responsive organisations

The psychological contract is a useful construct for viewing and managing the employment relationship. Employers should seek to understand and, through appropriate HR policies and practice, position the form of contract such that it is determined by and in turn supportive of organisational strategy and goals. Miles and Snow (1984) set out, in what has come to be regarded as a seminal work, a model categorising different business strategies and related HR policies and practice. They link types of business strategy, 'Defenders', 'Prospectors' and 'Analysers', with HR practices by categorising each in terms of whether the organisation would 'Make' or 'Buy' their human resources.

Rousseau (1995) develops the Miles and Snow model by linking the categories to the form of psychological contract. The Defender strategy (stable setting) is linked with a 'Make' HR practice (make and retain relevant talent) and a Relational psychological contract, whereas the Prospector strategy (dynamic environment) is linked with 'Buy' HR practice (buy new talent as necessary) and a Transactional contract. Rousseau goes on to suggest that the 1990s brought the emergence of a new strategy, the 'Responsive' organisation. Responsive firms have environments that are changing but where scarce human resources, talent, and high interdependence require co-ordination of efforts to respond to market changes and opportunities. Responsive organisations adopt a pragmatic, focused HR policy ('make with buy'), recognising that there will be a turnover of approximately 10–15 per cent, compared to 5 per cent and 25 per cent respectively in Defender and Prospector organisations. Responsive organisations seek to retain those with good performance and values by providing extensive training, continuous development and career progression, offering balanced/hybrid contracts for 'core' employees (generally fulltime) and transactional contracts for 'peripheral' employees, typically working on a part-time or sub-contract (contingent) basis.

There is a need and an opportunity to create a 'virtuous circle' of career management in which individual and organisational activities complement each other

(Sturges *et al*. 2002: 731). There is nothing inherently wrong with a relational or transactional form of psychological contract. The crux is that the form of psychological contract should reflect and reinforce organisational strategy, through appropriate HR policy and practice, in terms of both hard and soft measurable goals difficult to measure, culture and that where necessary organisations are able to negotiate and sustain hybrid variations in the norm to accommodate the wants and needs of talented individuals. Expecting the one (e.g. commitment and loyalty as in a traditional relational contract) but rewarding the other (e.g. substituting pay for attention, as in a transactional contract) is unlikely to lead to successful individual or organisational performance (Kerr 1975).

Conclusions and implications for the future

Environmental forces are driving changes in organisational and job structures and some employers and employees are exploring new patterns of relationship. Many new careerists adopting a Boundaryless or Protean career model will focus on short term, and possibly multiple, relationships, be active in self-direction and maintain portable knowledge, skills and competences and up-to-date networks of personal contacts.

At the same time, some of the relatively few empirical studies available report that the traditional career is 'alive and well' (Guest and Conway 2001) and that many talented executives still see their employment relationship primarily in terms of a relational rather than a transactional psychological contract (Osborn-Jones 2001).

Organisations should seek through appropriate HR policies and practice, to position the form of psychological contract such that it is determined by and in turn supportive of organisational strategy and goals. There is evidence of a more individual orientation, an emphasis on personal psychological satisfaction, but it is accompanied in many cases by a continuing preference and search for a satisfactory employment relationship. In a 'war for talent' organisations will need to remain sensitive and willing to negotiate and sustain hybrid contracts to meet the diversity of individual needs and wants. Satisfactory transactional terms dealing with quantitative rewards may be regarded as an essential preliminary, but other relational terms, that engender affective commitment, a 'want' to stay attitude, may be more important in harnessing the key qualitative aspirations of talented individuals to the interests of the organisation.

References and select bibliography

Arthur, M.B. and Rousseau, D. (eds) (1996) *The Boundaryless Career: A New Employment Principle for a New Organisational Era*, New York, Oxford University Press.

Bridges, W. (1996) *Jobshift*, London, Nicholas Brealey.

Cappelli, P. (1999) 'Career jobs are dead', *California Management Review*, Vol. 42, No. 1, pp. 146–67.

Cappelli, P. (2000) 'A market-driven approach to retaining talent', *Harvard Business Review*, Jan.–Feb., pp. 103–11.

Chambers, E.G., Foulon, M., Handfield-Jones, H., Hankin, S.M. and Michaels, E.G. (1998) 'The war for talent', *The McKinsey Quarterly*, Vol. 3, pp. 45–57.

Cooper, K. (2000) 'Work-life balance', *People Management*, May, pp. 35–36.

Drucker, P. (1999) 'Managing oneself', *Harvard Business Review*, Mar.–Apr., pp. 65–74.

Furnham, A. (1997) *The Psychology of Behaviour at Work*, Hove, UK, Psychology Press.

Goffee, R. and Jones, G. (1999) 'Organisation, culture and international HRM', in P. Joynt and B. Morton (eds), *The Global HR Manager*, London, CIPD.

Goffee, R. and Scase, R. (1992) 'Organisational change & the corporate career' *Human Relations*, Vol. 45, No. 4, pp. 363–85.

Gratton, L., Hope-Hailey, V., Stiles, P. and Truss, C. (1999) 'Linking individual performance to business strategy: the people process model', *Human Resource Management*, Vol. 38, No. 1 (Spring), pp. 17–31.

Guest, D. (1997) *The State of the Psychological Contract in Employment*, CIPD Report No. 16, Wimbledon, London, CIPD.

Guest, D. (1998a) 'Is the psychological contract worth taking seriously?' *Journal of Organisational Behaviour*, Vol. 19, pp. 649–64.

Guest, D. (1998b) 'Beyond HRM: commitment and the contract culture', in Sparrow and Marchington (eds), *Human Resource Management: The New Agenda*, London, Financial Times/Pitman Publishing, pp. 37–51.

Guest, D. and Conway, N. (2001) *Organisational Change and the Psychological Contract*, CIPD, London.

Hall, D.T. (1976) *Careers in Organisations*, Glenview, Illinois, Scot, Foresman.

Hall, D.T. (1996) 'Protean careers of the 21st century', *Academy of Management Executive*, Special Issue, Vol. 10, No. 4, pp. 8–16.

Hall, D.T. (ed.) (1996) *The Career is Dead-Long Live the Career: A Relational Approach to Careers*, San Francisco, Jossey-Bass.

Hall, D.T. and Moss, J.E. (1998) 'The new protean career contract', *Organisational Dynamics*, Winter, pp. 22–37.

Handy, C. (1989) *Age of Unreason*, London, Arrow Books.

Hendry, J. (1999) 'Cultural theory & contemporary management organisation', *Human Relations*, Vol. 52, No. 5, pp. 557–77.

Herriot, P. (1992) *The Career Management Challenge: Balancing Individual & Organisational Needs*, London, Sage.

Herriot, P. and Pemberton, C. (1997) 'Facilitating new deals', in C. Hendry and R. Jenkins (eds), *Human Resource Management Journal*, Special edition, Vol. 7, No. 1 (Dec.), pp. 45–56.

Herriot, P., Manning, W. and Kidd, J. (1997) 'The content of the psychological contract' *British Journal of Management*, Vol. 8, pp. 151–62.

Hiltrop, J. (1998) 'Preparing people for the future: the next agenda for HRM', *European Management Journal*, Vol. 16, No. 1, pp. 70–78.

Ibarra, H. (2000) 'Making partner', *Harvard Business Review*, Mar.–Apr., pp. 147–55.

Iles, P., Mabey, C. and Robertson, I. (1990) 'HRM practices and employee commitment: possibilities, pitfalls & paradoxes', *British Journal of Management*, Vol. 1, pp. 147–57.

Joynt, P. and Morton, B. (1999) *The Global HR Manager*, London, CIPD.

Kanter, R.M. (1989a) 'The new managerial work', *Harvard Business Review*, Nov.–Dec., pp. 85–92.

Kanter, R.M. (1989b) *When Giants Learn to Dance*, London, International Thomson.

Kanter, R.M. (1993) *Men & Women of the Corporation*, second edition, New York, Basic Books.

Kerr, S. (1975) 'On the folly of rewarding A, while hoping for B', *Academy of Management Journal*, Vol. 18, No. 4 (Dec.), pp. 769–83.

Komisar, R. (2000) 'Goodbye career, hello success', *Harvard Business Review*, Mar.–Apr., 161–74.

Makin, P., Cooper, C. and Cox, C. (1996) *Organisations & the Psychological Contract*, Leicester, The British Psychological Press.

Meyer, J.P. and Allen, N.J. (1997) *Commitment in the Workplace*, London, Sage.

Miles, R.E. and Snow, C.C. (1984) 'Designing strategic HR systems', *Organisational Dynamics*, summer, pp. 36–52.

Millward, L.J. and Brewerton, P.M. (2000) 'Psychological contracts: employee relations for the 21st century', in Cooper and Robertson (eds), *International Review of Industrial & Organisational Psychology*, John Wiley & Sons [ISBN: 0471858552].

Mirvis, P.H. and Hall, D.T. (1996) 'Psychological success and the boundaryless career', in Arthur and Rousseau (eds), *Boundaryless Careers*, New York, OUP.

Osborn-Jones, T.C. (2000) 'Emergent theories of career: searching for a new employment orthodoxy', *Henley Working Paper 2000/3*, Henley on Thames, Henley Management College.

Osborn-Jones, T.C. (2001) *Managing Talent: Exploring the New Psychological Contract*, Henley on Thames, Henley Management College.

Peiperl, M., Arthur, M., Goffee, R. and Morris, T. (2000) *Career Frontiers: New Conceptions of Working Lives*, Oxford, OUP.

Rousseau, D.M. (1995) *Psychological Contracts in Organisations*, London, Sage.

Rousseau, D. and Schalk, R. (2000) 'Learning from cross-national perspectives on psychological contracts', in Rousseau and Schalk (eds), *Psychological Contracts in Employment: Cross National Perspectives*, California and London, Sage.

Rubery, J., Earnshaw, J., Marchington, M., Cooke, F. and Vincent, S. (2002) 'Changing organisational forms and the employment relationship', *Journal of Management Studies*, Vol. 39, No. 5 (July), 645–72.

Scase, R. (2002) *Living in the Corporate Zoo: Life and Work in 2010*, Oxford, Capstone.

Scase, R. and Goffee, R. (1989) *Reluctant Managers*, London, Routledge.

Schein, E.H. [1968] (1978) *Career Dynamics: Matching Individual & Organisational Needs*, Reading, MA, Addison-Wesley.

Schein, E.H. [1985] (1990) *Career Anchors: Discovering your Real Values*, San Francisco, Calif., Jossey-Bass.

Sparrow, P. (1998) 'New organisational forms, processes, jobs and psychological contracts', in P. Sparrow and M. Marchington (eds), *HRM The New Agenda*, London, FT Management.

Sturges, J., Guest, D., Conway, N. and Mackenzie Davey, K. (2002) 'A longitudinal study of the relationship between career management & organisational commitment among graduates in the first ten years at work', *Journal of Organisational Behaviour*, Vol. 23, 731–48.

Sullivan, S.E. (1999) 'The changing nature of careers: a review & research agenda', *Journal of Management*, Vol. 25, No. 3, 457–84.

Sullivan, S.E., Carden, W.A. and Martin, D.F. (1998) 'Careers in the next millennium: directions for future research', *Human Resource Management Review*, Vol. 8, No. 2, pp. 165–85.

Truss, C., Gratton, L., Hope-Hailey, V., McGovern, P. and Stiles, P. (1997) 'Soft & hard models of human resource management: a reappraisal', *Journal of Management Studies*, Vol. 34, No. 1 (Jan.), 53–73.

Whittington, R., Pettigrew, A., Peck, S., Fenton, E. and Conyon, M. (1999) 'Change and complementarities in the new competitive landscape: a European panel study, 1992–1996', *Organisation Science*, Vol. 10, No. 5 (Sept.–Oct.), pp. 583–600.

Managing virtual teams

Shawn Ireland

The impact of organisational structures on performance has surfaced as a recurring theme throughout the book. The editors have selected the challenge of managing teams that are dispersed, diversified and physically detached as one of the major structural challenges of organisations in the 21st century. New technology and globalisation have propelled the management of virtual teams into the spotlight, hence this chapter is the focus of our attention. The writer proposes an important new concept – virtual team orientation (VTO) – as a means of developing and managing effective virtual teams.

Introduction

A colleague recently posed the following questions to senior managers participating in an international business leadership forum:

> In your experience, is there a difference between a group and a team? If so, what are the differences?

To our surprise, these two simple questions generated a one-hour debate examining the distinctions between groups and teams, their importance as business and management tools and their impact on business performance. For this group of managers, the need to deliver business results across multiple time zones, geography, national boundaries and cultures, often through the use of remote project teams, challenged their traditional notions of a team. The ingredients for successful teams – clear goals and objectives, level of trust, sense of interdependence and cohesiveness – (Babbington-Smith 1979; Blake *et al*. 1987; Schein 1988; Argyris 1990, 1992; Tyson and Jackson 1992; Katzenbach and Smith 1993) – proved inadequate to explain the requirements of virtual or remote project teams in their business settings. Most notable was the lack of consistent guidance on "best practice" for organising, deploying, supporting and evaluating the work of virtual teams.

A *virtual team* may be defined as:

> Multiple actors, separated by boundaries of time and/or distance, who leverage technology to conduct discrete interpersonal, social and economic exchanges of value to produce an outcome. Virtual team members have a common purpose, goal and approach to working together that hold them mutually accountable for their performance.

Emerging paradigm: virtual teams

The concepts of a *team* and *work-group* in a business context is supported by a well-developed body of research and literature in the study of group dynamics, leadership, organisation behaviour, team building and performance management (Argyle 1972; Dyer 1977; Adair 1986; Tannenbaum *et al.* 1992; Belbin 1993, 2003; Katzenbach and Smith 1993; Ray and Bronstein 1995; Higgs 1997). The literature has offered guidance and "best practice" for a generation of managers, learning and development professionals and the consulting industry. Whilst definitional variations exist in this literature between a *team* and a *work-group*, they offer the following distinctions:

- A *team* develops a common purpose, an approach to its work where members are interdependent, held mutually accountable and engage in relationship building opportunities to enhance performance. Relationship building is a principal building block of the team.

- A *work-group* has no critical business imperative or incremental performance requirement to function as a team. Members work together to share information, define tasks and collect information that enables decisions or actions to be taken. Task completion is the main focus of the work-group.

If we return to the definition of a virtual team proposed earlier in this chapter, the first core element – multiple actors separated by boundaries of time and/or distance who leverage technology to conduct discrete interpersonal, social and economic exchanges of value to produce an outcome – presents managers with a series of dilemmas, especially those managers with knowledge and experience in the study of *teams* and *work-groups*. In what specific manner may the use of technology and distance among members alter the structure and execution of the exchanges of value? What role does technology and distance play on influencing evaluation and accountability in the way a virtual team functions? Will the literature on *teams* and *teamwork* provide relevant guidance for practitioners and managers of virtual teams?

The second core element – commitment to a common purpose, goal and approach to working that hold team members mutually accountable for their performance – is supported by the results of research and literature examining the critical factors influencing team performance (Argyle 1972; Dyer 1977; Belbin 1993; Ray and Bronstein 1995; Adair 1986; Tannenbaum *et al.* 1992; Katzenbach and Smith 1993; Higgs 1997). This literature provides a rich and varied set of tools and guidance to assist managers in the development of teams.

The usefulness of guidance offered by the literature on teams and their development may prove less helpful to managers of virtual teams. This rests, in part, on the assumptions informing the notions of *teams* and *teamwork*. Four assumptions often emerge from the literature:

1 team members are co-located or are within a reasonable distance to support frequent person-to-person contact;

2 a team enhances project and/or business performance;

3 a commitment exists in the organisation to provide the time, resources and competencies to develop a team;

4 a team operates most effectively within the umbrella of an organisation structure.

Of particular interest is the first premise – teams are generally co-located or have opportunities for face-to-face contact. This is a critical element in developing a team or high performing team (Katzenbach and Smith 1993; Higgs 1997) yet creates a dilemma for managers using virtual teams. With the absence of co-location, will a virtual team develop the attributes of a high performing team? In particular, are these attributes even essential for virtual teams to be high performing?

In this chapter the role of virtual teams as a business and management tool is examined. Virtual teams are analysed within the context of existing guidance on teams and teamwork. This includes an exploration of assumptions informing the use of virtual teams and methods to critically examine those assumptions hindering their use as a management tool. The readiness of an organisation to embrace the use of virtual teams and the key organisational "core" competencies for successful deployment of virtual teams is explored. Critical elements supporting the success of virtual teams including selection criteria, starting a team and sustaining the work of the team are discussed with a view to defining initial principles of "best practice" for virtual teams. We conclude with an examination of future considerations for managers as they utilise virtual teams as a management tool.

This author's training and consultancy company has worked with virtual teams in diverse organisations ranging from Fortune 500 companies to government and international aid organisations for over 20 years. These organisations have used virtual teams in business and project delivery and as management development tools. This experience provides us with a rich and varied source of data, including first-hand personal accounts, to examine the impact of virtual teams on management practice. Whilst we rely on research and writing to anchor our ideas, these real-life experiences provide tangible support for insight, relevance and evidence as we pursue a path of conceptual development.

Assumptions

Initially, it was thought that managers and decision-makers would embrace virtual teams when they understood the value such teams bring to business performance.

This was based, in part, on studies examining the link between teams and business performance (Katzenbach and Smith 1993; Higgs 1997), the efficiencies of using teams and technology as a tool for enhancing team performance (Durante and Snyder 1996, 2001; Cohen and Gibson 2003) and on a drive in many organisations to leverage technology as a tool to gain competitive advantage.

In our practice, we found a series of long-standing assumptions informed managers' views on the nature and role of virtual teams. These assumptions can be summarised as follows:

- Virtual teams are a "cheap and cheerful" alternative to traditional teams or work-groups due to leveraging the use of technology.

- Virtual teams harness organisation talent in multiple locations.

- Technology equals cost savings; virtual teams are therefore more cost effective.

- Virtual teams diminish the need to address the "human" dimensions of team development.

The last assumption is of particular interest. The premise driving this assumption rests on two features – *face time* takes time, an ingredient in short supply for many managers – and distance diminishes emotional attachment. This presents managers with two dilemmas. What is the value of *face time* especially in the deployment of a virtual team? And how do we sustain the emotional attachment over long distances?

To explore the implication of these assumptions and dilemmas further, we have found it beneficial for managers to develop an opinion on five critical questions. These questions are:

1   Does the traditional notion of teamwork apply to remote or virtual teams?

2   Are we, as an organisation, comfortable using a virtual team to deliver high volume, focused business performance, rather than people being individually managed in remote locations?

3   Can we identify a set of performance management tools to ensure the success of a virtual team even though they may vary from the standard company system?

4   What unique competencies or skills are required in our organisation to ensure the success of virtual teams?

5   How does our organisational culture influence the support and use of virtual teams?

An exploration of these questions often provides managers with a degree of insight into the use of "teams" as a process for managing business across time zones and remote locations; the role performance management systems play in supporting or in detracting from working in teams and; an insight into the role and value of a virtual team as a viable tool to deliver business performance.

We offer five assumptions in support of the use of virtual teams as a management tool for delivering business performance:

1 Virtual teams are efficient vehicles for leveraging the talents of employees across the business.

2 Technology diminishes the need to co-locate teams enabling virtual teams to operate continuously.

3 Virtual teams are cost-effective tools to advance business strategies.

4 For large, complex projects, virtual teams provide an opportunity for managers to "step out of the box" in a competitive marketplace.

5 Virtual teams often require stretching the boundaries of organisational processes and systems to achieve results.

Each of these assumptions relies on managers adopting a more strategic or holistic view of how an organisation functions to deliver business outcomes and a less structured approach to the way they utilise the use of teams to achieve business strategies.

Traditional management and virtual teams

In a business environment requiring the combination of multiple competencies and experience across an organisation, a virtual team often produces better results than individuals (Durante and Snyder 1996, 2001; Cohen and Gibson 2003). Virtual teams, however, may challenge the basic notions underlying management practice, organisation systems, accountability and performance management systems.

The distinctions between established notions supporting management practice and leading virtual teams reflects a difference in orientation. We summarise these distinctions in orientation in Table 7.1.

These differences require managers to take a view on their level of comfort and readiness for utilising virtual teams, recognising the inherent conflicts this will pose. The use of a virtual team may diminish their level of control over daily activities, limit their flexibility to manage work flow and conflict with the organisational systems and structures designed to evaluate performance. To impose traditional levels of accountability and management practice may limit the inherent value of a virtual team. We do not advocate virtual teams to operate outside the requirements of management practice. Rather, a clearly defined agreement between management and members of the virtual team on how these issues will be addressed is required.

Table 7.1 Differences between virtual teams and management practice

Organisational Criteria	Virtual team	Management practice
Objectives/tasks	● Develop or optimise organisational talent from across the organisation ● Specific, targeted goals linked to business strategies ● Time limited, focused and leveraging the use of technology	● Work with known products, processes and organisational talent ● Multiple objectives and goals ● Optimise ongoing processes
People	● People with different experiences, competencies and values ● Temporary team composition based on business needs	● People with similar experiences and values ● Plan to optimise resource use over time
Systems	● Systems must be created or modified to integrate/ evaluate work	● Systems in place to integrate/ evaluate work
Risks	● Higher uncertainty of outcome, time lines and deliverables ● Disturbs status quo	● Higher certainty of outcome, cost, and deliverables ● Supports status quo

The benefits and risks of virtual teams to members, management and the organisation do not differ remarkably from the role played by intact teams or high-performing teams (Table 7.2 (overleaf)). From the perspective of virtual team members, the agreement to join a virtual team may be a career risk for they may cede control over assessment of their individual performance. Management may cede accountability and control, and organisations may cede control over institutional risk by diminishing systems and structures that support stability. In this context though it is important not to lose sight of the vital connection between risk taking and performance.

Virtual teams as a business and management tool: transforming perspectives and the virtual team orientation (VTO)

The successful deployment of a virtual team may raise any number of potentially difficult organisational issues. Managing these issues requires a brutally honest assessment of the contributing role virtual teams play in the delivery of business results, the readiness of the business to embrace virtual teams as a business and management tool, an appreciation and understanding of the technical, human and organisational dimensions of virtual teamwork, and agreement on the "added value" virtual teams bring to the strategic focus of business delivery.

Table 7.2 Benefits and risks of virtual teams to management practice

	Benefits for the organisation	Associated risks	Suggestions
Goal	Set challenging and innovative goals	Difficulties in executing multiple, divergent business goals across cultures and time zones at the same time	Focus on strategic clarity
	Leverage assets from across the business	Choosing wrong people, strategy or technology	Develop and evaluate alternative solutions
	Develop flexibility and agility across the business	Heavy political, competitive and time pressure	Support the creation of a virtual team culture in the organisation
Communication	Reduced communication effort through dispersed teams	Unclear loyalties, division of roles or tasks within the team	Team-based planning together with management
	Improved speed and flexibility of communication	Higher degree of uncoordination effort. Remote locations may not have technology infrastructure to support virtual teams	Communication audit, team-based decisions on best communication strategies and technologies
Change	Quickly react to market and customer requirements	Speed of work may overwhelm the entire organisation	Place greater importance on linking results to strategy
	Quickly shift to new technologies	Wrong solution or technology could be chosen	Develop and evaluate alternative solutions
Structure	Organisational structures to support flexibility and responsibility at all levels	Overburdening virtual team members with organisational structures	Agree boundaries and roles of the virtual team members
	Quicker release of resources	Conflict with management over role and priorities for virtual team members	Choose team members based on reputation and personality in addition to technical skills
	Formal authority is replaced with interpersonal, technical and entrepreneurial competencies	Changing the power structure will meet with resistance from some line managers	Stakeholder management

To address these organisational issues, consider two hypotheses:

1 For virtual teams to be successful, they must break the "rules" of the organisation.

2 Managing a successful virtual team is essentially a political process.

When these hypotheses are presented to diverse groups of managers, often there is agreement followed by spirited debate. The affirmative response to both hypotheses rests in recognition by managers that virtual teams, by their nature, require the creation of a revised set of taken-for-granted assumptions regarding the way work is accomplished in an organisation. These revised assumptions inform the basic notions of what constitutes virtual team "best practice" and the organisational "core competencies" required to deliver effective performance.

The decision to use a virtual team requires managers to acknowledge that the established notions of "management practice" may not be useful. Virtual teams expose complexities and ambiguities. The operating environment is less structured, organised and predictable. Furthermore, virtual teams will bring to the forefront paradoxes in deploying business strategies, and situations requiring a resolution between two or more opposing positions or ideas. Addressing the potential difficulties of remote communication, the availability of technology or media to communicate, multilingual demands, multiple stakeholder demands, regional or business unit strategic priorities, organisational systems and structures, legal requirements, regional management practices and local business requirements, require "stepping back" and examining the environment with a different perspective. Inevitably, many of these elements will merge, posing potential barriers to the work of virtual teams, where a solution requires a different set of "perspectives". In deploying virtual teams there are few universal rights and wrongs or clear answers to strategic dilemmas and no clearly defined "best practice" when working across business units, across functions and across cultures.

For these reasons, managers may view the use and role of virtual teams with some scepticism. The primary reason for this reluctance may be due to a lack of conviction that virtual teams are a valid delivery tool and that they do not deliver results more effectively and efficiently than other delivery methods. Further, there may be confusion over capabilities and requirements for effective use of virtual teams, and the degree of flexibility and risk a manager is willing to support as a result of deploying a virtual team.

This reluctance is understandable, given the performance demands managers face on a daily basis. Working with an unknown or untested management tool without ample guidance or the use of a "best practice" tool kit diminishes the likelihood of adoption. Overcoming this reluctance requires what Mezirow (1991) describes as a *perspective transformation* – challenging the habits of expectation supporting the perceiving and comprehending of new information or ways of understanding. Perspective transformation asks managers to engage in a process of critical self-reflection – examining those taken-for-granted premises or ways of thinking which create a perspective and then vigorously critiquing them. Variations in the development of perspective transformation as a learning process range from *self-scrutiny* (Brookfield 1987), *conscientization* (Freire 1970; Freire and Shor 1987), *libertory education* (Giroux 1983) and *reflection-in-action* (Schon 1987). The outcome of critical self-reflection is to examine new or simply different ways of thinking about the way we practise as a manager.

A short case study will help illustrate the points raised so far.

Case Study 1

Engineers from a regional technology company in the Middle East were organised as a virtual team to deliver a unique, state-of-the-art telecommunications metre system for multiple government clients. Key to the delivery was the use of high technology production facilities supported by technical experts from business units in other parts of the region. To achieve this goal required utilising, for the first time, a virtual team and expertise available only from two countries in the region with differing religious, political, cultural and economic interests. These requirements provoked resistance amongst team members leading to members asking to leave the project or diminishing their contribution. The intervention of an impartial third party as facilitator along with the use of case studies, critical incident reports and facilitated discussions with teams in a similar type of situation provided an opportunity to critique and discuss the implications of working as a virtual team and with other members of different backgrounds on this project. The virtual team debated the implications of working in this manner initially using remote technology and later in a face-to-face team meeting.

Overcoming a number of long maintained and cherished assumptions held sacrosanct by members proved difficult. A small number of team members reported discomfort, fear and emotional turmoil. Most team members found the discussions examining taken-for-granted assumptions uncomfortable yet helpful for revising their way of thinking about working as a virtual team. At the conclusion of the discussions, three teams members chose to be replaced. The project did not deliver the metre on time but the virtual team is now working on a second project together.

This experience provides insight into the use of perspective transformation. Most of these virtual team members found the *idea* of working with members from the new countries more anxiety provoking than the *actual* working together. The team also agreed that it was more comfortable as a starting point to work together on a "virtual" basis rather than meet face to face. They agreed to meet together at a later time to assess their performance working as a virtual team. This agreement provided a basic foundation for working together on the project.

Challenging taken-for-granted assumptions in culturally appropriate ways is key to perspective transformation. In essence, it is a "request" for managers or team members to step beyond the comfort of habits and consider different or new ways of approaching virtual teams. Managers have at their disposal a set of tools to support this process.

- *Critical incident reports* – The use of critical incident reports (Knowles 1980; Laird 1985; Nadler 1989) examines immediate or past performance against expectations by critically examining the factors helping and hindering the outcome. Critical incident reports provide a tailored, business-specific tool for addressing simple or complex problems faced by virtual teams.

- *Case study method* – The case study method (Knowles 1980; Laird 1985; Nadler 1989) is an oral or written record of a situation or event examined with the benefit of hindsight. A case study enables managers to apply critical thinking and analysis skills to gain new insights and perspectives on events.

- *Facilitated discussions* – Facilitated discussions (Laird 1985; Brookfield 1986; Freire and Shor 1987; Nadler 1989) offer managers an opportunity to examine performance outcomes against assumptions in the company of peers with a mutual interest. This form of discussion is collaborative in nature and will require a degree of personal courage and analytical ability.

- *Reflective questioning* – As a form of facilitated discussion, reflective questioning (Laird 1985; Bolton 1986; Nadler 1989) is an inquiry into an event designed to test ideas, stimulate thinking, challenge assumptions and clarify understanding. The goal is to arouse interest in an issue by eliciting opinions and feelings, the sharing of relevant experience and interests with answers leading to further questions of inquiry.

These tools may be supported by a number of organisational stakeholders. These can include management, peers and supervisors, experienced third parties, an internal or external facilitator or by a person who can provide feedback as a direct result of experience participating in or managing deployment of a virtual team.

Virtual team orientation (VTO) model

The *virtual team orientation* (VTO) model offers managers an opportunity to critically examine assumptions concerning the use and deployment of virtual teams in the present operating environment of the organisation. The assumptions may be similar or differ from those identified earlier in this chapter.

To this end, the VTO identifies key dimensions that directly contribute to the potential success of virtual teams within the confines of management practice. The VTO reflects the lessons we have learned over 12 years of working with virtual teams in a variety of business settings and organisational environments, providing a range of deliverables. The guiding principles supporting the VTO are derived from three elements: a growing body of research and writing on the impact of managing change in a fast paced business environment (Ghoshal and

Bartlett 1994; Collins 2001); the study of adult education and development (Guba and Lincoln 1981; Schon 1987; Barry and Rudinow 1990; Watkins and Marsick 1993; Ireland 1994); and the findings obtained from post-mortem review sessions with virtual teams that have been disbanded.

The credibility of the VTO rests on managers allowing virtual team members a sufficient level of participation to define the deliverable; place the deliverable within a strategic context, enabling the work of the team to have meaning and focus despite distance and time zone changes; have a view on the structures and tools for working as a team and managing its performance; and take a view of their work and deliverables within the climate of the business.

In more practical terms, the VTO provides an orientation for managers to assess the organisation's readiness to accept the use of virtual teams as a tool for delivering business. We accept that no organisation will be fully ready on each element. Furthermore, additional elements specific to industries and regions may alter the focus. The choice of these elements comes from lessons learned in working with virtual teams. This is not meant to be an exhaustive list but rather a starting point for managers to build their own set of elements. The critical issue for managers to address is their organisation's readiness, more or less, to leverage the use of virtual teams as a management tool.

The VTO addresses the following dimensions, presented in Figure 7.1.

Figure 7.1 Virtual team orientation model

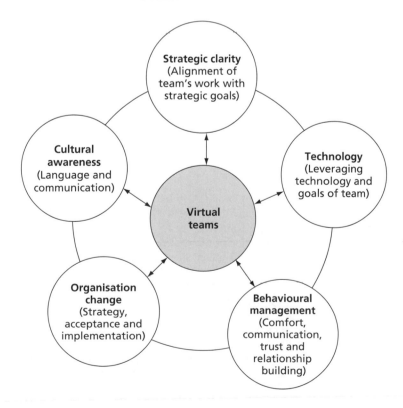

Strategic clarity

Virtual teams often function within a strategic vacuum fostered by the ambiguity created when people are tasked with working cross-functionally as a team. Distance, time zones, cultural norms, organisational and national politics will conspire to erode the continuity and clarity of the team's work, despite the best efforts of management to provide structure and consistency. Strategic clarity aligns the work of the team with how the business positions itself in the marketplace. In a competitive business environment, it links the work of the team to secure or sustain a competitive advantage in the marketplace. In other organisational environments, it connects the work of the team with the strategic imperatives of the organisation. In its basic form, strategic clarity diminishes the vacuum by linking the existence of the virtual team to the overall strategic imperative or intent of the business.

To secure any level of strategic clarity, it is critical for team members to have a global point of view on how the work of the team fits into the overall business strategy. Virtual teams often take independent actions and decisions outside the traditional organisation structures. The team has to operate and think more strategically especially in response to the immediate needs for action. Indeed, the more urgent and meaningful the outputs of the team, the more management will need to link the work of the team to the overall focus and direction of the business.

Securing strategic clarity requires the virtual team to negotiate a set of clearly defined, relevant and targeted performance goals within the business strategy. Furthermore, at the inception of the team, members need to address divergent or conflicting business unit goals/expectations within the team. This will require the team to take a view on placing their work within the broader context of the business, with potential local conflicts, such as management control of team members' time, accountability, performance management, superseded by the larger strategic imperative of the business. This also allows team members to link the actions of the team with the overall goals of the business. Finally, it sustains the motivation and momentum of their work over time.

Case Study 2

A co-funded regional development project in Eastern Europe supported by the EU and the United States Agency for International Development (USAID) required a virtual team to deploy the project from five capital cities. The delivery of the project was critical to establishing key targets for the redevelopment of the region. Due to the political, cultural and linguistic dimensions of the project, the team members initiated the project by meeting in person as a team prior to the launch of the project. Team representatives met with key stakeholders from organisations involved, with the specific goal of understanding how the project fitted into their mandate and the overall agency strategy. The team defined their goals, planning and delivery strategies as well as their performance criteria to reflect the purpose and intent of the sponsoring organisations. This was especially difficult as the team had to overcome conflicting goals, diverse expectations, cultural ambiguities and political/economic strategies influencing the sponsoring organisations and the receiving agencies.

> A project post-mortem revealed that framing the context of the project around the goals of the key organisations significantly modified the working structure, planning and implementation of the project, informed the types of technology used to communicate, shifted the choice of location, language and delivery methods, and required team members to negotiate local arrangements for project support and materials. It also informed the choice of evaluation criteria chosen by the team to judge their performance.

To gain strategic clarity within the context of the VTO, managers and team members are encouraged to address the following issues at the beginning of the team's life. The orientation process requires managers to take a view on six key questions:

1   In basic terms, what are the specific deliverables expected of the virtual team?

2   What gaps exist between local business strategy and the larger organisation strategy that impact the ability of the virtual team members to work together and/or achieve their goals?

3   What are the organisational and political constraints to the successful achievement of the deliverables?

4   Who are the stakeholders crucial to the team deliverable and what are their positions (opposed, neutral, supportive); and what stakeholder strategies will be deployed to assist the team in its working relationships?

5   To be successful as a virtual team what organisational practices must change? What must stop? What must be modified? And what must be created?

6   What leadership and management practices are required for the team to work effectively within the business culture?

You will see from the focus of these questions that the deployment of virtual teams requires a more holistic view of the strategic intent of the business to be able to understand the goals as they relate to the mandate of the team's task.

Key issues to address: What is the opinion of the management team about virtual teams acting independently yet within the confines of the overall strategic intent of the business? Will management feel confident supporting actions of a virtual team that do not sit within the traditional decision-making structures of the business?

Technical appreciation

Team members need to clarify and critically evaluate the accessibility, viability and credibility of communication alternatives. Due to the variety of locations, communication technology must be evaluated honestly for its suitability as a communication tool for use by virtual teams.

The choice of communication medium establishes the foundations for team success. Whilst some variations in teams do exist, our experience reflects the outcome of work conducted by Hofner-Saphiere (1999). Team members found the most effective technology to be email and telephone rather than more sophisticated technologies such as videoconferencing. According to the results of her research, 63 per cent of members rated email as the most useable technology. Most teams use two or more technologies inclusive of telephone, email, message mail and Lotus Notes. Real-time communication technologies are not essential to team success.

Additionally, written communication appears to be the medium of choice for most of the work of a virtual team. Whilst email remains the technology of choice, fax and mail have been used by a number of teams. Written communication can de-personalise the communication, especially when disagreements and the demands of the task create conflict amongst team members. Furthermore, it offers members a breathing space to reflect and examine the content of a communication that is often missing from the psychological intensity of face-to-face or telephone communication. This element of virtual team life may provide the foundations for a more focused approach to the task of a team's work, especially when a team is spread out over diverse geographical regions.

The development of a technology plan, agreed between the members and IT professionals, provides a roadmap for leveraging technology options. Based on the results of team performance to date, the specific components of a technology plan should reflect the organisation's expectations and tolerance for technology. It is worth remembering that when technology fails, a suitable back-up plan is essential to sustaining the work of the team.

Case Study 3

In the midst of a short term, business critical project for a global telephony firm, a series of typhoons battered the regions of the Pacific Rim ranging from Hong Kong to Tokyo. The storms eliminated basic electrical and telephone services for over three weeks in many areas. Team members in these regions were isolated from their colleagues in the rest of Asia and Europe depriving them of critical data essential to the delivery of the project. With no back-up plan, the team missed the deadline resulting in the loss of a market leadership position.

This company now builds contingency plans for communication and deployment of expertise required for all virtual teams.

Issues for discussion: What are the technological limitations and opportunities influencing standard work practice in the organisation? How will these limitations and opportunities impact the ability of the virtual team to sustain and deliver results? What are the preferred communication links between team members?

Behavioural management

People bring to a virtual team a range of psychological requirements (implicit/explicit needs, goals and expectations) that dictate the level of involvement and commitment to the work of a virtual team. We know that motivation is directly linked to the level of participation in a team especially around problem-solving, decision-making and resolving the business issues associated with the mandate of the team.

From the perspective of the members, four critical psychological dimensions need to be addressed. These include comfort, communication, trust and relationship building.

Comfort

In our review of virtual team performance, we have found a direct link between the performance of a virtual team and the psychological comfort of members. Virtual teams may require members to contribute a higher level of emotional energy or secure an "emotional investment" to achieve success. Members will provide the team with differing levels of emotional commitment – the level of emotional investment – to the task. This appears to have no correlation to culture or business environment. It is linked directly to the psychological needs of members in response to the ambiguities and clarity of the team's mandate.

Critical to decisively managing these psychological needs is providing "face time" at some point during the life of the team.

Communication

Not surprisingly, the level of communication (number of times the virtual team members interact with each other) has a direct impact on the success of the virtual team. At a deeper level of analysis, the most successful teams have made the effort to meet face-to-face at least once during the life of the virtual team, most often at an initial kick-off meeting. We have also found that the type of technology used by the team, the frequency and length of communication, the format of interactions, the frequency of interactions and the more focused the discussion, the more effective was the work of the virtual team.

Directly linked to communication is the sensitivity of managers to the difficulties faced in communicating remotely. In our work with virtual teams we have identified four peculiarities in remote communication.

Words are imprecise tools for communication. Often, we find the ideas we wish to communicate do not fit into words and sentences. This is especially common when we are communicating across languages – we are unable to say in precise terms what we mean. Remote communication, unlike face-to-face communication, relies heavily on the content of messages to convey meaning. It is critical for team members to take a few moments to reflect back to the other members the understanding of words, especially when they lack clarity, are ambiguous or based on jargon.

Distractions interrupt the attention and focus of team members. Depending on the location and use of technology, the emotional state of a team member, the time of day or the level of stress, members are easily deflected from concentrating on the work of the team. The average rate of speech for many languages is approximately 125–145 words per minute. This rate is slow for the brain, which can process information four times faster than we speak. The outcome, depending on the mode of communication, is that other items within themselves or in the immediate environment can preoccupy team members. It becomes essential for team members to clarify via technology the intent and purpose of the communication sent. This is true for voice or written communication.

The *meaning perspective* of communication between and among team members reflects an interaction between feelings, thoughts and behaviours of team members. When a police commander wishes to convey directions to a team of operatives on the street and does not want others to know the plans, they often send a coded message, that they hope will be understood only by the operatives. This reflects what happens in real world communication. Virtual team members report that they are often ambivalent about expressing themselves accurately. This is especially true when cultural and language sensitivities are active in a team. The result is that team members can find themselves speaking obscurely about ideas and even less clearly about feelings. In some cultures, we have been trained to speak indirectly on many topics or not to express our feelings.

Productive virtual teams have an agreed set of communication rules where members are given permission to do a "perspective check" when they feel they are becoming disconnected from the content of the work.

The presenting issue or content for discussion may not be the major concern of the team. Virtual teams often report that their meetings (via video/telephone or other technologies) are the most difficult part of the experience. People rarely initiate conversations focused on the matters of greatest concern. Everyone "travels incognito" to varying degrees. Before we get into a bath, we may test the water to make sure the temperature is right. A virtual team can provide an ideal opportunity for people to hide behind issues or difficulties and avoid dealing with the concerns they may have about a task or obligation. Teams often come up with solutions to minor problems while the more difficult issues and concerns are not addressed. Leaders of productive teams express an expectation that team members will support a "perspective check" in order to provide an opportunity to address concerns floating just below the surface.

Communicating a shared vision and goals are the glue that holds the team together. Members of virtual teams need to simply state and "communicate" a shared vision and goals for the mandate of the virtual team. Productive teams re-define their purpose and goals within the limits of the strategic goals of the business. The term "communicate" is stressed for it is more than just developing a vision and set of goals. It reflects a specific, clearly defined set of outcomes that are meaningful to team members and help define the level of commitment and energy required to be productive as a member.

Furthermore, due to the nature of working as a virtual team, members often want to know the performance expectations – what they are going to be held accountable for as a team and as an individual contributor. Indeed, the more urgent the need, the more likely the team will be able to fully develop and communicate a vision and goal consistent with the overall business strategy.

Trust – The dynamics of working with others unseen over periods of time, the tendency of technology to de-personalise relationships and the requirements of many adults to support their work relationships with some degree of emotional connection, place the role of trust at the centre of virtual team life. In this context we define trust as the team's ability to bring to the surface, in culturally appropriate ways, those differences in goals, expectations and opinions that can impact disproportionately on the work of the team. In the life of any team, disagreements, misunderstanding and mistakes will occur.

Building working relationships requires leaders of virtual teams to address the emotional and interpersonal issues when they surface. Our experience suggests that in order to build the requisite level of trust on a virtual team, leaders must foster working relationships that are characterised by a culturally appropriate level of openness or willingness to share and learn how to address emotional needs of members, with flexibility in approach to solutions and outcomes. In general, virtual teams operate with few rules, norms or precedents for how to work effectively as a unit. Fostering a willingness to share information across cultural and technological boundaries, addressing disagreements and problems immediately they occur and supporting a level of communication with respect and understanding, enable teams to push beyond the inevitable conflicts that emerge in any situation where people must work together.

It is crucial for managers to remember that people do not automatically work well together as a group or team despite a common culture or work setting. In particular, the use of technology creates unique challenges for the work of virtual teams. We can assume that the use of technology would necessarily de-personalise the work of conflict resolution and problem-solving. From observing high-performing virtual teams, when disagreements surface, the use of the written medium, coupled with time delays between communications, de-personalise the situation. This suggests that a sufficient level of trust and openness, coupled with the safety of distance and time, can be a benefit to working on relationship issues.

Case Study 4

A global technology-consulting firm with a strong, tightly knit family-based culture, deployed a virtual team of volunteer technical and marketing members to deliver a one-off integrated client solution in the record time of three weeks. The members with necessary expertise were located in Europe and the United States and had not worked together before. The leader of the team was based in California. Throughout the three-week deployment, the team interacted daily via videoconference. When the project commenced, the team leader noted that due to the tight delivery schedule, he would define the tasks, establish work schedules and milestones for each phase of the delivery and sought minimal feedback from team members. Videoconference meeting times were scheduled for 9:00 California time. During the three weeks, the full team was not present for video conferences, technical problems diminished voice and picture quality, other work continued during the videoconference, deadlines were missed by the US-based members, and conflicts over meeting times (due to time zone differences) were not addressed. The project was delivered on time by the European team but did not meet full customer specifications.

The most important finding to emerge from this team's post-mortem was the lack of enthusiasm and interest in the deliverable. The team reported feeling disconnected from the development process, leader and the client. Closer analysis revealed a lack of clarity on how the deliverable fitted into the nature of the business strategy, with no client contact and technology frustrating the US team members.

Involving virtual team members in defining and planning deliverables is essential, even on teams with short delivery schedules. This is especially important when team members do not have the opportunity to meet in person.

Relationship building

Selection of members for core teams often lacks any structure. One member reported being chosen for a team because he happened to be walking down the corridor between offices! Whilst this is the exception rather than the rule, productive team members have a good understanding of how the organisation works, the key stakeholder relationships essential to getting the work done, and have the ability to assess what is needed to make things happen. The critical ingredient here is the ability to establish and maintain relationships or networking. To this end we have been able to identify a set of individual member competencies critical to the relationship building requirement of a virtual team. These include:

- Problem-solving and decision-making;
- Interpersonal and cultural awareness;
- Enthusiasm for working on a virtual team;
- Time and support of management to contribute;
- A high degree of self-direction and motivation;
- An ability and desire to use technology as a source for working.

Since virtual teams tend to operate in an environment where few rules and precedents are available, leveraging relationships is often a key ingredient for getting the work done.

The difficulty with sustaining relationships on virtual teams rests in a basic human need to have time and contact to build trust and comfort with others.

The most significant barrier to virtual team success rests in lack of face-to-face contact, particularly in the early stages. Speaking with members of virtual teams during post-team review sessions, they report the level of commitment is directly related to the level of contact. Audio- and videoconferencing do assist in sustaining the basic relationship development but do not replace the need for occasional face-to-face contact. This may be the major drawback to the use of virtual teams where intensive work among the team members is required.

The importance of the emotional dimensions of relationship building in the creation of successful virtual teams has been noted earlier. This dimension is probably the most difficult for organisations and managers to assess. When we deal in the emotional realm of human interactions, the notion of logic, rational thinking and common sense take on a subtler, less concrete nature. We have encouraged leaders of virtual teams to develop their *third ear* to understand the undercurrents that may be influencing the work of the virtual team. Learning to listen to *internal discourse*, or self-talk, is the most effective way to listen with the *third ear*.

Case Study 5

You are sitting in a virtual project team review session with colleagues from Asia, North America and the Middle East. During the meeting you notice by the voice and choice of language that a colleague in the Middle East sounds tense and appears to be frustrated and impatient. You ask this colleague if there is anything they require or if any issues remain to be addressed. He declines to add any more detail to the discussion.

For many virtual team leaders and members, this situation would be overlooked as an event of insignificance. Indeed, if it is noted at all, it is often viewed and dismissed as a result of cultural or personality issues. The analysis of the reasons supporting the reaction of the colleague can be analysed from a number of different perspectives. For our purposes, the critical feature for virtual team leaders and members to develop a *third ear* is attending to the observation and taking what are deemed appropriate steps to manage the colleague.

Whilst no clear-cut "best practice" is available to assist in relationship building on virtual teams, various actions by managers and virtual teams can be beneficial. These are indicated in Figure 7.2 (overleaf).

Key issues to address: Can management create and 'communicate' a shared vision and common direction for the virtual team? Is management able to clearly articulate the expectations and accountabilities of team members in team performance? Does the present business performance management system support members' activities on a virtual team?

Organisation change

Successful virtual teams will require some level of structure. The key issues here are what do team members need to know, what is the frequency and style of

Figure 7.2 Relationship building strategies

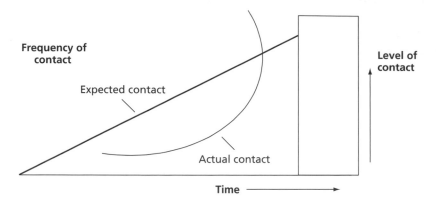

- support sharing of problems and conflicts related to project work
- establish formal communication controls
- encourage off-line communication
- reward successes/examine failures as a team
- agree dependencies
- clarify expectations, time/location/frequency of meetings
- agree autonomy
- define standards of team quality, performance and feedback
- assess technologies
- agree project management tools
- agree evaluation criteria
- schedule face-to-face meetings at regular intervals.

communication, what are the tools to manage conflicts, take decisions and deliver information to key stakeholders? Furthermore, due to divergent business goals across the team, members may feel compromised or torn between local business unit concerns and the larger strategic requirements of the virtual team.

Structure and control

Virtual teams require management to confront the paradox of ambiguity and lack of control in a business climate. This will mean recognising and accepting the complexity of the environment in which the virtual team works. Virtual team members will need to understand how the organisation gets things done, who are the key stakeholders and where power rests, who makes things happen. Within this environment, it will be essential for leaders of virtual teams to work with key local stakeholders to influence when required and to ensure the work of the team is supported when dual commitments and divided loyalties emerge. Productive teams define operating content and procedure, redefining when necessary, as the environment requires.

Linked to the success of a team is the organisation's support for rewarding team performance. Team leaders and members must clarify expectations of performance as a team. The difficulty here rests in the credibility of teamwork in the organisation as reflected in the performance management system used to measure success. If teamwork is expected but not rewarded, critical levels of commitment may be compromised. A successful virtual team is supported by a corporate performance management system placing a level of value on the members' and team's performance. Within this context, the virtual team is different from the sum of its parts, yet is intimately linked to individual performance.

Consider the following situation:

> ## Case Study 6
>
> A manager in a global oilfield business agrees to submit a bid for the installation of oilfield technology equipment in the field for a major client. The delivery of a bid required expertise from research centres and business units in a range of geographical areas. With a short time-line, limited resources and the daily demands of key staff in the field, the bid manager is confronted with organising and delivering a viable bid.

In theory, many organisations would organise a virtual team consisting of a series of experts and staff to contribute to the development of the bid via the use of technology. Some organisations even have in place a set of processes and structures to ensure the timely delivery of a bid to include a "stage and gate" development system and bid review sessions.

What actually happens? Managers report that these systems are used in principle but not in practice. In practice a small number of people work overtime, often doing special deals, calling in favours or using influence to get things accomplished. We call these systems espoused "as if" systems – systems which managers use in theory as a management tool but which are neither viable nor doable in practice.

Key issues to address: The management team's ability to accept ambiguity, handle the paradoxes and find resolution between two seemingly opposite positions or ideas, set aside the universal rights and wrongs of traditional styles of management across functions and cultures. Is management ready to accept the lack of control and the ambiguity that is fostered when deploying a virtual team?

Cultural awareness

Working across cultures requires team members to be aware of and appreciate the unique dimensions of national culture and work actions. Learned behaviours, automatic responses and psychological predispositions will necessarily influence the style of communication, what is communicated and the reaction to communication, especially when technology is involved.

Figure 7.3 provides a general summary of the interplay between culture and communication. Note the term *context culture* as the basic element influencing the communication requirements of team members. In this environment, we

Figure 7.3 Cultural and virtual team communication

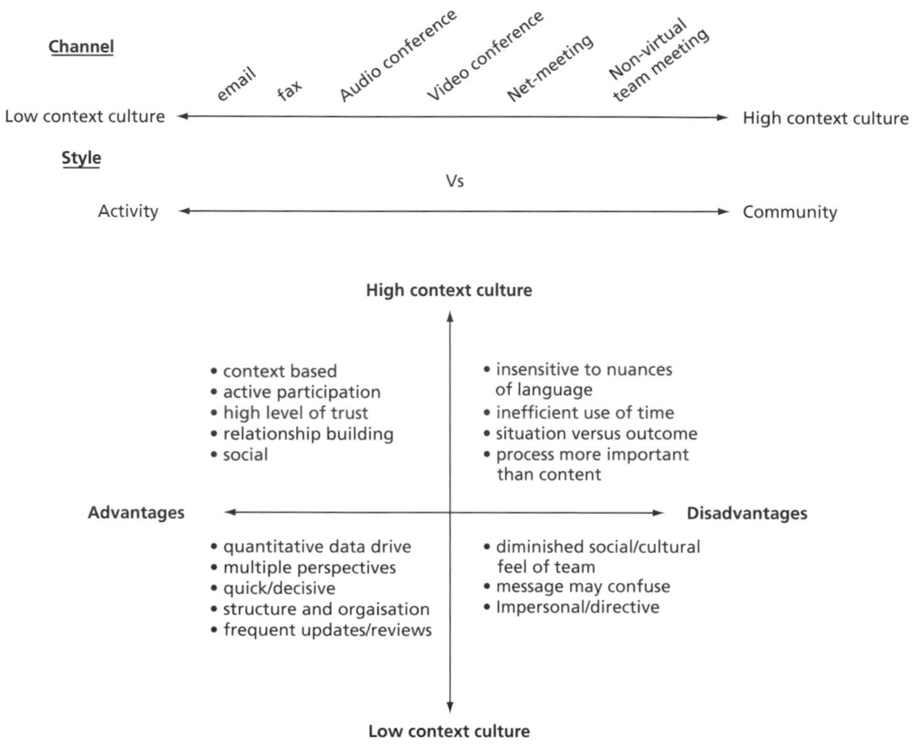

Channel

email   fax   Audio conference   Video conference   Net-meeting   Non-virtual team meeting

Low context culture ←————————————————————————→ High context culture

Style

Vs

Activity ←————————————————————————→ Community

High context culture

- context based
- active participation
- high level of trust
- relationship building
- social

- insensitive to nuances of language
- inefficient use of time
- situation versus outcome
- process more important than content

Advantages ←————————————————————————→ **Disadvantages**

- quantitative data drive
- multiple perspectives
- quick/decisive
- structure and orgaisation
- frequent updates/reviews

- diminished social/cultural feel of team
- message may confuse
- Impersonal/directive

Low context culture

Source: Adapted from Hofstede (1991), *Culture and Organizations: A Software of the Mind*.

define context culture as the expression of behavioural, psychological and cognitive dimensions informing cultural preferences.

Members of virtual teams should develop an appreciation of the effort required from all team members who do not speak the language of choice of the organisation. For those members who do not speak more than one language, the demands of working as a virtual team can be daunting.

Furthermore, unique behavioural and attitudinal components can influence the work of a virtual team.

Case Study 7

A small, French-based virtual team dedicated to dealing with client emergencies on a continuous basis in a global professional services firm, reported diminished coverage on Thursdays and Fridays in parts of the Middle East. Team members were not available on short notice when required. Due to cultural practice, Thursdays and Fridays were set-aside as days for religious retreat.

It is essential for virtual teams to take a view on the impact of cultural influences on the work of the team. Whilst this may be difficult for some members, the ability to highlight potential areas of conflict is essential to the work of the team.

Key issues to address: How rigid is management in requiring meetings to be conducted in the language of the business? Does management identify and support local cultural rules and norms as a condition for virtual team performance? Are virtual teams encouraged to coordinate activities around cultural requirements? What technical tools are available to overcome language barriers and does management support contributions from members where the language of business may not be their native tongue?

Application: success factors associated with the deployment of virtual teams

To summarise, we have identified a set of "core" factors that can inform "best practice" for successful virtual teams. These include:

- *Effective virtual team orientation* – provides a realistic review and outlook within the organisation for the support and role of a virtual team. This includes clarifying the value of the team's work to the larger business, a clear definition of team member contributions and participation, inclusive of expectations of team members and the team as a whole.

- *Participative planning as a team* – a business may provide members with a document to "communicate" the vision and goals of the project. This will enable the team to define their roles, rules for working and manner and scope of communication and technology, and provide the team with the opportunity to take decisions on execution. The key criterion here is that the *team* takes the lead on these activities with the support of management.

- *Effective communication* – clearly defining the tools for communicating whilst appreciating the common communication barriers that exist in human communication.

- *Relationship building* – recognising the emotional as well as cultural dimensions essential to develop the necessary discipline to work as a team.

- *Performance management* – team leaders and members need to set clear, detailed and task-specific performance goals. Productive virtual teams thrive on both members and the leader giving feedback formally and informally in culturally appropriate ways. Furthermore, will the business performance management system take into account the unique features of a virtual team?

- *Building of trust* – a level of trust is an essential ingredient to success when team members are dispersed across time zones and long distances. Consistency in words and actions, along with bringing to the surface those issues that keep it from working effectively, are critical success factors.

- *Stakeholder management* – virtual teams identify key stakeholders and their positions towards the work of the team. This involves defining the sources of power, which make things happen and who will have the most impact on the work of the team. Developing a stakeholder strategy provides agreed actions to influence the impact of stakeholders in the service of the teams' goals.

- *Networking* – understanding and managing the systems and structures in the organisation in service of the work of the virtual team.

- *Mentoring and career management* – people are often assigned to virtual teams by managers without consideration of the impact on career development and level of competencies to deliver results. Team members may become isolated from performance reviews or have managers unable to assess performance due to lack of oversight or contact with the work of team members. Team members and the team should keep records of their achievements.

- *Cultural sensitivity* – the work of many virtual teams is compromised by failure of team members to consider the impact of national and regional cultures. Cultural differences are not just based on nationality but on a unique set of behavioural, language and relationship variables.

- *Use of technology* – a critical assessment of the limits and opportunities of the organisation's technology assets to assist the work of the virtual team.

- *Managing the paradox of structure and adaptability* – productive virtual teams will require some level of structure. This requires negotiation with management to enable the team to develop its own structures, possibly outside the scope of standard organisation practice, to support the work of the team.

Future management considerations

We have focused on virtual teams as a business management tool. In the discipline of management and organisation development, virtual teams can also be a powerful tool for the development of business and behavioural competencies. A number of businesses are striving to meet new competitive challenges by utilising management and adult education practices to develop sustained competency development. This development need is in direct response to changes in the competitive business environment as well as to the need to measure the outcome via return on investment of the development initiatives. The deployment of virtual teams (global, regional or unit based) tasked with providing a deliverable to a business critical project links basic principles of adult education – adults learn by doing and adults learn by applying experience – to action-learning practice.

Figure 7.4 Performance development model

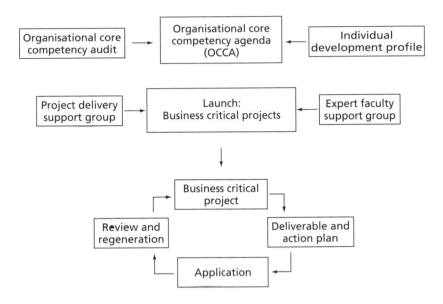

The performance development model (PDM), in Figure 7.4, is typical of this type of linkage between virtual teams and management development.

The PDM links ongoing development needs of managers with the strategic needs of the business. Furthermore, through the use of virtual teams, it optimises an organisation's capability to leverage human potential in service of the strategic goals of the business through use of action-based learning.

With the increased emphasis on developing management tools that better leverage the assets of a business, the use of virtual teams will become an increasing focus of management. Leading thinkers and decision-makers have been attempting to identify images of what a high performing organisation may look like in 10 years' time. The one common theme emerging provides a picture of a simpler, more flexible organisation less focused on command and control systems. The success of virtual teams, however, rests on management and key decision-makers understanding that to support productive virtual teams requires these elements today, not tomorrow.

The increased focus on virtual teams supports, not replaces, the more familiar organisation and management systems for achieving business success. Management will still be required to focus on the delivery of the business through roles and assignments, reporting relationships and management processes and policies. Decision-makers in key positions will continue to pay attention to where and how to compete in the marketplace and define an organisation around strategic imperatives. The critical role for senior management is to assess the best opportunities to deploy virtual teams, to pay careful attention to the requirements essential for team success and to establish an organisational climate that supports the development and performance of virtual teams.

References

Adair, J. (1986) *Effective Teambuilding*, Aldershot, Gower Publishing.

Argyle, M. (1972) *The Social Psychology of Work*, London, Pelican.

Argyris, C. (1990) *Overcoming Organisational Defenses*, Boston, MA, Allyn & Bacon.

Argyris, C. (1992) *On Organisational Learning*, Cambridge, MA, Blackwell.

Babbington-Smith, B. (1979) *Training in Small Groups*, Oxford, Pergammon Press.

Barry, V.E. and Rudinow, J. (1990) *Invitation to Critical Thinking*, San Fran, Holt, Rinehart & Winston.

Belbin, R.M. (1993) *Teams Roles at Work*, Oxford, Butterworth-Heinemann.

Belbin, R.M. (2003) *Management Teams: Why They Succeed and Fail*, Oxford, Butterworth-Heinemann.

Blake, R.R., Mouton, J.S. and Allen, R.L. (1987) *Effective Teams*, New York, John Wiley & Sons.

Bolton, R. (1986) *People Skills: How to Assert Yourself, Listen to Others and Resolve Conflicts*, New York, Simon & Shuster.

Brookfield, S.D. (1986) *Developing Critical Thinkers*, San Francisco, Jossey-Bass.

Brookfield, S.D. (1987) *Understanding and Facilitating Adult Learning*, San Francisco, Jossey-Bass.

Cohen, S. and Gibson, C. (2003) *Virtual Teams that Work: Creating Conditions for Effective Virtual Teams*, San Francisco, Jossey-Bass.

Collins, J. (2001) *Good to Great*, London, Randon House.

Durante, D. and Snyder, N. (1996) *Mastering Virtual Teams: Strategies, Tools and Techniques that Succeed*, San Francisco, Jossey-Bass.

Durante, D. and Snyder, N. (2001) *Mastering Virtual Teams: Strategies, Tools and Techniques that Succeed*, San Francisco, Jossey-Bass.

Dyer, W.G. (1977) *Team Building: Issues and Alternatives*, Reading, MA, Addison-Wesley.

Freire, P. (1970) *Pedagogy of the Oppressed*, New York, Continuum.

Freire, P. and Shor, I. (1987) *Pedagogy for Liberation: Dialogues on Transforming Education*, MA, Bergin & Garvey.

Giroux, B.A. (1983) *Theory and Resistance in Education: A Pedagogy for the Opposition*, South Hadley, MA, Bergin & Garvey.

Ghosal, C. and Bartlett, S. (1994) "Linking organizational context and managerial action: the dimensions of quality management", *Strategic Management Journal*, Vol. 15, 91–112.

Gibson, C. and Cohen, S. (2003) *Virtual Teams that Work: Creating the Conditions for Virtual Team Effectiveness*, San Francisco, Jossey-Bass.

Guba, E.G. and Lincoln, Y.S. (1981) *Effective Evaluation*, San Francisco, Jossey-Bass.

Higgs, M. (1997) *An Investigation into Competencies, Characteristics and Process Factors Associated with Senior Managerial Team Performance*, Unpublished Doctoral Dissertation, Henley Management College.

Hofner-Saphiere, D. (1999) *Understanding Virtual Teams*, San Francisco, Jossey-Bass.

Hofstede, G. (1991) *Culture and Organizations: A Software of the Mind*, London, McGraw-Hill Publishers.

Ireland, S. (1994) *Furthering the Practice of Parenting Education: Developing Skills of Critical Self-reflection in Parenting Programs*, Unpublished Doctoral Dissertation, New York, Columbia University.

Katzenbach, J.R. and Smith, D.K. (1993) *The Wisdom of Teams*, Boston, MA, Harvard University Press.

Knowles, M.S. (1980) *The Modern Practice of Adult Education: From Pedagogy to Androgogy*, Englewood Cliffs, New Jersey, Prentice-Hall.

Laird, D. (1985) *Approaches to Training and Development*, second edition, Reading, MA, Addison-Wesley.

Lipnack, J. and Stamps, J. (2000) *Virtual Teams: People Working across Boundaries and Technology*, second edition, MA, John Wiley & Sons.

Mezirow, J. (1991) *Transformative Dimensions of Adult Learning*, San Francisco, Jossey-Bass.

Nadler, L. (1989) *Designing Training Programmes: The Critical Events Model*, New York, Addison-Wesley-McGraw.

Ray, D. and Bronstein, H. (1995) *Teaming Up*, New York, McGraw-Hill.

Schein, E.H. (1988) *Organisational Psychology*, Englewood Cliffs, NJ, Prentice-Hall.

Schon, D.A. (1987) *Educating the Reflective Practioner*, San Francisco, Jossey-Bass.

Tyson, S. and Jackson, T. (1992) *The Essence of Organisational Behaviour*, third edition, Englewood Cliffs, NJ, Prentice-Hall.

Tannenbaum, S.I., Beard, R.L. and Sales, E. (1992) "Team building and its empirical developments", in K. Keley (ed.), *Issues and Theory in Industrial/Organisational Psychology*, London, North Holland.

Watkins, K.E. and Marsick, V.J. (1993) *Sculpturing the Learning Organisation*, San Francisco, Jossey-Bass.

Managing rewards

Helen Murlis

Part II is concluded with an evaluation of the developing trends in a key area of people management – rewards. This topic has always aroused the interest of employees, managers and HR specialists, probably due to the difficulties of designing and implementing reward strategies and systems that satisfy all stakeholder preferences. How people benefit from their relationship with the organisation and, implicitly, how they are motivated, is a powerful reflection of the social forces, both from within the organisation and from the external environment. This chapter provides an insight into many of these forces and the likely direction of reward strategies in the future.

Introduction

Rewards can be the 'oil' or the 'grit' in the people management process. Reward literacy has become a key skill not just for HR professionals, but for anyone who takes real accountability for managing their people. To understand how rewards can be designed and managed effectively as well as creatively in future, it is important to start with business strategy and then consider how organisations can best implement, maintain and review reward policies that will motivate and maintain a diverse workforce.

This chapter describes how organisations in the private sector and public service (and beyond) need to approach reward strategy development and the kinds of actions they may take to implement change successfully. These observations enable us to identify what the future business world may hold for reward strategies.

New reward strategies and changes to existing strategy should reflect and support any proposed strategic changes in the way any organisation and its people are to be managed, and provide reward and recognition for achieving successful change. Alignment between reward and change strategies is crucial.

Reward has proved not to be a good area for fads and quick fixes. New developments in reward need care as well as creativity to make sure management aims and intentions are communicated effectively. Nor is reward an area where 'best practice' can safely be implemented – 'best fit' to the organisation, its circumstances and state of development is much more important for success.

The practicalities of achieving these goals mean that organisations should:

- Start with a hard look at what they are paying for now and assess what they have in terms of actual and 'implied' reward strategy.

- Evaluate how reward and recognition fit the development of their overall strategy.

- Map and plan for the reward strategy development process that is best aligned with the way they operate.

- Consider how current and prospective employees view their employment 'deal' when making work and career choices.

- Develop a 'road map' for implementation and maintenance, with steps and timescales.

Two issues are critical here:

1 First, in most organisations, the processes of reward design and implementation ideally ought to involve all stakeholders and be delivered within a culture that is as inclusive and positive as possible.

2 Second, innovation and change to reward strategy (e.g. to enable greater individual flexibility and career choice and movement), ought to be designed with a clear vision of the benefits being sought – and managed to achieve those benefits.

What is reward strategy?

Reward strategy defines what an organisation wants to pay people for. Strategies provide specific directions on how an organisation will develop and design pay, benefits and related programmes to ensure that the behaviours and contributions needed to support the achievement of operational goals are rewarded appropriately. They should be clearly linked to strategy for the effective management and development of people to ensure the organisation has the capability to deliver its overall strategy.

All organisations have a reward strategy; this can either be 'implied' from what has developed over time and is there now, or developed specifically to match new or changing demands. Recent research in the UK by the Chartered Institute of Personnel and Development (2003) found that just over 70 per cent or private sector organisations have a formal, business focused reward strategy.

Strategies that are 'implied' rather than 'defined' (like many traditional private sector and public service reward strategies of the last century), may exhibit some or all of the following features:

● Assumptions that length of service and experience in jobs reflect incremental growth in individual contribution – everyone develops at the same speed. (In the UK, this concept is now extremely dubious in terms of legislation concerning Equal Pay and Equal Value and may need to be replaced. In other countries, the discriminatory issues around women who take career breaks and lose seniority in traditional, long pay scales with annual fixed increments may be less challenged.)

● Promotion to the next job above are the only real reward for doing well – rather than rewarding breadth of experience and performance.

● Progression into general management is rewarded, but other ways of progressing – such as acknowledged technical expertise – is not.

● Traditional working patterns are rewarded – rather than recognising and paying for flexibility at work, and the acquisition of new skills and competencies or the maintenance of deep expertise.

● Individuals are incentivised at the expense of team achievement by focusing only on personal targets in bonus scheme design.

● Processes for assessing salary market competitiveness no longer reflect current sources of competent staff.

Defined reward strategies, developed to serve future needs, embrace issues such as:

● Rewarding people for learning new skills and capabilities in current roles.

● Recognition that the pace of individual development can vary.

● The need to reward behaviours associated with successful work in broader roles for example emotional intelligence competencies for managers and also for customer facing, 'front-line' roles.

● Changing career patterns, new ways of working and the growth of current or new technical specialisms.

● Measuring differences in roles and levels in larger organisations by using an agreed analytical and transparent approach to ensure fair rewards for different kinds of skills and responsibilities. (Understanding how one job relates to another – and why it is paid at a particular level – is as important to perceptions of fair treatment as ever!)

● Equality proofing policies and practice to ensure that a more diverse workforce can be attracted, developed and progressed.

- Recognition of the importance of work – life balance and for taking account of the varying life cycle needs of different employees (e.g. care responsibilities for children in poor health). In many countries parents of young children have the legal right to ask for flexibility in working patterns and that organisations may no longer provide different employment conditions for part-timers.

- Considering rewards on a 'total reward' basis, i.e. considering the balance between everything that employees see as rewards for their work (their employment 'deal') and seeking to be competitive within what they can afford.

- Choice – providing frameworks that allow people to choose, within legal and sound boundaries, the way in which their rewards are delivered – allowing a measure of customisation to reflect the differing personal requirements of different stages of career and kinds of work.

- Building line management capability to manage and communicate reward policies more effectively – often an area where good, progressive policies founder and fail.

Part of a wider approach to change

Despite views often expressed by those not familiar with reward technicalities, changing reward strategy should *not* be used as the main lever for organisational change. Experience over the last 20 years or so in the UK with adopting performance-related pay as a major engine for performance improvement suggests that this is rarely, if ever, successful. Pay does not manage performance – people do. And quality of performance management has far greater impact.

> The place of reward strategy lies in supporting change, helping to enable progress by recognising willing acquisition of new skills and behaviours and the delivery of the outcomes needed to achieve a new organisational strategy.

To understand where reward and recognition fit in this wider context, it is useful to work from a recognised and respected framework for looking at all the elements that need to be addressed for change to be successful. The conceptual basis of the framework given below comes from the Burke and Litwin work on organisational change (1992).

This has been adapted by the Hay Group, an international human resources consultancy organisation, to help a wide range of organisations understand where they stand currently on reward strategies, and identifying the main elements of future transformation. Figure 8.1, shows seven main elements (or levers) for successful change and how they are dependent on each other. Leadership influences the whole process. It makes clear the reality that reward and recognition are part of, and dependent upon, other elements of the change agenda.

Figure 8.1 The key elements of successful organisation change

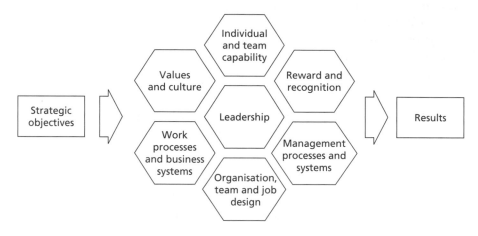

Source: Developed by Hay Group from Burke and Litwin (1992).

Many organisations use frameworks like this to check that they have fully considered the change agenda. This helps them check their change capability and the interlocking support mechanisms.

This model *starts with strategy* by asking:

● What are the organisation's key challenges and opportunities for the future?

● What are the key capabilities required to achieve these?

● How far has the strategy been translated into the key things that have to happen?

● Whether there is an integrated plan to align resources and systems with the strategy?

It reviews *leadership* in terms of whether:

● There is a compelling vision that inspires the organisation;

● Current leaders act according to this vision;

● They create clear expectations of others;

● Obstacles are eliminated;

● Leadership styles are effective.

It provides for the assessment of *values and culture* in terms of:

● The values and behaviours that support success;

● Whether there is consensus around these values;

- The extent to which behaviour matches these values;

- The extent to which excellence in leadership is valued;

- How much the organisation values people.

It also scrutinises *work processes and business systems* to assess:

- Which work processes are critical to delivery of the strategy;

- Whether these are efficient and effective;

- The extent to which there is clear process ownership;

- Whether people delivering specific processes are clear on overall requirements;

- How far business systems and policies are aligned with work processes;

- The extent to which information flows to where it is needed when it is needed.

And reviews *organisation, team and job design* in terms of:

- Whether the grouping of resources supports overall strategy;

- How effectively people and teams work together;

- How challenging jobs/roles are;

- The extent to which the structure efficiently supports the required work processes (e.g. does the current work structure/hierarchy reflect changing working practices?);

- Whether work is performed where it makes sense;

- How far roles are correctly assigned and clearly understood.

It examines *individual and team competence* to assess:

- Clarity on excellence in different organisational roles;

- Which individual and team competences are needed for success – and whether these have been adequately defined/explored;

- Whether there is an adequate talent pool in the organisation or accessibility to it;

- The extent to which there is a process to identify and learn from superior performance within the organisation and externally in its business sector;

- Whether outstanding people have been matched to key roles (do good people get the roles that best play to their strengths?);

- How high current levels of performance are and how variations in performance are handled or tolerated (e.g. how well/swiftly is underperformance handled?).

Assesses *management processes and systems* to review:

- How well people management systems are integrated (e.g. linking training and career development);

- The appropriateness of selection systems (e.g. how many entry points should there be and does the organisation select good people at each point?);

- Whether succession systems are adequate (do the right people get to the top?);

- How appropriate are development systems for upcoming business challenges;

- How well good performance is encouraged and developed – is performance management a dishonest annual ritual, or has it evolved to become the way in which performance is focused, developed and delivered through the year?

- How well managers add value;

- Links to and alignment with business planning processes and other management systems.

And finally, it scrutinises *reward and recognition strategy and policies* to check:

- Whether the reward structure in terms of base salary and variable pay is well aligned with strategy and values (is the organisation paying for the right things, e.g. personal contribution, effective teamwork, sales which help grow market share, professional excellence, innovation, growing skill and knowledge to meet new demands);

- If the organisation can attract and keep the right people at the right stage in their career (e.g. success in attracting good graduates, key specialisms, a diverse workforce able to deliver high quality customer service in their local community);

- The balance of reward focus between internal equity, fair recognition for delivering results and external salary market pressures (e.g. for IT specialisms);

- Whether there is a clear link between rewards and the measurement of contribution (are people paid more as they perform better against agreed business goals and development targets and add to their skill base? Are there processes in place to ensure fair and consistent rewards?);

- How far rewards really encourage or discourage people to learn, develop and practice new capabilities;

- Whether progression through levels in the career and pay structure is clearly linked to larger or broader roles with value-added activities and contributions.

And, taking an overall perspective, to see *results* in terms of;

● Building the value-added contribution required by all stakeholders with an interest in the organisation's success (e.g. shareholders, employees, management, clients/customers, trade unions and the local community);

● Delivery of the results needed to sustain and improve performance;

● Meeting financial targets (e.g. effective investment, sound cost management);

● Having an organisational climate that is focused on delivery and supports the desired results – sustainability (e.g. maintaining a well led, highly motivated and engaged workforce, committed to making the business vision a living and developing reality).

Doing the right things in the right order therefore means first having a 'Business Strategy' as well as having the main strands of an HR strategy of which reward should be part.

Developing a strategy for reward and recognition

Figure 8.2 illustrates a typical reward strategy development and implementation process and the way in which the different elements are linked together.

Figure 8.2 The reward strategy development 'map'

Source: Developed by Helen Murlis from Armstrong and Murlis (1998) and Armstrong and Brown (2001).

This shows what has to happen and in what order to get from having a reward philosophy through to implementation of new or updated approaches to reward. The way in which this process is developed should help all the people involved to understand what has to go into the strategy and why, who is responsible and what the benefits will be.

Essentially, the process involves:

- *Diagnosis* – looking at the business, HR, cultural and reward context to assess future needs and priorities – what is the case for change and why?

- *Setting and agreeing principles* – priorities and direction for the reward strategy and implementation process.

- *Detailed design* – of the changes to existing practices and new practices needed to deliver the strategy.

- *Testing the designs and building capability* – among HR professionals, line management and employees to implement and work with the new practices and planning the transition from existing practices, including modelling and costing planned changes.

- *Implementation* – to a planned schedule – accompanied by review of how the whole thing is going and 'fine tuning', adapting the design and practices to meet changing or new demands.

Many years of experience in reward strategy development confirm how critical it is to involve both the people covered by any new policy and those who will manage it.

Senior management needs to be involved in and lead change, supporting their people as they all learn to work with new reward practices. Employees and their representatives need to feel their views and needs have been respected and addressed. Successful reward strategies are those that are well understood where the logic and benefits are clear, and where capability has been built to operate the different elements effectively. As Duncan Brown, stresses in the 2003 CIPD Reward Management Research Report 'Without extensive employee communication and involvement to create understanding and trust, without effective line and performance management, then the written reward strategy goals that many organisations now have can never be delivered in practice.'

Understanding the broader reward 'deal'

Organisations are increasingly recognising that individual employees, too, have a part to play in reward strategy development. A very important element of the diagnosis and design background is understanding what employees at all levels, see and want as their total reward package, that is the 'deal' that attracts people to an employer and makes them want to stay. Employers need to get to the heart of this to become and stay an 'employer of choice' for the kinds of people they need. Developing an 'employer brand', is the means by which opportunities differentiate their employment offer from those of their competitors. To do this properly, organisations need to use a systematic means of finding out what, realistically, current and potential employees look for and find motivating. The framework shown in Figure 8.3 starts from the basic reality that when people are really engaged in and committed to their work they are able to perform better and make a fuller contribution.

Figure 8.3 The main things employees want from their work

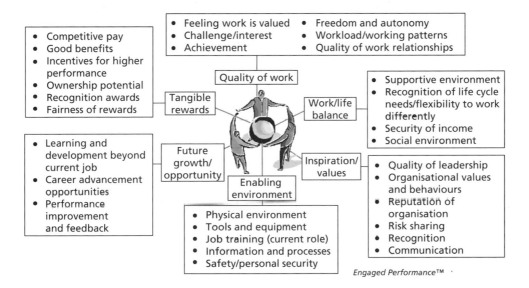

- Feeling work is valued
- Challenge/interest
- Achievement
- Freedom and autonomy
- Workload/working patterns
- Quality of work relationships

- Competitive pay
- Good benefits
- Incentives for higher performance
- Ownership potential
- Recognition awards
- Fairness of rewards

Tangible rewards

Quality of work

Work/life balance

- Supportive environment
- Recognition of life cycle needs/flexibility to work differently
- Security of income
- Social environment

- Learning and development beyond current job
- Career advancement opportunities
- Performance improvement and feedback

Future growth/ opportunity

Enabling environment

Inspiration/ values

- Quality of leadership
- Organisational values and behaviours
- Reputation of organisation
- Risk sharing
- Recognition
- Communication

- Physical environment
- Tools and equipment
- Job training (current role)
- Information and processes
- Safety/personal security

Engaged Performance™

This was developed by the Hay Group from many years of working with employees of all kinds to discover what is important to them about their work and careers and the way they are rewarded. It covers the whole 'deal' needed to enable people to contribute 'Engaged Performance™', and has proved helpful to organisations in public and private sectors in prioritising HR and reward strategy development and in being more responsive and creative in developing new approaches. Some elements matter more in some organisations than others. Ownership potential (i.e. the opportunity to have a financial stake in the business) clearly matters more in the private sector and feeling your work is valued more in most parts of the public service. The kinds of issues explored using this model and some examples of the things that matter to employees include:

For *Inspiration and values*:

- How well leaders/managers provide effective and motivating leadership for example use of emotional intelligence in handling change or facing a crisis;

- How well the organisation defines and lives by a clear set of values;

- Level of respect for the organisation in the community;

- How well responsibility for risks is taken/shared;

- The degree to which individual and team achievement and contribution is given recognition;

- The quality of communication to staff, for example whether it is clear, timely and uses appropriate media.

For *Future growth and opportunity*:

- How effectively personal development and learning are encouraged and supported for example clear training and development maps and courses, coaching and mentoring to 'fast track' development;

- The extent to which career opportunities exist and people are encouraged to develop and progress;

- How clear people are about what is expected from them and how much they get effective feedback on how they are doing.

For *Work-life balance*:

- How much the environment is one in which people feel considered and cared for? Do managers know about their employees' backgrounds and any pressures from home they have to face?

- How far can people get a sensible balance between work demands and their life outside work?

- How secure people feel about their continuity of employment and income?

- The degree to which positive social interaction between employees is encouraged both at work and in the community.

For *Tangible rewards*:

- The degree to which cash rewards reflects pay available for similar work elsewhere, for example basic pay, annual and long term incentive scheme design, pay progression opportunities, shift pay and overtime, market premia and large town allowances.

- The competitiveness of benefits provisions; for example, pensions and death-in-service benefits, private medical cover, childcare provisions, sick pay, annual leave, company cars, sports and social facilities.

- The extent to which pay and benefits are believed to be fair in comparison to others doing similar work, performing at the same level in the same workplace.

- The degree to which employees are given opportunities to participate in the ownership of the business – share schemes; profit sharing, gainsharing.

- How much and how well the employer provides cash or non-cash recognition awards/prizes for specific achievements. Is this a culture that celebrates success?

- The availability and effective design of incentives to encourage and reward excellence.

For *Quality of work*:

- How far people feel their work is valued for its impact on the success of their employer and outside in the community;

- How much challenging and interesting work is on offer (e.g. opportunities to broaden role, travel or work on a new project);

- Level of opportunities and encouragement for personal achievement;

- How far people are encouraged to take independent decisions and actions (e.g. the balance between essential frameworks to maintain quality of delivery and personal discretion to innovate and take calculated risks);

- The manageability of the workload expected (e.g. working patterns, shift patterns, team resources for specific tasks – is there a culture of presenteeism/long hours – which over time becomes stressful);

- The extent to which interesting, stimulating and beneficial relationships are available with colleagues at work.

For *Enabling environment*:

- The effort the employer puts into providing and improving the physical working environment (e.g. state of decoration and quality of facilities provided – an agreeable and welcoming entrance to the premises, good working light, ergonomically designed furniture, pleasant staff restaurant);

- The extent to which appropriate and effective work tools and equipment are provided (e.g. the most up-to-date and reliable IT (an ultralight laptop?) or other equipment);

- How well the employer provides training and development as well as support to people to do their current job well (e.g. online learning opportunities, specific courses, updates on new software, customer service training to help with the handling of challenging 'clients');

- The effort the employer puts into designing and providing for ways of working and the information needed to do the current job well for example company 'knowledge maps' on the intranet;

● How well the employer safeguards employees against hazards and minimizes exposure to personal risk associated with their work (e.g. effective briefing for travel to countries with different local and work cultures, clear safety procedures, protective uniforms).

People's views and priorities around these six elements vary considerably depending on what they believe most needs doing to improve the employment environment and where they are in the organisation. Money is part of this picture, but it may not be the dominant driver. High-quality leadership (people have a habit of joining organisations and leaving bosses), having a job that individuals believe is worthwhile, and opportunities to progress can be as or more important. Increasingly too, the ability to have a reasonable work-life balance is seen as very important.

Some examples of the kinds of responses organisations make when they have completed a survey and/or focus group diagnostic covering the elements of 'Engaged Performance™', are:

> A multinational services company used the research to launch a new reward strategy and communicate this in terms of saying that the organisation has really listened to the feedback it has had and is concerned to get its market positioning and 'employer brand' right. This marks the beginning of improvements not just to the reward package, but also to the way policies are explained and managed by line managers as well as HR.

> A major financial organisation developed a work–life balance programme that provided for flexible working and so took account of family commitments such as school holidays, time to care for elderly parents, time out for study, short sabbaticals to enable world travel. A key element that went with this was achieving a behavioural change among senior management to ensure that they were discouraging the working of long hours and raising the importance they attached to leading a more balanced life (e.g. going home early occasionally to pick up their children from school and feed them, working from home).

> A high-technology company worked on improving communications to employees about reward policies and practices to ensure that the details and benefits were better understood – improving the level of detail for each policy on the corporate intranet; and issuing annual total remuneration statements so that people had an up-to-date picture of their reward package.

> A government agency focused on simplifying performance related pay so that employees were clearer what they were being paid for and why and improving performance management processes, changing the emphasis from an annual report on achievement of objectives to a more continuous process which gave equal focus to personal and career development.

> A research based organisation developed career groups or job family based pay structures within broader pay bands to allow more clarity on career progression and enable specialists to progress to strategic professional roles rather than being plateaued if they do not want a line management role.

> A local authority introduced choices In benefits for example allowing employees to trade a week's holiday for cash when they were not able to take the full six weeks because of work pressures.

> An IT services company trained line managers to handle and communicate annual pay reviews more fairly and effectively to help them motivate and encourage their staff.

> An engineering company produced a career planning guide so that staff could see what competencies they would need to learn to do different jobs or gain promotion in their current job family.

> Changing the dress code at work – providing more modern, better quality 'smart casual' work wear for employees in customer service roles, based on full consultation with staff – for example in financial services and retailing – reflecting the culture and image the firm wanted to have in its marketplace.

> Development of a recognition scheme for teams in a call centre, where the criteria for success were defined by the staff and the rewards tailored to what the team wanted within a given budget.

What might the future look like?

The future of reward practice is as likely to be concerned with doing what exists now better as it is with extraordinary new developments. Progress tends to be incremental – few reward strategists are 'trail blazers'! The key trends that seem to be developing at this time generally involve integration with other HR policies and focus on:

- *Improving the evidence base* – understanding what the preferred reward deal is for different kinds of employees and responding to this within the budget required to compete effectively. Sophisticated diagnostics are increasingly being used both to find areas for innovation and to track progress or the need for change. The CIPD research, published in May 2003, illustrates clearly how companies such as Nationwide in financial services and Selfridges and Tesco in retailing use research to inform and improve the way they manage and reward their people.

● *Greater openness about reward policy* – forced by two things. First, pay and benefits information from a range of sources is accessible on the Internet – market data is no longer available only to employers through confidential salary surveys. Taboos around discussing pay levels, benefits entitlements and different organization policies are becoming much less prevalent. Secondly, increasing legislative requirements (most recently in the UK through Equal Value legislation) that allow employees to ask about the pay level of equivalent individuals of the opposite sex who may be getting a more favourable deal is raising pressure to run salary policies that are defensible when exposed.

● *Job evaluation in its place* – recognition that the reported demise of job evaluation has proved wrong. Surveys in 2003 by the CIPD and e-reward in the UK confirm that this underpinning to the measurement and management of relativities is alive and well, but in need of regular maintenance. Organisations have long been stripping away unnecessary bureaucracy and ensuring that this process supports flexibility rather than imposing rigidity, what they could do more of is getting the best out of the investment. The thinking behind sound approaches to job evaluation is important to effective organisation design. Regularly updated job and role data is key to many HR processes including organisation design, performance management, training needs analysis, succession planning and recruitment.

● *Getting to grips with rewarding career development* – by matching reward levels and progression to career patterns – based on more effective mapping of skills, competencies, accountabilities and performance criteria that apply to the roles and levels in specific groups – the 'job family' approach – which provides most effectively for specialist career ladders. This is one of the newer applications of job/role measurement – which is typically used to measure role levels and help ensure that equal value considerations are properly respected. Success here depends on having sound role information and ensuring that families do not become silos which restrict lateral and diagonal movement to enable career development and change of track. A clear picture of career and salary progression opportunities needs to be supported by development guides and self-managed learning opportunities.

● *Pay structures that match organisational needs* – there has to be the iron hand of cost control in any pay structure. Highly capable managers, able to manage and progress people within defined pay budgets can more easily work with broader grades and flexible structures than those new to the idea and not yet conversant with its benefits – with freedom comes responsibility! The lessons of the fashion for broad banding of the 1990s have shown that what is taken out in structure needs to be put back in terms of management capability, notably in quality performance management and commitment to development. The market as well as organisation design do not always require this – 'fit for purpose' is an important consideration.

- *Being more imaginative and creative with rewards for 'engine room' staff* – employees in retail, manufacturing, call centres, public service delivery – who may not be promoted more than a level or two over their working life. This involves introducing provisions such as non-cash rewards such as 'chill-out rooms' with good sound systems for young staff in call centres, team charity fund-raising competitions run by local supermarket staff which bring community involvement and recognition, and company social events involving families which reinforce an open and more caring culture. It can also involve recognition schemes with cash or non-cash rewards.

- *Growing use of flexible remuneration* – allowing employees to make reward choices that reflect their lifestyles. This typically gives options around level of pension, health care, company cars (cash/car trade-offs), leave (buying/saving/selling days above a given threshold) and other choices related to specific benefits. The term 'mass-customisation' is appearing as IT-based administration systems make the whole process more accessible and cost effective. 'Flex' approaches are even beginning to appear in parts of the UK public sector with the benefit that employees are much more aware of the total value of their reward package. The CIPD (2003) and other surveys confirm this trend.

- *Greater realism over what performance rewards can and cannot deliver* – combined with a stronger focus on the quality of performance management. In many places there is a new perception of equity focused on comparable pay for equivalent contribution. But several years of low inflation in the UK and elsewhere have reduced the value and impact of performance related base pay increases. Non-consolidated, non-pensionable cash bonuses now have more impact as long as base pay is reasonably competitive. These are being given to reward individuals who continue to add value even though they are at the top of their pay band. Improvements in the understanding of both business and behavioural performance measures and the relationship between them, as well as in the quality of management feedback, are key to real motivational impact. Where robust measures can be developed or exist (e.g. in retail and service businesses), customer views on performance are being included in performance assessment. Rewards based on these approaches are really payment for contribution over the longer term rather than short-term performance – much as delivery continues to matter in all sectors.

- *Greater realism about the practicalities of team rewards* – Team rewards sound like a good idea and one that supports the value of effective teamworking. They can work well where teams are relatively small and really control their own performance outcomes. But, as many organisations are finding, they are much harder to design and implement as well as fund in large complex organisations with many interdependencies. And they do not really serve as a means of avoiding individual performance pay. Individual performance still has to be managed and developed and high performing employees may still want individual recognition for their efforts and contribution.

● *Increasing awareness of the importance of emotionally intelligent processes* – for managing reward and recognition – with a view to reducing the number of wasted opportunities for motivation found in the reward practices of many organisations. Words and psychology matter and bland, formal approaches can all too easily demotivate. This point is critical for all communication about reward policy and in the handling of annual salary review. Using these to encourage continuing engagement and personal contribution is an obvious 'win'. This is one of the key findings to emerge from the CIPD/Bath University study (2003) – what the authors call 'organisation process advantage' – gained from strong values and an inclusive culture and enough line managers able to bring HR policies and practices to life – living the values rather than delivering a duty. This is not something that can be legislated for and it has to be led from the top by imaginative and empathetic senior teams.

● *Continuing improvement in the use of IT* – to support reward design and administration and, through organisational intranets, communicate policies, entitlements and choices to employees, with links to development and performance management processes, the world of e-HR is coming into its own. Again design based on consultation over employee needs is critical to success.

● *An increasingly tough approach to governance and probity in executive rewards* – as major shareholders use their growing reward literacy to question 'excessive' current remuneration provisions and 'oversized' payoffs to those who have underperformed but are influential. There are some real conflicts here with views on what should be as against what is happening. In major multinational organisations in sectors such a pharmaceuticals, petrochemicals, FMCG and financial services this is an area of 'international' remuneration market pressures combined with the scarcity of talented leaders – executives able to stand at the helm of major organisations. There is also a concurrent need to conform to perceptions of current practice in levels and reward elements to compete and meet executive expectations of their worth, especially when they are being head-hunted. Falling stock markets, underwater options (i.e. options that are worth less when they are due to be exercised than they were when granted initially) and market uncertainties since the end of 2001 are complicating the picture for the long-term incentive plans.

Non-Executive Board Remuneration Committees favour aligning executive effort with sustainable corporate performance. A new regime seems to be in the process of emerging.

Whatever happens over the next few years, reward practice will not stand still and reward management will continue to be a challenge. This challenge will, in this author's view, better be met if reward is treated holistically rather than as 'compensation engineering'. Treating reward purely as an economic transaction is to miss the point. In any developed economy, people work for meaning as well as money and the work they do at least partly defines who and what they are. Reward management can make this positive or negative by the degree to which employees feel valued for their efforts. Oil or grit? Above all, it is important to know.

Future people management issues

This chapter has focused on the development of reward strategies and their link to strategic human resource management and business transformation. These strategies will impact significantly on line and project managers and require them to be more 'reward literate'.

The discussions here have indicated how important it is to respond appropriately to changes in the business environment and the employment market. Managers need to be increasingly sensitive to pick up overt and subtle changes in their people's attitudes to reward. As a vital conduit of information to senior and HR management, operational managers can play a key role in helping to shape organisational responses to reward pressures. Whilst the HR function may ultimately be responsible for proposing and developing suitable approaches to reward, their proposals and subsequent policy implementation will need to take into account feedback obtained from employees through their managers, through research and through surveys and/or focus groups to fine-tune understanding.

It is likely that greater employee acceptance and commitment to reward strategies will emerge if there is a transparent system of consultation. Managers will have greater confidence in implementing reward systems if these are seen as helping build a genuine sense of employee engagement both with their employer and the work they do.

This will require a detailed understanding of reward management principles, something that needs to be incorporated into company management development programmes alongside building a real, practical understanding of what motivates people at work.

References

Armstrong, M. and Brown, D. (1999) *Paying for Contribution*, London, Kogan Page.

Armstrong, M. and Brown, D. (2001) *New Dimensions in Pay Management*, CIPD.

Armstrong, M. and Murlis, H. (1998) *Reward Management: A Handbook of Remuneration Strategy and Practice*, fourth edition, London, Kogan Page.

Brown, D. (2001) *Reward Strategies: From Intent to Impact*, CIPD.

Purcell, J., Kinnie, N. and Hutchinson, S. (2003) *People and Performance: Unlocking the Black Box*, CIPD.

Reward Management (2003) *Survey Report*, CIPD, Feb.

Thompson, P. (2002) *Total Reward*, CIPD, pp. 21–23.

Thompson, P. (2003) *What is happening to Job Evaluation Today, e-reward*.

Warner Burke, W. and Litwin, G. (1992) 'A causal model of organisational performance and change', *Journal of Management*, Vol. 18, No. 3, pp. 523–45.

Part

III

Management competencies for future success

The emotionally intelligent leader

Malcolm Higgs and Victor Dulewicz

"Leadership" has emerged as a third major element in the corporate performance triangle to accompany technical and management capability. Many organisations have invested heavily in leadership development programmes, recognising that discretionary performance is achieved through leadership skills and competencies. This chapter opens our third, and final section, by building on the performance management theme established in the earlier two sections. The emergence of "emotional intelligence" as an effective approach to identifying and developing leadership potential has perhaps been one of the major advances in recent years in our understanding of leadership. Professor Malcolm Higgs and Professor Victor Dulewicz explain the concept and indicate how this approach to leadership fits with the future HR agenda.

Introduction

The idea that something called "Emotional Intelligence" plays a bigger role in accounting for individual success than "traditional" measures such as Intellectual Competencies (IQ) has grabbed the attention of the media and the business world. Why should this be? A major reason for this is that organisations are increasingly recognising that the quality, capability and style of their people plays an important part in their long-term success. Therefore, a way of understanding what it is that drives individual success can help organisations build a better talent pool to support their growth and performance strategies.

The media interest may well have arisen from the resonance of the idea with people's real life experiences. We can all think of "super-intelligent" people who are hopeless in dealing with the business world (or even everyday life). At the same time most of us can think of people who do not display traditional signs of high IQ or educational attainment, but are more rounded individuals who enjoy considerable success. Richard Branson is a very good example of such a person. An idea which confirms this is bound to receive considerable attention.

However, in the media there appears to be considerable confusion around the nature of Emotional Intelligence and indeed directly contradictory descriptions. For example, *The Times* carried two articles around six weeks apart which explored the idea as applied to leading politicians. In the first of these all of Bill Clinton's personal, and related political, problems were attributed to a low level of Emotional Intelligence. In the second, Clinton was quoted as an example of an individual and politician with outstanding Emotional Intelligence!

Many of the articles seem to have focused on Emotional Intelligence as being to do with the "soft" aspects to behaviour and personality. These are typified by the headline in one major UK newspaper; "Soft and Cuddly Bosses make it to the top". The illustration of successful leaders provided under this headline included individuals who were neither "soft" nor "cuddly" in terms of other descriptions of their behaviours!

The level of attention that Emotional Intelligence has been receiving, together with the apparent confusion around the nature of the idea, led the authors (working at Henley Management College) to explore the topic in more detail and to conduct a number of research studies.

In reviewing what was being covered in both the popular media and the academic journals we found that we had a number of important questions to answer. These were:

● What is Emotional Intelligence?

● What evidence is there from the business world to support the claim that it is an important factor in explaining individual success?

● Is there a relationship between Emotional Intelligence and leadership?

● Is Emotional Intelligence an element of the personality we are born with (and have to live with) or can it be changed and developed?

The answers to these questions are explored in this chapter.

What is Emotional Intelligence?

The idea that individual success (particularly in terms of success in careers or in the business world) is not adequately explained by "traditional" measures of intelligence is certainly not particularly new. Psychologists have been looking at "other forms of intelligence" since the 1920s. The term Emotional Intelligence is one which pulls together this earlier research. It has been presented in a way which has captured people's interest by Daniel Goleman (an American psychologist). In spite of this history of research it is difficult to find a concise definition of Emotional Intelligence. On examination it appears to be a composite of a number of elements of an individual's personal capabilities and related behaviours. From our review of earlier research we identified that Emotional Intelligence was concerned with:

● *Self-awareness* – Knowing what you are feeling and being able to handle those feelings without having them swamp you.

- *Motivation* – Being able to motivate yourself to get jobs done, be creative and perform at your peak.

- *Empathy and interpersonal sensitivity* – Sensing what others are feeling and handling relationships effectively.

Reflecting further on this research we arrived at a broader definition of Emotional Intelligence as being:

"Achieving one's goals through the capabilities to:

- manage one's own feelings and emotions;

- be sensitive to the needs of others and influence key people; and

- balance one's motives and drives with conscientious and ethical behaviour."

On investigating this further in our own studies, which are discussed below, we identified seven elements which make up an individual's Emotional Intelligence. These are described in Figure 9.1.

Figure 9.1 The seven elements of Emotional Intelligence

1 *Self-awareness* – The awareness of your own feelings and the ability to recognise and manage these.

2 *Emotional resilience* – The ability to perform well and consistently in a range of situations and when under pressure.

3 *Motivation* – The drive and energy which you have to achieve results, balance short- and long-term goals and pursue your goals in the face of challenge and rejection.

4 *Interpersonal sensitivity* – The ability to be aware of the needs and feelings of others and to use this awareness effectively in interacting with them and arriving at decisions impacting on them.

5 *Influence* – The ability to persuade others to change their viewpoint on a problem, issue or decision.

6 *Intuitiveness* – The ability to use insight and interaction to arrive at and implement decisions when faced with ambiguous or incomplete information.

7 *Conscientiousness and integrity* – The ability to display commitment to a course of action in the face of challenge, to act consistently and in line with understood ethical requirements.

Source: Higgs and Dulewicz (2002).

In practice there are differing views on the nature of Emotional Intelligence. (We will now refer to Emotional Intelligence as EI.) Some (such as Salovey and Mayer 1990) see it as an ability, like IQ, which is hard to change. Others, such as Daniel Goleman (1996), see it as a set of competencies which can be seen in similar ways to other competency frameworks. These represent two ends of a scale of views. Our own view is more aligned to a third group, including Reuven Bar-On (2000), who see EI as being a combination of personal factors. Within this framework, which lies around the middle of the scale, some of the elements are developable and others more difficult to change.

In our view it is important to look at all of these elements separately rather than consider Emotional Intelligence (sometimes referred to as "EQ") as an overall measure (like IQ). Indeed, when one looks at the seven elements one realises that, for many individuals, there are inevitable conflicts between them. For example, an individual who has a high level of "Motivation" is not necessarily going to have a natural tendency to exhibit either "Interpersonal Sensitivity" or "Conscientiousness". In thinking about these contradictions, and tensions, between elements which we need to keep in balance, helps us to understand the reason why high Emotional Intelligence is such a "prized" capability. If we look at the elements we can identify an overall view or model of performance, which helps us to understand why Emotional Intelligence is both potentially important and difficult to develop. From our initial research we have identified that the seven elements of Emotional Intelligence fall into three groupings which are:

1 *Drivers* – Those elements which motivate and drive our behaviour (i.e. motivation).

2 *Constrainers* – The aspects of Emotional Intelligence which rein in our behaviours (i.e. conscientiousness and integrity).

3 *Enablers* – The aspects of Emotional Intelligence which help us to keep drivers and constrainers in balance and achieve overall performance (i.e. interpersonal sensitivity, self-awareness, intuitiveness, emotional resilience and influence).

The way in which the balance of these elements is presented in practice is shown in Figure 9.2.

Figure 9.2 A model of Emotional Intelligence

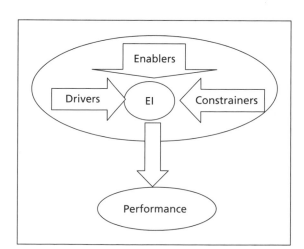

In looking at these seven elements, it is clear that Emotional Intelligence is about more then being "soft and cuddly". There are some clearly "harder" (i.e. non-interpersonal) elements (e.g. Motivation, Intuitiveness). The new idea and implication introduced by these seven elements, is the need to *balance* apparently contradictory "hard" and "soft" behaviours. This has been summarised as being able to exhibit "Tough Love".

When we understand the real nature of Emotional Intelligence the apparent contradictions in the media described above can be explained, for example the two views of Bill Clinton's Emotional Intelligence could have arisen from journalists having different elements in mind when writing their descriptions.

What is the evidence for Emotional Intelligence?

The core proposition presented by Daniel Goleman was that a combination of at least average IQ and well-developed Emotional Intelligence accounted for success of individuals to a far greater extent than differences in IQ alone. A lot of the evidence to support this proposition has been drawn from educational research amongst both school children and university students. This has been brought together with physiological research which has been examining the development of the human brain and, in particular, the role of the "emotional site" within the brain. Finally, the understanding of the concept of Emotional Intelligence has been expanded by linking the above research to developments in therapy and counselling. In the initial presentation of the idea, there was very little rigorous evidence that the core proposition held up in the business world. This prompted us to attempt to examine the idea in an organisational context.

Our starting point for this research was a seven-year study of managers who had attended the Henley Management College General Management Course. The data we had on these managers (one hundred in total) included personality questionnaires, competency data and, importantly, information on their rate of advancement within their organisations over a seven-year period. Subsequently we were able to identify subsets of the competency data which closely matched the elements of Emotional Intelligence. We were also able to construct from the competency data, a measure of Intellectual Competencies which related to IQ. Finally, a third subset of the competency data related to more "traditional" management competencies. We labelled this measure "MQ" (Managerial Competencies). On analysing the data we found that whilst IQ accounted for about a quarter of the variation in individual "success" (as measured by "rate of advancement"), Emotional Intelligence accounted for over one-third of the variation and MQ a little under 20 per cent. Furthermore, when we looked at a combination of IQ and Emotional Intelligence, we were able to account for more than 50 per cent of the variation in "success". This provided some compelling evidence that Emotional Intelligence is an important factor in accounting for the success of managers in terms of their progress within an organisation. Interestingly, the combination of IQ, EQ and MQ accounted for

Figure 9.3 Broader model of performance

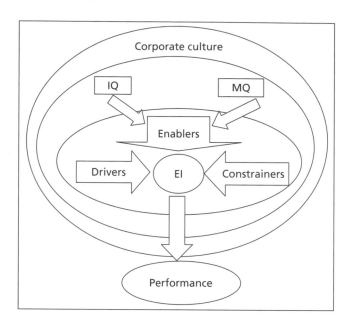

just under three quarters of the variation in "success". It is likely that a lot of the unexplained variation will be explained by differences in organisational culture. This has led us to develop a broader model of performance and EI which is shown in Figure 9.3. Encouraged by these initial findings, we have now carried out a range of studies using both self and 360-degree versions of an EI questionnaire which we have developed (Dulewicz and Higgs 2000) and found not only strong evidence for linkages between Emotional Intelligence and performance, but job satisfaction and stress (the higher the levels of Emotional Intelligence the lower the levels on stress measures).

The clear evidence now available highlights that Emotional Intelligence is a significant factor which should be considered in the development of managers. The interest in the idea, and its potential significance, expressed by organisations appears to be well founded.

Can you measure Emotional Intelligence?

Given that Emotional Intelligence represents a collection of characteristics and behaviours which organisations would benefit from developing in their people, it is important to have a means of measuring it. There has been much debate about the feasibility of measuring Emotional Intelligence through a direct test or questionnaire. However, we decided to develop such an instrument, initially using data provided by more than 200 managers who were participating in a range of programmes at Henley Management College. This research resulted in the production of a psychometric test which reliably measures a manager's

Emotional Intelligence and, most importantly, identifies their strengths and weaknesses in relation to each of the seven elements of Emotional Intelligence. Further, work with much larger samples of managers has confirmed the reliability of the measure. The original questionnaire was based on an individual self-assessment. However, an additional version involving rating by others (a 360-degree assessment) has also been developed together with separate versions for non-managerial employees. These questionnaires are now available from Assessment & Selection for Employment (ASE), a major psychological test publisher, and are being used in a wide range of both private and public sector organisations (see Dulewicz and Higgs 2000, for details).

Can Emotional Intelligence be developed?

If, as the research literature suggests, Emotional Intelligence contributes significantly (other things, especially IQ, being equal) to "life success" and, ultimately, corporate success, then the question arises as to whether Emotional Intelligence can be developed, or is it a more enduring personality trait. There is strong consensus within the Emotional Intelligence literature that it is a developable trait or competency. In particular, Daniel Goleman has stated unequivocally that Emotional Intelligence is amenable to development, although he emphasises that traditional classroom training is not appropriate, and that it is a lengthy process.

From our experience we would tend to agree with him, up to a point. When we look at Emotional Intelligence we tend to find that it is the Enablers in our model which are most readily developable (e.g. Self-awareness, Interpersonal Sensitivity and Influence). It would seem that both the Drivers (e.g. Motivation) and Constrainers (e.g. Conscientiousness) are associated with more deep-rooted personal traits and are thus more difficult to change. However, we do find that individuals are able to develop means of coping with "shortfalls" in these areas, by building skills in relation to behaviours which reduce the overall impact of the elements on their work performance. In addition, in these areas individuals are able to benefit from development which will enable them to fully exploit their existing capabilities.

This concept of "secondary development" may be best illustrated by considering an example. Managers who are low on Emotional Resilience are likely to find that their performance is badly affected by a build-up of pressure or backlog of work, or by being faced with complaints about their delivery of work on time. A "coping strategy" for dealing with this may be to improve their abilities to involve others in projects and to delegate work effectively. For such a manager, development aimed at improving their delegation and project management skills would result in reducing the level of pressure and complaints. Following this line of development would be unlikely to raise their Emotional Resilience to *very* high levels. However, it would help them to cope more effectively with a number of situations in which the low level of Emotional Resilience would impact badly on their work performance and to exploit the capability they do have.

Whilst the idea that Emotional Intelligence can be developed was theoretically sound, we were keen to explore the practical realities. From several studies with team leaders and managers, undertaking planned development, we have indeed found evidence that their Emotional Intelligence (as measured by our questionnaire) has improved. From the above evidence, and our earlier comments on the development of other elements of Emotional Intelligence, it follows that an individual's competencies in this area can either be developed directly or through a planned process of "secondary development". However, we do emphasise that building competency in terms of Emotional Intelligence is not something which can be achieved through a "quick fix" training solution. Developing Emotional Intelligence requires sustained effort. Furthermore, whilst training courses may have a role to play in building a person's understanding of the nature of Emotional Intelligence and potential effective development actions, the real results will be achieved through sustained personal actions which are appropriately planned, monitored and guided. Effective development in this area is, no doubt, helped enormously by working with an individual coach or mentor.

Leadership and Emotional Intelligence

As we have noted above, Emotional Intelligence has become a "hot topic". Another significant "hot topic" today is leadership. Indeed, we would propose that the underlying reasons for interest are similar and the two areas are related. In exploring this proposition it is helpful to begin by exploring how our understanding of leadership has developed.

For centuries we have been obsessed with leaders, and with identifying the characteristics required for effective leadership. In more recent times (i.e. the latter part of the twentieth century), the topic of leadership has been studied more extensively than almost any other aspect of human behaviour. Many have pointed out that, in spite of the plethora of studies, we still seem to know little about the defining characteristics of effective leadership. A major difficulty in arriving at a definitive understanding of leadership is that the more the leaders one encounters, the more difficult it is to describe a typically effective style of leadership.

However, such problems do not appear to have stemmed our interest in continuing the search. In order to attempt to make sense of leadership in today's context, it is helpful to consider some of the critical issues facing organisations that appear to be driving our current interest in leadership. It would seem that these fall into the following broad groupings:

- *Changes in societal values* – the underlying need to engage employees in a different way in order to secure their commitment.

- *Changes in investor focus* – investor decisions are increasingly influenced by "intangibles" such as the quality and depth of leadership, the ability to implement strategy, and the ability to develop a "boundaryless" organisation.

- *Making change deliver* – It has been widely estimated that 70 per cent of change initiatives fail (Higgs and Rowland 2003).

- *Burn-out and stress* – around 60–65 per cent of employees see their immediate manager as the major cause of their dissatisfaction and discomfort with their job (Alimo-Metcalfe 2001).

- *Playing to a wider audience* – increased exposure of leaders to the media, clients and a wide range of other stakeholders.

An emerging perspective on leadership

The diverse, and often contradictory, findings on the nature of effective leadership frequently share two common factors. These are:

1 the focus is on top-level leaders;

2 the measure of success employed to judge success is financial performance of the business being led.

In broad terms, however, what we have learned about leadership from these studies is that the problems central to effective leadership – motivation, inspiration, sensitivity and communication have changed little in 3000 years. Focus on people aspects is critical. This suggests an alternative means of assessing the effectiveness of leadership behaviours in terms of the impact of leaders' behaviours on the followers. A further problem in understanding leadership is that the extensive literature on leadership, and changing schools of thought and models, contain much reworking of earlier concepts. Perhaps the frustration with the inability of leadership research to provide a clear picture is rooted in a belief that there is a fundamental truth which is yet to be discovered. However, the view of "sense-making" proposed by Weick (1995) provides a potential new way forward. Weick proposes that:

> Social and organisational sciences, as opposed to physics or biology do not discover anything new, but let us comprehend what we have known all along in a much better way, opening up new, unforeseen, possibilities of reshaping, re-engineering and restructuring our original social environment.

Viewing leadership in this way suggests a potential change in the measure of leadership effectiveness from hard business results to the impact of leaders on their followers. This alternative viewpoint has been suggested by some writers. For example, de Pree (1989) in his book *Leadership is an Art* proposes:

> The measure of leadership is not the quality of the head, but the tone of the body. The signs of outstanding Leadership appear primarily among the followers.

He goes on to suggest that the real measure of leadership is the level of people capability which leaders build into an organisation.

Looking at leadership through the eyes of followers is not in itself new (having first been suggested in the 1960s). However, in today's context it provides an emerging view which appears to make sense if we accept that the leader's role is to build capability. Some examples of what has been found by adopting this view are given below. What these examples share, in addition to the followers' views, is that they focus on what leaders do. The first example is the research carried out by Kouzes and Posner, who identified the following key activities:

- *Challenging the process* – a constant questioning of why things are being done in a certain way combined with openness to having their own actions challenged;

- *Inspiring shared vision* – engaging others with a vision of how things can be and how progress may be made;

- *Enabling others to act* – working on a belief in the potential of people and creating the conditions to enable people to realise their potential;

- *Modelling the way* – acting as a role model and demonstrating integrity in terms of congruence of words and actions;

- *Encouraging the heart* – providing recognition tailored to an understanding of the needs and personalities of each person.

A further example of the "emerging school" is provided by the research of Goffee and Jones (2000), who identify the following behaviours of effective leaders:

- *Approachability and vulnerability* – being willing to expose personal weaknesses, thus revealing their humanity and approachability;

- *Intuitive in dealing with "soft" data* – using "soft" data to judge the nature and timing of interventions;

- *Tough empathy* – empathising genuinely, but realistically, and caring about what people do;

- *Reveal differences* – capitalising on what is unique about themselves.

As we highlighted above, organisations are concerned with finding ways to implement change effectively. Our third example of the "emerging school" looks at change leaders. Higgs and Rowland (2001a,b) conducted a study to determine the competencies of effective leaders of change, and included a measure of their ability to build capability into their overall assessment of effectiveness. The areas of competence which they identified, the "change leadership competency" model, were:

- *Creating the case for change* – Effectively engaging others in recognising the business need for change.

- *Creating structural change* – Ensuring that the change is based on depth of understanding of the issues and supported with a consistent set of tools and processes.

- *Engaging others* – In the whole change process and building commitment.

- *Implementing and sustaining changes* – Developing effective plans and ensuring good monitoring and review practices are developed.

- *Facilitating and developing capability* – Ensuring that people are challenged to find their own answers and that they are supported in doing this.

In looking at studies such as these, it becomes clear that this "emerging school" sees leadership as being a combination of personal characteristics and areas of competence. In the studies outlined above, the common observation is made that leadership is based on exercising a relatively small number of areas of competence in a way which reflects the personality of the leader.

A potential model of leadership

Having looked at leadership from a "sensemaking" rather than discovery perspective, a pattern is beginning to emerge. One part of this pattern is that the personality of the leader is a determinant of his/her effectiveness. The second element of the overall pattern is that effective leaders are differentiated from other leaders through the exercise of a relatively small range of skill or competence areas. The way in which these skills and competencies are exercised is not prescribed, but is the function of the underlying personality of the leader. Indeed, this combination suggests that effective leadership requires being yourself, with skill.

This relatively simple statement has significant implications for the way in which we view leadership. Building on this view, it is possible to suggest a model which reflects the research and thinking on leadership emerging from a "sensemaking" viewpoint. This model is shown in Figure 9.4.

Figure 9.4 An emerging model of effective leadership

• Envision • Engage • Enable • Inquire • Develop	Areas of competence

• Authenticity • Integrity • Will • Self-belief • Self-awareness	Personal characteristics "Being yourself"

The elements in this model are explored briefly below:

Areas of competence

- *Envision* – the ability to identify a clear picture of the future which will inform the way in which people direct their efforts and utilise their skills;

- *Engage* – finding the appropriate way for each individual to understand the vision and, hence, the way in which they can contribute;

- *Enable* – acting on a belief in the talent and potential of individuals, and creating the environment in which these can be released;

- *Inquire* – being open to real dialogue with those involved in the organisation and encouraging free and frank debate of all issues;

- *Develop* – working with people to build their capability and help them to make the envisioned contribution.

Personal characteristics

- *Authenticity* – being genuine and not attempting to present yourself in an inauthentic way; being open, and not acting in manipulative way;

- *Integrity* – being consistent in what you say and do;

- *Will* – a drive to lead, and persistence in working towards a goal;

- *Self-belief* – a realistic evaluation of your relevant capabilities and belief that you can achieve required goals;

- *Self-awareness* – a realistic understanding of "who you are"; how you feel and how others see you.

Emotional Intelligence and leadership

In the earlier sections of this chapter, we outlined the growing interest in Emotional Intelligence, and our evidence for its reliability and validity in relation to explaining individual success and performance. More recently a number of writers in this area have been making assertions that Emotional Intelligence is strongly linked to effective leadership. Daniel Goleman, in making the case for Emotional Intelligence, asserts that whilst Emotional Intelligence is more important than IQ and technical skills for all jobs, it is significantly more important for leadership roles. Indeed, in an interview on BBC radio in 1999, he went further and suggested that the higher one progresses in an organisation, the more important Emotional Intelligence becomes. We were interested by this claim and in whether or not it could be borne out by any evidence. In thinking about this we realised that we had competency assessment data on around 100 Directors, CEOs and Chairmen. Using a similar approach to the one we adopted in our original research, we were able to calculate measures of EQ, IQ and MQ for this sample. If Daniel Goleman's claims were to hold, we would have expected to find that the Chairmen/CEOs would have higher levels of Emotional Intelligence than other Directors. Indeed, as can be seen from Table 9.1, it is what we found. Interestingly, there was also a difference in terms of IQ but not for MQ.

Table 9.1 t-test of differences between Chairman/CEO and other directors

Measure	t-value	Difference	Significance level
Overall EQ competencies	−2.07	Significant	0.04
Overall IQ competencies	−2.97	Highly significant	0.01
Overall MQ competencies	−1.70	Not significant	–

Within our original research sample of General Managers we were able to identify which participants were directors and thus able to compare directors with managers. We would now expect the directors to have higher levels of Emotional Intelligence than the managers. Again, as can be seen from Table 9.2, this is what we found. In particular it appeared that the directors were higher on two elements of EI (Interpersonal Sensitivity and Emotional Resilience) as well as the total EQ score. Once again, no differences were found on MQ, although Chairmen and CEOs were higher on IQ.

Table 9.2 t-test differences between Directors and Managers (from seven year-follow-up study)

Measure	t-value	Difference	Significance level
Overall EQ competencies	−2.66	Highly significant	0.01
Sensitivity competencies	−2.86	Highly significant	0.01
Emotional resilience competencies	−2.82	Heavily significant	0.01
Overall IQ competencies	−0.12	Not significant	–

While the results from these studies provide good support for the links between EI and hierarchical levels of leadership, it is important to emphasise that leadership is not exclusively (or even predominantly) related to organisational level. In order to explore the suggestion that EI might be related more broadly to leadership, Higgs and Rowland conducted a content analysis of the transformational leadership models and the work of authors classified above as being in the emergent theory area. Based on this work, they mapped the authors' EI elements on to a range of leadership models. An example of this mapping is shown in Table 9.3. From this it is clear that there is a theoretical

Table 9.3 Relationships between leadership "models" and Emotional Intelligence

Elements of Emotional Intelligence	Leadership models and frameworks					
	Transitional/ transformational (Bass 1985)	Leadership Constructs Alimo-Metcalfe and Alban-Metcalfe – TLQ (2001)	Goffee and Jones (2000)	Kouznes and Posner (1998)	Kotter (1990)– What leaders do	Bennis (1998)
Self-awareness		• Self-awareness	• Reveal differences • Selectively show weaknesses			• Develop self-knowledge • Develop feedback sources
Emotional resilience			• Tough empathy	• Challenges processes • Enable others		• Balance change and transition • Learn from adversity
Motivation	• Charismatic leadership	• Achieving, determined	• Tough empathy	• Challenge processes • Model the way	• Motivating and inspiring • Setting directions	• Role model
Interpersonal sensitivity	• Individual consideration • Charismatic leadership • Intellectual stimulation	• Consideration for the individual • Sensitive change Management	• Tough empathy • Selectively show weaknesses	• Challenge processes • Inspire shared vision • Enable others • Model the way • Encourage the heart	• Aligning people	• Open style
Influence	• Charismatic leadership • Individual consideration	• Networking	• Reveal differences • Tough empathy	• Inspire shared vision • Enable others	• Aligning people • Motivating and inspiring • Setting direction	• Open style
Intuitiveness	• Intellectual stimulation	• Decisive, achieving	• Intuition	• Inspire shared vision • Encourage the heart		• Capacity to concentrate • Curious about innovation
Conscientiousness and integrity	• Individual consideration	• Integrity and openness	• Tough empathy • Reveal differences	• Model the way • Encourage the heart	• Aligning people	• Role model

case for a broader link between EI and leadership. To test the relationships empirically, Higgs and Rowland (2001a) conducted research using the change leadership competency model (see above) and the authors' EI questionnaire with a sample of managers. The results of this research are summarised in Table 9.4 and show strong relationships between the change leadership competencies and all but one of the elements of EI.

Table 9.4 Results of analysis of EIQ versus change leadership competencies (CLCQ)

Change leadership competencies	Elements of Emotional Intelligence							
	Overall EI score	Self-awareness	Emotional resilience	Motivation	Interpersonal sensitivity	Influence	Intuitiveness	Conscientiousness
Creating the case	√	√		√	√	√		√
Structural change		√		√	√			
Engagement		√			√	√		√
Implementation	√	√	√	√	√	√		
Facilitation	√	√	√	√	√			
Overall change competency	√	√		√	√	√		√

To explore the relationship between Emotional Intelligence and leadership in a more general leadership context, and to explore its possible application in identifying leadership potential, an early exploratory study was conducted in the context of a development centre. The development centre involved the participants engaging in a range of group exercises and discussions as well as role plays and individual exercises over a three-day period. In the development centre the participants were observed by a trained team of assessors who rated their leadership potential against a set of pre-determined criteria.

At this stage the study is very limited as only 20 participants have been through the centre. However, as a part of the centre all have completed the authors' EI questionnaire. The results of the centre observers' assessments of each criterion as well as the overall assessment rating were compared with the participant's Emotional Intelligence scores. Exploratory analysis of the results showed that just under a third of the variations in the overall leadership potential rating was explained by the EI elements. A review of the centre criteria showed that three were more related to thinking abilities and knowledge. When these three criteria were removed from the analysis, just under 40 per cent of the variation in the overall leadership potential rating was explained by the EI elements. This exploratory study, together with the others reported above, shows that evidence is beginning to emerge to support the claim that Emotional Intelligence and leaderships are related. Furthermore, the findings of Higgs and Rowland provide evidence of a relatively high degree of relationship between Emotional Intelligence and the "Emerging Model" of Leadership outlined in Figure 9.4.

The concept of "being yourself with skill" implies a mix of intra- and inter-personal competence. The concept of intra- and inter-personal attributes also appears in the Emotional Intelligence literature. Figure 9.5 shows how the elements in the authors' model of Emotional Intelligence may be grouped in terms of Intra- and Inter-personal attributes.

Figure 9.5 EIQ-M inter- and intra-personal components

EIQ element
Intra-personal
Self-awareness
Emotional resilience
Motivation
Intuitiveness
Conscientiousness and integrity
Inter-personal
Inter-personal sensitivity
Influence

In reflecting on Figure 9.5, and the research into links between Emotional Intelligence and Leadership described, there is potentially a link to the model proposed above (Figure 9.4) which attempted to capture the components of the "Emerging Leadership" model. Figure 9.6 outlines how these two models may be related.

Figure 9.6 Mapping Emotional Intelligence onto the "Emerging Leadership Model"

	Elements of areas	EI elements	Other elements
Areas of competence	**Envision** ● Identifying future picture ● Identifying linkages to current people ● Understanding needs of people	● Interpersonal sensitivity	● IQ ● MQ
	Engage ● Identifying linkage of vision to individuals ● Communicating case to individuals ● Finding compelling arguments	● Interpersonal sensitivity ● Influence	● MQ
	Enable ● Belief in talent of individuals ● Understanding how to release individual potential ● Ensuring individuals believe they can contribute	● Interpersonal sensitivity ● Influence	● MQ

	Inquire ● Open to views of others ● Listening ● Empathising ● Explaining your perceptions ● Listening to challenges	● Interpersonal sensitivity	● IQ

	Develop
	● Understanding strengths of others
	● Understanding individuals
	  performance barriers
	● Listening to others
	● Explaining links to future vision
	  of strengths
		● Interpersonal
		  sensitivity
		● Influence
			● MQ

Personal characteristics	**Authenticity** ● Non-manipulative ● Honest ● Vulnerability	● Conscientiousness and integrity	● Openness
	Integrity ● Consistency in words and actions	● Conscientiousness and integrity	

	Will
	● Desire to lead over long term
	● Desire to make a difference
	● Persistence in working towards a goal
		● Motivation
		● Conscientiousness
		  and integrity
			● Achievement
			  motivation

	Self-belief ● Realistic self-evolution ● Confidence in own capabilities	● Intuitiveness ● Self-awareness	● Locus of control
	Self-awareness ● Understanding own feelings and emotions ● Understanding impact of yourself on others	● Self-awareness	

A summary of this expanded model of leadership, which captures the relationships, is shown in Figure 9.7.

Figure 9.7 Revised emerging model of effective leadership

	Leadership	EI element	EI focus
Areas of competence	● Envision ● Engage ● Enable ● Inquire ● Develop	● Interpersonal sensitivity ● Influence/sensitivity ● Influence/sensitivity ● Inter-personal sensitivity ● Inter-personal sensitivity	Inter-personal

Personal characteristics
"Being yourself"
	● Authenticity
	● Will
	● Integrity
	● Self-belief
	● Self-awareness
		● Conscientiousness and
		  integrity
		● Motivation
		● Conscientiousness
		  and integrity
		● Intuitiveness
		● Self-awareness
			Intra-personal

From Figure 9.6 it is clear that whilst Emotional Intelligence is clearly linked to the "Emerging View" of leadership, it does not provide the whole picture. It is evident that aspects of IQ and MQ have a part to play. Perhaps a more comprehensive way of identifying the nature of leadership is by examining the combination of EQ, IQ and MQ. Further work, built on this thought, may lead us to a proposition that leadership capability (LQ) can be seen as follows:

$$LQ = EQ + IQ + MQ$$

Conclusions and future considerations

Whilst the research on leadership is vast and diverse it has, to date, been inconclusive and often contradictory. The search for leadership has come along a very "long line" and almost certainly has a longer one to follow. The shift from an obsessive focus on business results and willingness to accept a reworking of earlier theories as a part of "sensemaking" helps to establish an emerging framework which appears to facilitate the learning process and to stimulate new research.

Research to date has shown some interesting developments when combining an "emerging leadership" perspective with Emotional Intelligence. If the thoughts and research in this chapter are borne out, both in practice and through further research, then we are potentially facing new challenges in selecting and developing our new leaders. Alongside the greater focus on the context of leadership and the importance of different leadership profiles and styles for different contexts, especially regarding levels of change, there is likely to be a greater importance placed on the potential of EI as a tool for developing leadership styles.

The fact that Emotional Intelligence can be developed has to be good news in the broader context of leadership development presented in this chapter. Whilst much of the motivation to develop will come from within the individual, it is important that within the organisation a culture evolves which will reward and reinforce the new behaviours. The potential benefits of developing the Emotional Intelligence of leaders and potential leaders within an organisation will only be realised if the organisation ensures that a supportive culture is in place. Without this, individuals who do build their Emotional Intelligence may well be tempted to take their new capabilities to an organisation which truly values them.

References and further reading

Alimo-Metcalfe, B. and Alban-Metcalfe, A. (2001) "The development of a new transformational leadership questionnaire", *Journal of Occupational and Organisational Psychology*, Vol. 74, No. 1, pp. 1–27.
Bar-On, R. (2000) "Emotional and social intelligence", in R. Bar-On and J.D.A. Parker (eds), *The Handbook of Emotional Intelligence*, San Francisco, Jossey-Bass.
Bass, B.M. (1985) *Leadership and Performance beyond expectations*. New York: Free Press.
Bennis, W. (1998) *On Becoming a Leader*, London, Hutchinson.

De Pree, M. (1989) *Leadership is an Art*, New York, Bantam Doubleday.

Dulewicz, V. and Higgs, M.J. (2000) *EIQ-Managerial User Guide*, Windsor UK, NFER-Nelson.

Goffee, R. and Jones, G. (2000) "Why should anyone be led by you?", *Harvard Business Review*, Sept.–Oct., pp. 63–70.

Goffee, R. and Jones, G. (2001) "Followership: its personal too", *Harvard Business Review*, Dec. 2001, p. 148.

Goleman, D. (1996) *Emotional Intelligence: Why It Can Matter More Than IQ*, London, Bloomsbury Publishing.

Higgs, M.J. and Dulewicz, V. (2002) *Making Sense of Emotional Intelligence* (Second edition), Windsor, NFER-Nelson.

Higgs, M.J. and Rowland, D. (2001a) "Does it take Emotional Intelligence to lead change", *Journal of General Management*, Vol. 27, No. 3, Spring 2002.

Higgs, M.J. and Rowland, D. (2001b) "Developing change leaders: assessing the impact of a development programme", *Change Management Journal*, Vol. 2, No. 1, Aug., ISSN 1469-7017.

Higgs M.J. and Rowland, D. (2003) "Is Change Changing?" Henley Working Paper Series HWP0313.

Kotter, J.P. (1990) "What leaders really do", *Harvard Business Review*, May–June, pp. 37–60.

Kouzes and Posner (1998) *Encouraging the Heart*, San Francisco, Jossey-Bass.

Salovey, P. and Mayer, J.D. (1990) "Emotional Intelligence", *Imagination, Cognition and Personality*, Vol. 9, pp. 185–211.

Weick, K.E. (1995) *Sensemaking in Organisations*, London, Sage.

Chapter 10

The culturally fluent manager

David Rees

A major consequence of the development of a globalised business system is the need for managers to work effectively within and between multi-cultural environments. This chapter proposes that a key competency of the future line, project and HR manager will be tied to the ability to work effectively across cultures. This competency is termed 'cultural-fluency'.

Introduction

> As you step on board the Cairo-bound plane at Singapore's Changi airport, feelings of excitement for your overseas assignment are tinged with apprehension and foreboding. It's not that you do not feel confident in your technical capabilities as an IT project manager – you have an impressive CV. You've done well over the last 10 years, gaining regular promotions in this large global pharmaceuticals company, resulting in your present senior position. And you have handled many projects in foreign places.
>
> No, it's just that feeling you get when you are about to work in a different cultural environment. The day-to-day behaviours are one thing – communication, interpersonal styles, protocols and social etiquette. But behind these more obvious differences are the ways in which organisations function. How are people managed, who really holds power and influence, who are the real stakeholders?

Most managers can probably identify with this situation and the feelings generated. It is often argued that as humans we tend to be creatures of habit, preferring environments that we know and are comfortable with. Change always challenges us to 'give up the old ways' and move to a new mindset.

In the example above, the ability to do things differently is certainly required – maybe conforming with local customs or using alternative styles of communication. But this does not mean that individuals have to 'unfreeze' existing behaviours and then 'refreeze' new behaviours in a permanent sense (after Lewin 1947). Rather, our example serves as a scenario managers are increasingly likely to face, operating in a range of cultural environments that will demand great flexibility and adaptability.

As the business world becomes increasingly global, the likelihood is that we will no longer be exposed to a small number of business cultures during our professional lives. Rates of change are accelerating and this could mean that managers will be managing people within and across a large range of cultural environments with increasing frequency.

The implications for managers are profound. Not only will they face the challenges of working in and out of a myriad of cultures themselves – they will also have to lead their teams and individuals in similar circumstances.

Hall (1995) uses the phrase *cultural literacy* to describe the capability of companies from different cultural styles to get along with one another. Her 'Path to Cultural Literacy' is shown in Table 10.1.

Table 10.1 Path to cultural literacy

0 Our way is their way.
0 Their way is different, it's wrong.
1 Our way is "X", their way is "Y".
2 Both their way and our way have strengths and weaknesses.
3 Cultural synergy We can learn from them, they can learn from us.
4 Cultural flexibility We can bridge differences during our interactions by adjusting our behaviours.
5 Cultural literacy With this partner we bridge this way: with that partner we bridge in another way.
6 Cultural mediation We can prevent conflict, diffuse it and keep it from escalating, and resolve it where already present.

Source: Hall *Managing Cultures* (1995).

Hall and various scholars (see, e.g. Lessem and Neubauer 1994; Berry 1980; Olie 1990) have discussed various situations requiring cultural change at the organisational level.

Many authors have articulated the need for specific skills in approaching cross-cultural interactions (see, e.g. Guy and Matlock 1991; Marx 1999; Lewis 2000).

Other writers (see, e.g. Garrison and Rees 1994; Hickson and Pugh 1995; Garrison 2001) have identified an understanding of political and economic systems as a pre-requisite for senior managers carrying out their duties in culturally variable arenas.

It is the thesis of this chapter that managers will need to develop extraordinary competencies for addressing these aspects of inter-cultural working.

The expression used here to indicate this collective managerial capability is *cultural fluency*.

Cultural fluency

Based on its Latin root, *fluency* suggests a flowing movement – something easy in motion or shape. Often used in connection with linguistic ability, fluency in understanding, moving between and working within different cultures is a capability firmly on the future manager's competency agenda. A definition is thus proposed below.

The culturally fluent manager

Our proposed definition of this managerial competency is:

The repertoire of cultural awareness, knowledge and skills needed by managers to perform effectively across cultural boundaries.

A start to unravelling the complexity of the culturally fluent manager can be made by identifying the key features of international and corporate cultures (Figure 10.1).

Figure 10.1 The component capabilities of the 'culturally fluent' manager

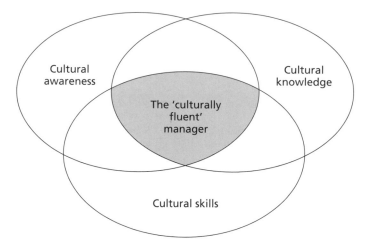

Source: Based on Rees (2002) 'Cultural fluency – leveraging the benefits of diversity'.

International culture

A common-usage phrase of describing culture is *the way we do things around here*. Holden (2002) confronts many of the classic definitions and approaches offered by the well-known contributors such as Hofstede (1980) and Adler (1991). Instead, Holden develops a *social constructionist* approach, quoting Haastrup (1996) 'where culture is conceived as being made up of relations, rather than as stable systems of form and substance'.

As Holden states, under this approach people's identification with different cultures are subject to change and boundaries between communities become fluid. An important implication emerging from this contention is that cross-cultural interactions cannot be predicted with any certainty.

This chapter's author takes this viewpoint as the intellectual basis for proposing the *culturally fluent manager* model.[1]

Essentially, when managers are facing situations of cultural difference they are required to become aware and understand shared sets of values, attitudes and behaviours.

As Jacqui sets off for her Cairo assignment we can think of several culture-bound issues that may affect her success as a project manager – technical and managerial status, qualifications, age and gender; the organisational climate and management style under which she will operate; the whole concept of project management as a business philosophy; the local and cross-border environments in which she will be working.

Additionally, in her role she will have to manage a number of cultural issues related to the project stakeholders. Do customers understand her approach to service delivery? Do project team members view time management in the same way? Is project planning seen as a valuable tool for effective performance?

Culture, business performance and the role of the manager

Throughout this publication so far there have been many references to the critical role that organisational culture plays in achieving corporate performance. We are deeply interested in understanding business cultures because extensive research and operational experience has demonstrated the links between how things get done in an organisation and subsequent performance achievement. Indeed, it is suggested by many observers that corporate culture is the one true competitive differentiator as it is so hard for others to copy or imitate.

Certain managerial capabilities can also create this differentiation. It is argued that for international managers *cultural fluency* is one such managerial competency. These competencies can be activated at different levels – strategic, operational and personal.

Let us consider these levels with some examples.

Cultural fluency: strategic level

The following three scenarios all have a *cultural fluency* challenge. Can you spot them?

Your South African organisation has fundamentally changed its business strategy. For over 100 years the company has brewed beers but as profits declined over the last decade it engaged in a strategy of vertical integration. Finally, it has decided to divest itself of beer production altogether to focus on running hotels. What do you envisage as your company's greatest challenge for ensuring the new strategy is successful?

As a former state utility, your UK power-generating company is finding it tough to compete with other players in the domestic market for electricity production. In response, the senior management team has approved a new strategy of international project development. Your commercial team has identified a tender invitation to build and operate a new power plant in North Africa. To share the risks of this venture you decide to bring in a partner for this project. How will your company choose its partner?

Aggressive competition in the Asia-Pacific telecommunications market has led to consolidation through mergers and acquisitions. Your company, a major player in this marketplace, has decided to make a bid for a rival almost equal in size. A due diligence team is now conducting an assessment of the other organisation's assets. Who will be in the team and what will they be evaluating?

Look again at those questions:

- your greatest challenge at a time of business transformation?

- your partner selection method?

- your merger strategy?

In each of these cases, 'culture' becomes a *strategic* issue – managing change, corporate decision-making, 'valuing' people assets and organisational resources.

The first scenario is a challenge for senior executives to align their corporate culture with the business strategy. In changing the market focus you can be sure that customer demands will change, too. Changing customer demands will certainly mean 'doing things differently'. This may impact on how the company will be structured in future, what kind of people will be hired, the behaviours people will need to adopt – and much more.

At this senior level, managers will need to:

- define, position and understand their own culture and that of their organisation;

- define, position and understand other corporate cultures;

- define and measure the cultural gap between their organisation and its competitors.

These activities will produce a type of 'gap analysis'. Gaps can be measured formally – with a specific measurement tool – or informally through the judgement of the individual manager. Figure 10.2 illustrates this concept.

Figure 10.2 Identifying the culture gap

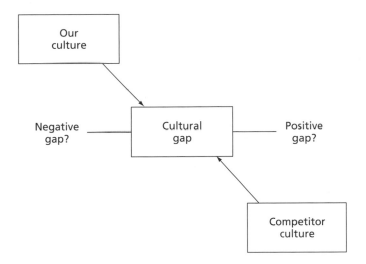

Further, executives may also consider that frequent cultural change becomes a competitive strategy in its own right. Instead of culture being a product of strategic change it actually becomes the transformational driver.

The second scenario reflects a situation where this firm chose an inappropriate partner – and paid a huge penalty! A French partner was selected, creating a very negative impression in the minds of the customer. This led to the UK power-generator being discounted from further participation in the deal and with it the loss of perhaps 30 years revenue flow and profit from the project (Figure 10.3).

Figure 10.3 Case study example: loss of business through cultural misunderstanding

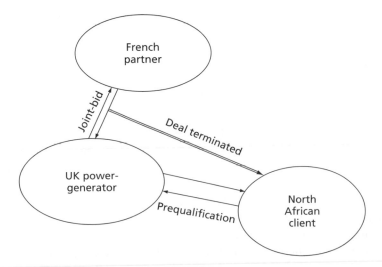

The third scenario is representative of the consolidation that many industries now find themselves facing. This is a world of mergers, acquisitions and strategic alliances – and culture again rears its head as a challenging feature of corporate integration to get right. Table 10.2 offers selected research studies to demonstrate this point.

Table 10.2 International mergers and acquisitions, alliances, partnerships and JV's: 'the failure' factor

1997 – Imperial School of Management found . . .
'a statistically significant negative relationship between differences in management style and inferior post-deal performance amongst 129 UK companies.'

1998 – Booz-Allen and Hamilton found . . .
'only 10% of strategic alliance members reached a level of real understanding of a partner's structure, culture, work environment, reward systems and promotion programmes.'

1999 – US survey found . . .
'nearly all 180 respondents faced serious problems in managing the HR aspects of M&A's. 50% felt management had not paid adequate attention.'

These studies illustrate the need for senior managers to ensure that culture is elevated to a strategic priority.

Cultural fluency: operational level

Many years ago a major American corporation decided to re-structure its world-wide operations along a matrix model of organisation. This approach has many advantages – speed of response, sensitivity to customer demands, swifter time to market and so on. However, when this structure was rolled out in Italy the story was very different. There was a high degree of local discomfort over the new arrangements and this affected performance adversely. What was the problem?

Of course, it was a cultural issue! Figure 10.4 shows the matrix structure becoming a dilemma for people who are used to doing things differently and being organised differently.

Here, the way people were organised reflects a strong sense of belonging to a family group. By a long way, Italians place 'family values' as a major priority in how they live and work. There is strong loyalty to 'one papa and one mama' that a hierarchical system of organisation sustains. A matrix management system brings complexity to lines of reporting and performance appraisal. This can create uncertainty and confusion for both employees and managers whose relationships have dramatically changed.

What can we learn from this? Not that matrix management (or any other management system, for that matter) is inherently 'good or bad', 'better or worse', 'right or wrong'. It reminds us again of a challenge for managers – to be able to identify such dilemmas and take into account such cultural preferences.

Figure 10.4 US electronics company matrix organisation structure

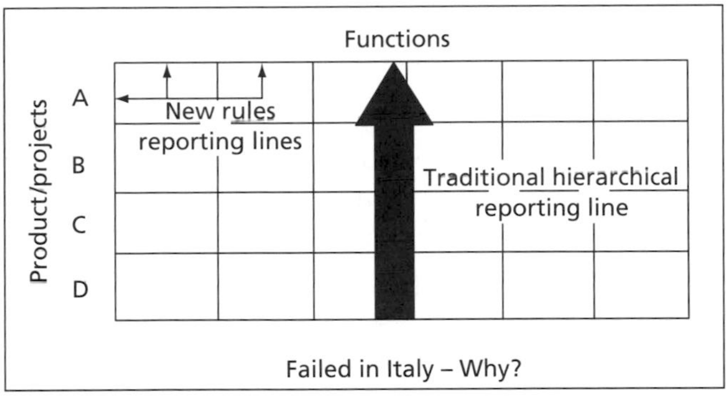

Costs

Organisational re-structure costs – ?

Impact on operational performance – ?

Second re-structuring costs – ?

Managers, whether they are local or headquarters-based, need to develop an awareness that there can be potential cultural conflicts. They have to possess skills to influence senior managers of the difficulties their decisions may create.

Once more, this represents an opportunity to gain performance advantage over those competitors who do not possess this ability to work *with* different cultures, effectively.

This ability is not restricted to the international dimension. The same type of scenarios can be considered when working cross-functionally. How capable is the manager in recognising the differences – sometimes very subtle differences – between the way different departments, divisions and business units operate? How good is the manager at identifying, proposing and implementing cultural change – if that is required? Or, if change is not possible, how effective is the manager at developing strategies for working with other cultural norms? How capable is the manager at influencing and persuading his or her team members of the need to change their behaviours to work across, within and alongside varied cultural environments?

This leads us to consider the personal attributes of cultural fluency.

Cultural fluency: personal level

Earlier, three key characteristics of cultural fluency capability were proposed:

1 'Awareness' relating to the recognition of your identity as a member of one or more cultural groups, and a recognition that other groups may be culturally different.

2 'Knowledge' referring to an understanding of how and why cultures are different.

3 'Skills' indicating the capabilities you possess to work effectively in and across different cultures.

These personal cultural fluency competencies are needed at all management levels.

At the strategic level, executives will need a deep grasp of the significance of the organisation's culture and its linkage to business results. Further, they will need to ensure that this culture supports operational strategies and that all personnel understand what behaviours are required of them. They will also need to demonstrate exceptional skills in dealing with a range of culturally diverse stakeholders. These could be regulators, trade unions, government bodies, finance providers and international clientele.

At an operational level, managers will need to understand the cultural expectations from the top and ensure these are met through their roles as team leaders. Particular competencies are required in managing customer and supplier relationships, managing across functions and managing culturally diverse teams.

Cultural fluency: interpersonal skills

Rapport

Probably the key skill is the ability to build rapport with others. 'Rapport' is all about developing effective relationships and is best achieved through careful observation and active listening. You are trying to gain a platform of mutual trust and respect with another party. This is demonstrated by tangibly showing others that you understand how and why they see things as they do.

During transformational programmes a lack of trust is usually cited as one of the biggest resistance factors in making change successful (see various authors including Carnall 1990; Binney and Williams 1997). In the formation of alliances, joint-ventures and partnerships, trust and respect is essential to establish between the members at an early stage. Doing business in overseas territories requires rapport to be built and sustained over long periods of time. Do you have the ability to look at a problem or issue from one perspective – your own – then orientate your view of that same situation through a 180-degree shift? It's not easy!

A favourite perception exercise runs as follows:

One afternoon three people were walking through a forest...

One was an artist
One was a lumberjack
One was a botanist

What did they see...?

This ability to shift one's perspective is all about maintaining a balance of view.

The 'Cultural Balance' as Figure 10.5 shows some examples of shifts that may be required in the context of organisational and management systems.

Figure 10.5 The cultural balance

The cultural balance	
You do not sign the contract as speedily as we would like...	...but I understand that you prefer to build a good relationship first.
Your organisation is very hierarchical and produces much bureaucracy...	...but I realise that your status and authority is very important in your society.
Young people are promoted early on in their careers in my company...	...but I appreciate that you value wisdom through age and experience in yours.
We express our emotions openly during business meetings...	...but I am aware that you keep your feelings private.
I like to do presentations with interactive participation...	...but I know that your style is more about listening and giving tangible respect.

Source: Cultural Fluency Training & Development Ltd (2003).

Some of the difficulties in achieving this shift include:

● having no experience of this situation;

● relating everything against our own norms;

● not understanding why people behave like this;

● being uncomfortable with ambiguity;

● becoming judgmental;

● jumping to conclusions;

● preferred comfort zone is our own cultural environment.

As with many of these competencies, programmes of training and development can significantly improve individual performance.

Leadership styles

Managers need to have a repertoire of leadership styles at their disposal that can be applied to various situations they find themselves managing. This resource – and the skill to implement it – is a real hallmark of managerial cultural fluency.

In some cultural environments, a highly directive style may be entirely appropriate; in other situations a strongly supportive style may be better. The ability to adapt and change style when required is a feature many organisations need in their management ranks.

Conflict-handling/negotiation

Similarly, a range of approaches that can be easily and quickly accessed to help solve conflicts and ensure successful negotiations are valued competencies. This means understanding not only immediate 'win–lose' positions but future scenarios as well. The 'rules of the game' need to be clearly understood.

Emotional Intelligence

This contemporary concept is very relevant to the capability of the culturally fluent individual. It can take enormous emotional maturity to deal with situations where behaviour and attitudes are completely at odds with your own. Trying to put the past behind you (or your employees) can mean dealing with substantial cultural baggage. Moving from one cultural position to another may require a high level of EQ.

Communication

This may be at a pure linguistic skill level or it may be more a question of interpersonal style. The methods and approaches used to communicate will undoubtedly have a major impact on the ability to influence situations. At an extreme (e.g. an overseas work assignment or a privatisation programme) this could necessitate the learning of a completely new language or way of interacting. The way in which presentations are made in different cultural environments could easily become a success differentiating factor.

Attitudes

A positive attitude to getting things done in culturally diverse situations becomes a crucial personal attribute.

Tolerance of ambiguity, a sensitivity to how others feel, and a patient approach become important mindset features of the culturally fluent manager.

Assessing your personal level of 'cultural fluency'

New tools are being developed to measure these capabilities and these are referred to later. You may like to assess your own levels of cultural fluency from an international perspective using the template in Figure 10.6. (The inspiration for this has come from 'The cultural learning curve' in *Cross-Cultural Team Building* by Berger 1996.)

Figure 10.6 Assessing your level of cultural fluency

	Total non-cultural fluency	Some awareness	Active awareness	Some understanding	Active understanding	Some skills	Culturally skilled	Culturally fluent
Understanding how, when and where to apply the awareness, knowledge and skills I have								GLOBAL ROAMER
I love travelling, got lots of experience and like to communicate in the way they do							SEASONED TRANS-NATIONALIST	
I enjoy multicultural experiences and I try to 'act local'						RAPPORT-BUILDER		
The reasons for cultural differences are understood					LEARNED TRAVELLER			
I can clearly see cultural differences, I know some of the reasons for this				WILLING LEARNER				
Cultures are different, I don't understand why but I'm interested			INQUISITIVE TOURIST					
I know people are different but I don't see the need to change my behaviour		DAY TRIPPER						
No knowledge, awareness or skills for dealing with other cultures	STAY AT HOME							

Level of cultural fluency competence

Source: Based on Berger, *Cross-Cultural Team Building* (1996).

The culturally fluent organisation

We have been considering the specific managerial capabilities for the culturally fluent manager but the enterprise needs to develop itself as a 'culturally fluent' organisation. This is an organisation that is aware of its own culture, knows what its culture should be to succeed, and has the capabilities for cultural change. Cultural diversity is positively embraced.

Managing cultural diversity

This is a challenge for a number of reasons:

- It takes time to learn about other cultural norms and behaviours. It can take longer to resolve conflict. Protocol and etiquette issues may extend process time within teams.

- Which cultural norm will prevail? In which direction do we change behaviour?

- Existing prejudices and stereotypes.

- Lack of commitment, involvement, confidence.

- Self interest.

- Fear of losing power, influence and control.

- Patronising behaviour.

- Under or non-existing human resource strategy on cultural diversity.

Cultural diversity is becoming an important issue for organisations because:

- this can be a source of competitive advantage for an increasingly global business;

- the right people, often people coming from different cultural backgrounds, need to be attracted;

- particular skills and experience – such as language fluency and international travel – are at a premium for most international businesses;

- multicultural teams are the direction in which many companies are moving;

- many businesses want to be thought of as good, responsible employers;

- as a tangible representation of the company's business philosophy it needs to demonstrate a positive image to the world.

The benefits of cultural diversity

- a wider, richer pool of diverse resources and capabilities become available to respond better to changes in the business environment;

- opportunities to introduce more creativity and imagination to the product/service offer;

- culturally diverse teams can work better with increasingly culturally diverse customers, suppliers and partners;

- culturally diverse teams may stimulate more productive ideas and solutions;

- customers are increasingly making 'ethical' purchasing decisions based upon a company's social attitudes;

- reputation damage through the mis-management of cultural diversity comes at a potentially heavy price;

- cultural diversity can bring a new dynamic to the work atmosphere – energising, motivating and enriching.

Take stock of where you think your organisation is. Assess where you feel the organisation's cultural fluency strengths and weaknesses lie. What actions do you feel the organisation need, to take to ensure that cultural issues do not become an impediment to success?

For many organisations around the world this 'paradigm-shift' has been extremely difficult to implement – especially in the international context. In Europe most companies are only slowly realising the benefits of developing themselves as *culturally-fluent* transnational organisations. Too often they have de-prioritised cultural understanding and awareness, usually dismissing these as unimportant topics.

Further, their recruitment, selection and career development strategies do not place a high value on cultural skills. These skills are seen as 'soft' rather than 'hard' and hence technical capability assumes a higher value. This is in conflict with the majority of traveller's tales that suggest deals are being 'won' or 'lost' according to how culturally fluent people are.

Management role

Managers are, of course, in a unique pivotal position. They themselves are products of the cultural bedrock of their societies and the resulting organisational systems. In turn, their task is to manage operations within the prevailing cultural norms of the enterprise. In other words, they have a responsibility to administer the activities of the company according to prescribed sets of rules, regulations, processes, procedures and systems. But they also have an opportunity to influence and implement change depending on a variety of factors including their ability to challenge the prevailing corporate culture.

Building a *culturally fluent organisation* is going to be a major management challenge for many businesses.

Cultural training and development

Clearly, specific training and development programmes will have to be initiated to help people achieve appropriate levels of competency. The aggregate of these skills and competencies across the whole organisation, the transformation of structures, processes and procedures, and the change of mindset from monoculturalism to multiculturalism identifies the *culturally fluent* organisation.

Managers will be expected to identify these competency needs as part of their managing people responsibilities and, like other competency development needs, these will be determined using training needs analysis.

Solutions should be built upon a clear identification of needs. When these are fully understood, appropriate programmes can be targeted for individuals and teams.

An example of how a cultural fluency training and development programme could look for a business entering new overseas markets is shown in Figure 10.7.

- *Strategic cultural fluency* – These roles often involve strategic relationships across cultures – international business development, M&As, alliances and partnerships. Effective management of these relationships calls for special awareness of cultural behaviour at a senior level.

Figure 10.7 Cultural training and development planning

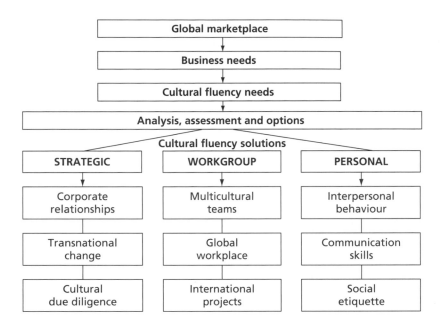

Source: Cultural Fluency Training & Development Ltd (2003).

- *Workgroup cultural fluency* – Leading multicultural teams and international projects requires a repertoire of skills and techniques. The lifespan of global teams may be short, demanding excellence in team formation, development and closeout. Project managers need to acquire dexterity in managing multicultural stakeholders.

- *Personal cultural fluency* – Individual performance in handling working relationships and social etiquette can be enhanced through the acquisition of specific skills and knowledge. Interpersonal behaviour can be improved through foreign language learning, international English training and non-verbal communication skills.

For major projects, significant programmes of training may be required to help manage cultural diversity between stakeholders.

Conclusion

In conclusion, then, this chapter has placed on the future people manager's agenda the need for organisations to take managing culture seriously as a potential differentiator of competitive success.

Enterprises will have to be increasingly agile in making changes – both strategic and tactical – to the way in which they do things in response to changes in the business environment. They will need to be proactive in meeting cultural challenges, not simply reacting to new situations. As social values and attitudes change, organisations must be ready to face new cultural demands. The fast-developing global legal environment will add to the pressure for speedy cultural changes.

As enterprises amalgamate, consolidate and break up at ever-increasing rates, cultural flexibility and adaptability will become a key corporate attribute. We have identified the need to build 'culturally fluent' organisations.

Managers will play key roles in meeting these challenges. They will need to be equipped with outstanding abilities to deal with cultural change. We have termed these people 'culturally fluent' managers.

Future implications for managers

The development of culturally fluent organisations requires culturally fluent managers. For many managers, particularly those not yet working in an international capacity, there may be a skills and competency gap to be filled.

Many organisations have placed such organisational and management development initiatives as a low priority but there is clear evidence that cultural fluency competencies will be greatly in demand in the future. We have witnessed rewards and premiums being offered to attract talent with such capabilities.

There is also evidence, however, that many large multinationals see the development of these competencies as essential for future career progression.

Note

1. It is not the purpose of this chapter to engage in a detailed explanation of theories of culture but for readers interested in pursuing the topic in more detail Holden's book is an admirable point of reference.

References

Adler, N. (1991) *International Dimensions of Organisational Behaviour*, PWS-Kent Publishing.

Berger, M. (1996) *Cross-Cultural Team Building*, McGraw-Hill.

Berry, J.W. (1980) 'Social and cultural change', in H.C. Triandis and R.W. Brislin (eds), *Handbook of Cross-Cultural Psychology*, Vol. 5, 211–79, Boston, Allyn & Bacon.

Binney, G. and Williams, C. (1997) *Learning into the Future*, Nicholas Brealey.

Carnall, C. (1990) *Managing Change in Organisation*, Prentice-Hall.

Cultural Fluency Training & Development Ltd (2003) Internal Training Resources.

Garrison, T. (2001) *International Business Culture*, Elm Publications.

Garrison, T. and Rees, D. (1994) *Managing People Across Europe*, Butterworth-Hienmann.

Guy, V. and Matlock, J. (1991) *The New International Manager*, Kogan Page.

Haastrup, K. (1996) *A Passage to Anthropology: Between Experience and Theory*, Routledge.

Hall, W. (1995) *Managing Cultures: Making Strategic Relationships Work*, John Wiley & Sons.

Hickson, D.J. and Pugh, D.S. (1995) *Management Worldwide*, Penguin.

Hofstede, G. (1980) *Culture's Consequences*, Sage Publications.

Holden, N.J. (2002) *Cross-Cultural Management: A Knowledge Management Perspective*, Person Education.

Lessem, R. and Neubauer, F. (1994) *European Management Systems: Towards Unity Out of Cultural Diversity*, McGraw-Hill.

Lewin, K. (1947) 'Frontiers in group dynamics: concept, method and reality in social science', *Human Relations*, 1.

Lewis, R.D. (2000) *When Cultures Collide*, Nicholas Brealey.

Marx, E. (1999) *Breaking Through Culture Shock*, Nicholas Brealey.

Olie, R. (1990) 'Culture and integration problems in international mergers and acquisition', *European Management Journal*, Vol. 8, No. 2, pp. 206–15.

Rees, D. (2002) 'Cultural fluency – leveraging the benefits of diversify', in *Henley Manager Magazine*: The alumni magazine of Henley Management College, Issue no. 10, Autumn, Henley.

The learning manager

Elizabeth Houldsworth

Our third selection of future people management capabilities focuses on the role managers will have in developing the skills, knowledge and competencies of others. Organisational and individual learning has proved to be a major topic of interest, largely because this has become a key weapon in achieving competitive advantage. Part I identified the value of human and intellectual capital as the source of most organisations added value in the future. This chapter brings the theme of learning to the level of this individual manager.

Introduction and context

Much has been written about learning at an individual and organisational level. Within the space available, this chapter does not attempt to recount the whole story. Instead, it takes the view that for managers and staff within organisations the issue of development is key, as the quote from John Browne indicates:

John Browne, CEO British Petroleum, said:

> Learning is at the heart of a company's ability to adapt to a rapidly changing environment. It is the key to being able both to identify opportunities that others might not see and to exploit those opportunities rapidly and fully . . . In order to generate extraordinary value for shareholders, a company has to learn better than its competitors and apply that knowledge throughout its business faster and more widely than they do. (see Prokesch, 1997)

The suggestion in the reference is that organisations need to effectively foster and direct learning at an individual level in order to achieve company learning and value for stakeholders. Pfeffer's influential work (1998) has already suggested that extensive training is a key high performance management practice, which in turn drives learning and development and associated business benefits of cost reduction and increased customer satisfaction (Figure 11.1).

For the individual people manager, the context for this emphasis upon development is a changing psychological contract, where organisations offer less and less jobs for life and as a result employees invest more and more in their own intellectual capital. Learning has been elevated from

Figure 11.1 The importance of training and development in high performance management practices

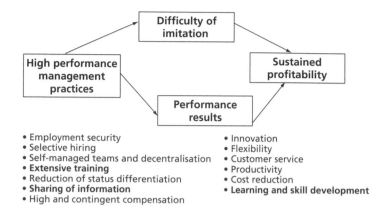

- Employment security
- Selective hiring
- Self-managed teams and decentralisation
- **Extensive training**
- Reduction of status differentiation
- **Sharing of information**
- High and contingent compensation

- Innovation
- Flexibility
- Customer service
- Productivity
- Cost reduction
- **Learning and skill development**

Source: Pfeffer, *The Human Equation – Building Profits by Putting People First* (1998).

something that was done at school, as a result of external influences (we had to go and teachers directed the process), to something that all adults should be striving to achieve on an ongoing and lifelong basis.

For line and project managers, the terminology for their accountability will often be training and development. We shall define training here as: *The intentional intervention to help an individual to become more competent at work.* The literatures on both learning and training and development are vast and it is beyond the remit of this chapter to consider them fully. Given our main concern here is with people and project managers, our focus as the chapter unfolds will be largely upon the evolution and the current practice of management development as well as suggesting ways it may develop in the future.

Management learning developments and approaches

Following the Second World War and the fact that the officer training in the Services had impressed many people, there was a movement towards implementing similar methods in education and in management. In 1947, in the first report to recommend a national system of management education, Colonel Urwick did stress that 'there is no implication in this report that young men and women can be trained as managers in industry and commerce by following certain courses of study' therefore stressing the need for practical experience. In 1946, the Administrative Staff College (now Henley Management College) was established in the UK, the result of an initiative by a group of people with experience in industry, commerce and public service, with support from the Nuffield Trust. In 1947, the British Institute of Management was established and launched its Diploma in Management Studies. Not until the 1960s was there more widespread interest from British Universities. The 1963 Robbins Report recommended the setting up of two postgraduate business schools in the UK and in the same year Lord Franks proposed that these be at London and Manchester. Lord Franks in 1963 set the target of 2000 MBAs per annum and only in the late 1980s did these figures begin to be realised, then exceeded with the MBA qualification becoming almost a prerequisite for middle and senior management positions.

As this industry around management learning has developed, John Burgoyne is one author who has reflected extensively on the subject. In 2002 he built on earlier writing (Burgoyne 1975, 1977; Burgoyne and Stuart 1977) in order to provide a 'mapping' of the variety and alternatives of theoretical perspectives on learning for managers. The chapter he wrote in 2002 provides a useful overview of the field and a sense of timing and chronology. Burgoyne points out that in describing the differences in learning theory there is a historicity to them, with the theories and practices and the people who developed them belonging to different time periods and eras. He describes fourteen schools of learning, summarised in Table 11.1, and in addition his chapter describes how the approaches contain different conceptions of self.

Table 11.1 Fourteen schools of thought about learning

Learning theory	Self
1 Conditioning and the connectionist approach	A mechanical view of self
2 The trait modification view	A specification view of self
3 The information transfer approach	A recorder view of self
4 The cognitive school	A knowing view of self
5 The systems theory approach	The discovery view of self
6 The humanistic and existential approach	An essential view of self
7 Social learning theory	An identity view of self
8 Psychodynamics and related approaches	A mystical view of self
9 Post-modernism	The decentred and fragmented self
10 Situated learning theory	The communal self
11 Post-structuralism	The 'vacant' self
12 Activity theory	The contextualised self
13 Actor network theory	The co-evolving self
14 Critical realism	The hermeneutic self

Source: Burgoyne (2002).

We shall not deal with all of these schools of thought in detail here. Burgoyne suggests that although they do not fall into a neat chronology, it is possible to identify a rough ordering (Table 11.2). This allows a sequencing to emerge, suggesting how conceptions of learning and self have developed over recent history.

Although the views about self provide a very interesting insight, we are more concerned here with understanding the experience and requirements of people managers in terms of managing learning (of self and others) within their organisations. We shall therefore concentrate on the most prevalent approaches. In 1988, Binsted reviewed Burgoyne's earlier writing in which he suggested seven schools of thought about learning. Binsted suggested that of these seven, three could be picked out as core:

1   the conditioning,

2   the cognitive, and

3   the experiential.

If we combine these with the contents of cluster A in Table 11.2 (which we interpret as being the longest established in terms of management development provision), we emerge with the five schools which we shall go on to describe as key to the experience of learning managers within organisations today. It is important of course to acknowledge that there are (at least) nine

Table 11.2 Suggested clusters showing development of learning theories and concepts of self

Cluster	School nos.	Name of school/approach	Views of self based on clustered schools
A	1–4	Conditioning, Trait Modification, Information Transfer Cognitive	An individualised, passive and machine-like view of learning and the self
B	4–6 & 8	Cognitive Systems Theory Humanistic and existential Psychodynamics	An individualised but purposive view of the self as a learner
C	7 & 10	Social Learning Theory Situated Learning	A social view of self – individual as existing in relation to other people
D	9, 11–14	Post-modernism Post-structuralism Critical realism	Learning as a system- or context-located phenomenon with the person/self as a node in this process, with variations of status in relation to learning. Learning seen in a system-wide context. Totality of this not only social, but technical and ecological as well.

Source: Adapted from Burgoyne (2002).

other schools of thought which have been popular in management development over the past 30 years, or are currently gaining momentum. (E.g. Cluster B captures the learner-centred and psycho-dynamic approaches, typically emerging in the 1970s.)

Five key schools of learning

Conditioning theories are based upon a stimulus/response view of learning where reinforcement, practice and feedback are the appropriate learning principles. This approach, according to Burgoyne (2002) is the basis of a large amount of empirical experimental research and theorising. Although this way of thinking about learning has been criticised for is mechanistic nature, it is appropriate for certain types of skill development and rote learning. The drill and practice type learning of 'times tables' are familiar to most of us from school and exemplify the behaviourist tradition of stimulus-recall type development. It may not as an approach be generally appropriate for management *development* in its true sense, but plays a role in training programmes, for example, Health and Safety, where compliance and certain responses to key situations are required.

Cognitive theories are based on ideas of an experiencing learner who builds up complex maps of the world, which can be added to (assimilation) or modified when new experience 'does not fit' (accommodation). The 'cognitive maps' are not just the accumulation of facts and data, but the representation of patterns and relationships among and between them (Burgoyne and Stuart 1977). The approach is concerned with grasping the wholeness of what is being learned. Here knowledge is essentially personal and subjective, in contrast to the 'information transfer' model. This school also embraces concepts such as insight and is useful for managers who need to integrate new learning into their work and need to recognise and be able to operate within different situations.

For management development, experiential approaches are often selected. The experiential school encompasses the concepts of holistic learning and learner autonomy and choice. It sees learning as a natural process of growth as opposed to a teaching-based activity. Early approaches to management development saw an emphasis on sharing experience and less on content. Indeed the Syndicate method was devised for this purpose. Revans's action learning emerged as an approach to help managers to 'help themselves' via practical problem-solving around real-life issues (see Revans 1971, 1980).

The work of Malcolm Knowles follows a similar theme. During the 1980s he popularised the notion that for adults, the learning requirements are rather different to those found in the classroom. Knowles' ideas were not new, he built in particular on the earlier examples advanced by Lindeman (1926). The principles of adult learning which Lindeman and, later, Knowles (1984) expounded suggest that:

● Adults are motivated to learn as they experience needs and interests that learning will satisfy. Therefore, these are the appropriate starting points for organising adult-learning activities.

- Adults' orientation to learning is life-centred. Thus, the appropriate units for organising adult learning are life situations, not subjects.

- Experience is the richest resource for adults' learning and the core methodology of adult learning is the analysis of experience.

- Adults have a deep need to be self-directing as such, the role of the teacher is to engage in a process of mutual enquiry with them, rather than to transmit his or her knowledge to them and evaluate their conformity to it.

- Individual differences among people increase with age. Adult education must make optimal provision for differences in style, time, place and pace of learning.

According to Knowles the rationale for learning is likely to be around a real 'life' need. There may, of course, be exceptions – we may embark on a course in ancient history because we are fascinated by the subject matter, but the principles suggest that we are likely to study car mechanics, for example, if we cannot afford a new vehicle. Try this out for yourself, using the process below:

> *Try out these ideas for yourself*:
> Jot down 2 or 3 things which you have learnt in the past two years.
>
> *Having reflected on some things you have learnt, now for each one make a note of the driver for that learning*:
>
> Thing learnt?   Why (and perhaps how) the learning was achieved?

    Information transfer approaches regard the product of learning as stored information. Here the learning processes are around transmission, organisation, storage and retrieval. This perspective therefore leads to an interest in organising knowledge and helping the learner access information. When this way of thinking is dominant, teaching staff are primarily valued as subject experts, teaching methods are one-way knowledge transfer and examination is primarily on the basis of information recall. In terms of our own experience at school, many of us learnt ways that were subject and tutor focused. Management programmes that send out lengthy reading lists beforehand and where the subject area is divided into territories are likely to be information-transfer-based (Burgoyne and Stuart 1977).

    Such information transfer approaches have also been the driver for the migration of *content* onto technology-based delivery mechanisms. Birchall and Woolfall (2003) have considered how Corporate e-learning is being designed and implemented in order to deliver business benefits. Table 11.3 summarises the benefits being sought by organisations from e-learning provision. It suggests that potential cost savings are seen as a common driver for e-learning. The dominant learning approach would appear to be information transfer, sharing the largest body of knowledge with the largest group of people at the most reasonable cost.

Trait modification views of learning are based on the concept that the learner is describable as a set of characteristics and learning is a change in the profile of these characteristics. The approach is often associated with psychometric traditions (e.g. Myers Briggs type indicators). In the applied world of training, according to Burgoyne (2002) there tends to be reference to 'knowledge', 'skills' and 'attitudes' as three broad categories of trait which define learning goals and outcomes. This approach also raises the question of characteristics that affect

Table 11.3 Benefits sought from e-learning

Improved resource utilisation
Travel time and accommodation savings
Procurement savings
Cost-effective micro training courses
Economies of scale possible
Just-in-time (JIT)
Scalability
Rationalisation of offerings

Geographical reach
Flexibility – any place, any time
Provides access for people in remote locations
Better support of field staff at customer premises
Rapid transfer of knowledge including best practice
More training to more people

Effectiveness of delivery
Faster roll-out and employee development
More focused training and development
Consistency of information
Lean training to support lean organisation

Organisational benefits
Getting better overall performance from technology
Support for staff at workplace – JIT training improves problem-solving capability
Helps to attract good quality talent
Demonstrates real commitment to employee development
Cost-effective delivery of promised life-long learning

Enhanced learning
Self-paced learning
Increased self-management capability
Enhanced individual choice by providing an alternative approach for learning

Source: Adapted from Birchall and Woolfall (2003).

the learning process itself, either directly through the idea of learning style or indirectly through the proposition that personality characteristics may influence how learning takes place. This is illustrated in the fairly commonplace usage of the learning style frameworks of Kolb (1976a,b) and Honey and Mumford (1986). Kolb viewed learning as a series of experiences with cognitive additions, rather than as a series of pure cognitive processes. He saw learning as a circular process in which concrete experience is followed by reflection and observation. This, in turn, leads to the formulation of abstract concepts and generalisations, the implications of which are tested in new situations through active experimentation. Honey and Mumford's later work (1986) examined learning styles in the context of management. Their learning styles questionnaire with its 80 questions based upon managerial behaviour has become commonplace within organisations. The four styles contained within their model are summarised by way of an example below:

1 **ACTIVISTS** are those who learn by doing. They are enthusiastic about new opportunities to learn and enjoy a degree of risk and challenge. They are not concerned about making a fool of themselves in asking questions or volunteering for something new.

2 **REFLECTORS** are those who learn by standing back and thinking things through. They are often creative, coming up with ideas by listening to others, sharing thoughts and considering all the alternatives. They also see the total picture, understanding how issues are connected and seeing longer-term implications.

3 **THEORISTS** are those who learn through logic, facts and figures. They are curious and like to understand all that they work on. Well planned, precise and thorough, the THEORIST has a preference for 'academic' approaches.

4 **PRAGMATISTS** are those who learn through seeing the applications of theory. They are practical and well organised, setting goals and making plans of action to ensure things are done on time.

The whole approach of profiling people and jobs and the majority of competency approaches (as described later) are based on trait modification approaches. These approaches have become very popular within organisations and as a result we shall devote the next section to understanding more about them.

Use of competency-based development approaches

As an example of the trait modification approach to learning, competencies have become one of most common ways of identifying and planning development needs. They take a place in both performance reviews and in training plans. These often form the basis for career progression and high potential recognition.

The background to the popularity of competencies in the UK lies in the mid-1980s. In 1987, the Constable and McCormick Report set out to uncover the reasons for the UK's lack of competitiveness. They suggested the skill base within their organisations could no longer keep pace with the developing business climate. Factors that underlined this were:

- the failure of large-scale change programmes to deliver the necessary changes in individual behaviour;

- a growing link between business performance and employee skills, such that sustained business performance can only be achieved through improved management capability;

- the need of individuals to upgrade their skills to keep pace with continual change.

In response to these needs, a structured approach to managerial training and development geared around an emerging set of 'Industry Standards' was advocated. Hence the Management Charter Initiative was born in the UK with its use of occupational competencies. This approach to management development focused upon 'outcomes' – that is the ability to perform a task satisfactorily. The 'Review of Vocational Qualifications in England and Wales' in 1986 suggested a vocational qualification should be 'a statement of competence, clearly relevant to work. Standards of occupational competence were defined across all sectors of industry'.

At about the same time within the UK, an approach to competencies was gaining momentum, which had grown out of the research of McClelland (1973) and captured in his article *Testing for Competence Rather Than for 'Intelligence'*. This approach, first deployed and popularised by the Hay Group (with its links to McClelland) adopts a 'process' approach. Competencies are defined as behavioural characteristics and attributes a person exhibits in order to be successful at work for example influence, team work, analytical thinking. Although NVQs continue as a qualification route in many fields within the UK, their popularity within management education has dwindled. Within most organisations the 'default' since the late 1990s has been to seek to define 'behavioural' models with competencies arranged in a number of clusters as illustrated (Figure 11.2).

Once the competencies which are important for an organisation's success have been identified, they may be used to underpin a whole range of company processes, as illustrated below in Figure 11.3. It suggests some of the ways in which competencies may be deployed within organisations. Many people will already have been trained as managers in competency-based recruitment techniques such as focused interviewing. For competencies to be effectively used in performance management, further preparatory work will be required. A starting point for this is likely to be the profiling of roles in terms of their competency

Figure 11.2 Sample contents of a competency model

Personal effectiveness	Cognitive	Achievement	Influence	Management
Self-control	Technical/ professional expertise	Achievement orientation	Influence and impact	Directiveness
Self-confidence	Information seeking	Innovation	Organisational awareness	Developing others
Dealing with failure	Analytical thinking	Concern for order and quality	Relationship building	Teamwork and co-operation
Organisational commitment	Conceptual thinking	Initiative		Team leadership
Flexibility		Customer service orientation		
Interpersonal understanding		Discretionary effort		
Listening and responding				

Figure 11.3 Possible application of competency models within organisations

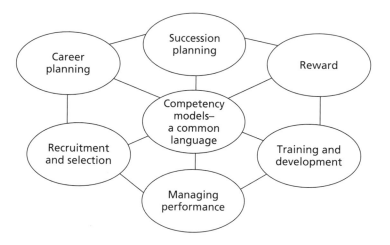

requirements, in order to facilitate gap analysis between the job holder and their current or future role.

In order to apply a competency framework, each individual competency or attribute is usually described as having a number of different levels of display (Figure 11.4).

Competency levels equate with 'just noticeable difference' scales and are intended to help managers and their direct reports better codify their performance against the framework (for more detail see Spencer *et al.* 1994).

Figure 11.4 Illustrative competency levels

Achievement Drive is a concern for working well against a standard of excellence

1 Wants to do well the job in hand. Works to set standards.

2 Sets standards for self.

3 Makes changes in own work methods to improve performance.

4 Sets stretching goals for self for example improving efficiency by specific measure.

5 Tries new things and new goals, at the same time limits risk.

6 Takes action over a period of time to succeed in an entrepreneurial activity.

If you do not have a competency model for your own role you may like to complete the quick exercise below.

Applying competencies to your own role

List the top 6–8 competencies for your role (refer to those in Figure 11.2, if you do not have an organisational model)	Indicate here the relative importance of this competency to your role. Do you need a high level of it, for example level 5 for achievement drive, or is it a behaviour which may be displayed at a lower level, but is required very frequently

Once the competency and levels have been identified for a given role, it is possible to use the appraisal and development discussions to capture any areas for improvement. The example in Figure 11.5 shows how this might be captured on a computer-based system.

The example depicts a role profile for a position described here as being in job band S2ii. It indicates the required level of each competency for the current role as well as those required for promotion to the next level. It also tells us how the current incumbent has been assessed in terms of their existing personal competency level against the job requirements. A gap exists between the levels required for:

● customer focus (level 3 is required for the role and the individual's personal level has been rated at 2 in this competency);

● decision-making (level 2 is required and the individual's personal level has been rated at 1);

● business and communication understanding (level 2 is required and the individual's personal level has been rated at 1);

Figure 11.5 Illustrative computer-based competency role profile

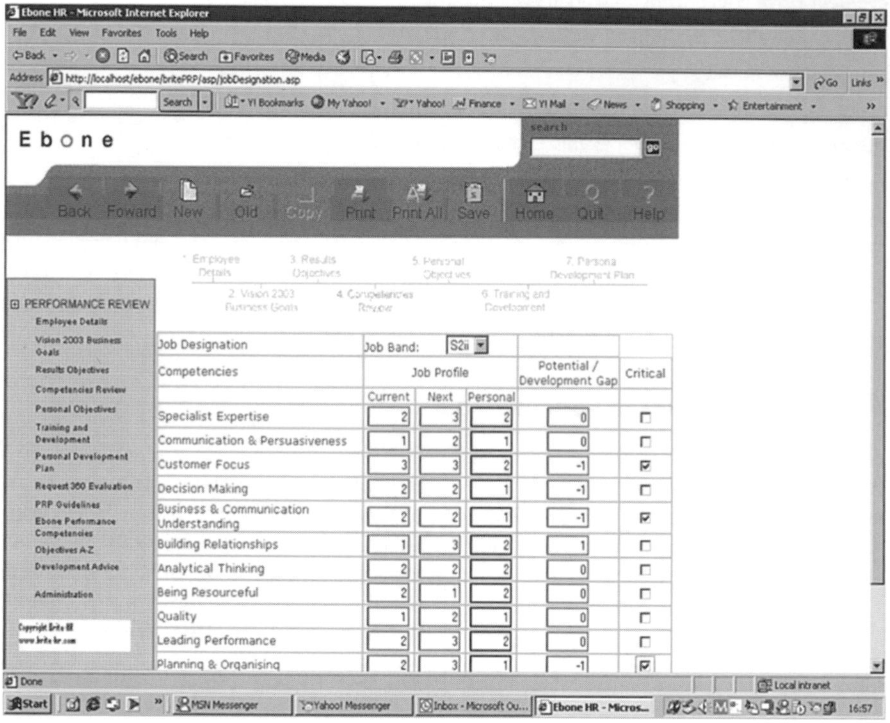

Competencies	Job Profile: Current	Job Profile: Next	Job Profile: Personal	Potential / Development Gap	Critical
Specialist Expertise	2	3	2	0	☐
Communication & Persuasiveness	1	2	1	0	☐
Customer Focus	3	3	2	-1	☑
Decision Making	2	2	1	-1	☐
Business & Communication Understanding	2	2	1	-1	☑
Building Relationships	1	3	2	1	☐
Analytical Thinking	2	2	2	0	☐
Being Resourceful	2	1	2	0	☐
Quality	1	2	1	0	☐
Leading Performance	2	3	2	0	☐
Planning & Organising	2	3	1	-1	☑

Source: An illustration provided Courtesy of Brite-HR.

- planning and organising (level 2 is required and the individual's personal level has been rated at 1).

The occurrence of 'gaps' between job requirement and an individual employees personal competency profile may be used as a part of the performance review process. More immediately it can be used to help create a competency-based development plan along the lines of the one in Figure 11.6.

Figure 11.6 Illustrative competency-based development plan

DEVELOPMENT PLAN FOR: ***Relationship Building***

Suggested development activities

- ***For key priority accounts identify key individuals/decision makers.***
- ***Develop long-term contact plan with these key individuals, anticipate any questions and concerns and prepare for them.***
- ***Keep a log of contact activity, who I spoke to, what it concerned, when I should contact them again.***
- ***Review the content of this with Ken and with the team every month for the 10 key accounts.***

The example suggests relationship building as a key development area for an individual employee. It divides this into four activities, requiring the individual to put in place a process around key account planning in order to better manager relationships with clients and ensure more repeat business.

Developing competencies is different to learning new content or subject knowledge. Recognising this fact, many organisations have sought to put in place competency-based development guides. These help learners and their line managers by providing suggestions for each competency and usually contain a range of on-the-job and off-the-job training and developments. They make the point that attending training programmes is only one option and not always the best for modifying behaviour at work.

In this chapter we have so far considered how management development has evolved along with the associated schools of thought about learning which have been influential. The evolution appears to have mirrored advances in learning and educational theory. For example, the last half of the 20th century saw a switch away from the 'sheep dip' type training of the 1950s and 1960s, which were typified by systematic training for large cohorts. More learner-centred approaches became in vogue following the work of Carl Rogers and David Kolb in the 1970s. In the 1980s, with Malcolm Knowles' work on adult learning, it came to be recognised that adults learn in ways that are different to children and therefore require a different set of learning support. In particular, 'learner focused' tailored support came to the fore with learning resource centres being established. The 1990s saw the increased emphasis upon lifelong and self-managed learning as well as the emphasis upon competency development and more recently web-enabled approaches. The final part of the chapter will now seek to consider possible future directions, particularly how the use of new technologies is changing the way we both work and learn.

Looking to the future

One of the major drivers of changing learning delivery mechanisms has to be the technological support now available. An earlier section has considered the reasons why organisations suggest they adopt e-learning. The dawn of a new millennium has seen the continuation of earlier massive changes in both culture, society and education, based around these new technologies. According to Steeples and Jones (2003) the explosive growth of the Web has been a major driver of educational changes at all levels. The Internet has emerged from its military beginnings and a period of academic development into a general, social and commercial resource in the 1990s (Steeples and Jones 2003). Speaking of changes within universities, Spender (2000) has said:

The process is technology driven. Just as steam and electricity changed the way we organised society, . . . we are now caught up in the digital revolution.

Steeples and Jones (2003) say that the network society which has emerged, has impacted on the debate about skills as well as highlighting the needs of a knowledge-based economy. Similarly, Burgoyne and Williams (2002) suggest in their report that the initial drivers for e-learning adoption: cost-reduction, replacement and improved geographical reach should now be replaced with approaches which link e-learning to a firm's knowledge management systems, strategies and business models.

The future does indeed look set to involve harnessing technology to a greater degree not just to deliver content but also to support individual learning and organisational knowledge management. Research suggests in particular that one of the areas for the increase could well be that of virtual networks of collaboration, both within and across organisations. Such approaches to learning are grounded in the social learning and situated learning schools of learning which Burgoyne (2002) has described. These schools are captured in cluster C of Table 11.2 presented earlier. They reflect a view of learning that recognises that individuals exist and learn in relation to others. This is perhaps not surprising given the virtual and distributed environments in which many people and project managers are working. Themes of particular interest which are emerging from research are practice-based perspectives (Brown and Duguid 1991) collective and situated learning (see Lave and Wenger 1991; Wenger 1998) and learning in virtual teams (Sole and Edmonson 2002).

If we look at a few examples, one researcher, Tsoukas (1993) has described a reality for people managers which involves a variety of communication technologies being deployed to co-ordinate spatially distributed activities. The implication is that this is very different to more 'traditional' environments where face-to-face interactions on a daily basis are managed under the same roof. Tregaski (2003) conducted a study on three foreign-owned subsidiaries in the UK. Her findings similarly suggest that location is important for collaboration, and 'face-to-face' contact facilitates the achievement of this.

Similarly, Sole and Edmonson (2002) have described some of the likely challenges facing project managers and managers of distributed teams. Their in-depth qualitative study saw virtual teams grapple with differences in time zones as well as non face-to-face communication media. They quote an engineer as saying:

> On each of these dispersed projects, our big challenge is that we just don't get together as a team because we're spread so far apart. So it forces us to collaborate....But to do that in non-traditional ways where we can't just have a meeting or work with each other across the hall.

Their findings suggest that spending time together helped to create a foundation for team effectiveness beyond the current task in hand. In addition re-location and co-location across the dispersed teams was found to be an effective strategy for team learning. Therefore, moving people physically, if not for the duration of the project, at least for a period was encouraged to allow for participation in certain key events.

Technologically supported approaches, therefore, appear to be on the increase and also to be moving beyond the distribution of content. The suggestion from these examples is that networked technologies may play an increasing role in supporting the distributed nature of working and learning which is becoming an organisational reality for many people managers.

In summary

This chapter has sought to explore a number of different themes. We started by considering the evolution of management development and some of the schools of thought and approaches which have served to shape the terrain. We have suggested that the management of such learning and knowledge can serve as the glue to unite a range of the aspects related to the management of people. The chapter has described the sort of competency-based approach that people managers are likely to be required to deploy, given their current popularity within organisations. It has concluded with a look at the future, acknowledging the role of the Internet and the future increased influence networking technologies will have in work and in learning in the future.

References

Binsted, D. (1988) 'Open and Distance Learning and the use of new technology for the self-development of managers' in M. Pedler *et al.* (eds), *Applying Self Development in Organisations*, Hemel Hempstead, Prentice-Hall.

Birchall, D. and Woolfall, D. (2003) *Corporate e-Learning: Delivering business benefits*, Grist Ltd.

Brown, J.S. and Duguid, P. (1991) 'Organisational learning and communities of practice: towards a unified view of working', *Learning and Innovation, Organisation Science*, Vol. 2, No. 1.

Burgoyne, J. (2002) 'Learning theory and the construction of self: what kinds of people do we create through the theories of leaning that we apply to their Development', in M. Pearn (ed.), *Individual Differences and Development in Organisations*, Chichester, John Wiley & Sons Ltd.

Burgoyne, J. and Williams, S. (2002) 'He who rides the tiger cannot dismount – implementation of e-learning within company strategies', *Proceedings of 3rd International Conference on Networked Learning*, Sheffield.

Burgoyne, J. (1975) *Learning Theories and Design Assumptions in Management Development Programmes*, CSML Publications, University of Lancaster.

Burgoyne, J. (1977) 'Management learning developments', *BACIE Journal*, Vol. 31, No. 9.

Burgoyne, J. and Stuart, R. (1977) 'Implicit learning theories as determinants of the effects on management development' *Personnel Review*, Vol. 6, No. 2, pp. 5, 14.

Constable, C. and McCormick, R. (1987) 'The Making of British Managers', A Report for the BIM and CBI into Management Training, Education and Development, British Institute of Management and Confederation of British Industry, London.

Franks, L. (1963) 'British Business School Report', *British Institute of Management*, London, Staple Press.

Honey and Mumford (1986) *The Manual of Learning Styles*, second edition, Maidenhead, Peter Honey.

Knowles, M. (1980) *The Practice of Adult Education*, Chicago, Follett.

Knowles, M. (1984) *The Adult Learner: A Neglected Species*, Houston, Gulf Publishing.

Kolb, D.A. (1976a) 'Management and the learning process', *California Management Review*, Vol. 21, No. 3, pp. 21–31.

Kolb, D.A. (1976b) *The Learning Style Inventory Technical Manual*, Boston, MA, McBer & Co.

Lave, J. and Wenger, E. (1991) *Situated Learning: Legitimate Peripheral Participation*, Cambridge, Cambridge University Press.

Lindeman, E.C. (1926) *The Meaning of Adult Education*, New York, New Republic.

McClelland, D. (1973) *Testing for Competence Rather than for 'Intelligence'*, American Psychologist.

Pfeffer, J. (1998) *The Human Equation – Building Profits by Putting People First*, Harvard Business School Press.

Prokesch, S. (1997) 'Unleashing the power of learning: an interview with British petroleum's John Browne', *Harvard Business Review*, Vol. 75, No. 5.

Revans, R.W. (1971) *Developing Effective Managers*, London, Longman.

Revans, R.W. (1980) *Action Learning*, London, Blond & Briggs.

Review of Vocational Qualifications in England and Wales (RVQ) Working Group Report, April 1986.

Robbins, Lord, Chairman of the Committee on Higher Education, appointed by the Prime Minister 1961–1963. Report 'Higher Education' presented in 1963, London, HMSO.

Rogers, C. (1969) *Freedom to Learn*, Ohio, Charles Merrill.

Rogers, C. (1977) 'Personal thoughts on teaching and learning', in M.C. Wittrock (ed.), *Learning and Instruction*, pp. 600–602.

Sole, D. and Edmonson, A. (2002) 'Situated Knowledge and Learning in Dispersed Teams', *British Journal of Management*, Special Issue, Vol. 13, Sept.

Spencer, L.M., McClelland, D. and Spencer, S. (1994) 'Competency assessment methods: history and state of the Art', Hay/McBer Research Press. Paper First Presented at the American Psychological Association Annual Conference, Boston, MA, 13 August 1990.

Spender, D. (2000) *The Role of a University in a Dot Com Society: What is it?* http://collaborate.shef.ac.uk/nl2000.html.

Steeples, C. and Jones, C. (2003) *Networked Learning: Perspectives and Issues*, Springer Verlag.

Tregaski, O. (2003) 'Learning networks', *Power and Legitimacy: International Journal of Human Resource Management*, May, Vol. 14, 3.

Tsoukas, H. (1993) 'Ways of seeing: topographic and network representations in organisation theory', *Systems Practice*, Vol. 5, pp. 441–56.

Urwick, Colonel Lord (1947) 'Education for Management', Report of a Special Committee appointed by the Ministry of Education, London, HMSO.

Wenger, E. (1998) *Communities of Practice: Learning, Meaning and Identity*, Cambridge, Cambridge University Press.

Managing mentoring and coaching

Richard McBain

The book's final chapter addresses the current and future developments of a managerial activity that has been present, usually informally, since the development of the modern organisation and is now increasingly formalised. It is suggested that mentoring and coaching provide perhaps the greatest opportunities for managers to obtain discretionary performance from their teams and colleagues.

Introduction

The tremendous recent growth of interest in mentoring and coaching has been driven primarily by the need for organisations to provide focussed learning and development opportunities in order to increase actual and potential performance. Coaching and mentoring have been described as 'the most tangible, practical and if carried out effectively, possibly the most useful forms of on-the-job development' (Doyle *et al.* 2001). Informal coaching and mentoring activity probably occurs in some form in every organisation. In addition many organisations now actively support coaching practice and 'formal' mentoring programmes.

Organisations as diverse as the UK Civil Service, ICI, KPMG, Motorola and Procter and Gamble use coaching and mentoring to support the performance of their people and achieve a wide range of objectives. This chapter will begin by considering the changing context in organisations and in human resource management, which are impacting upon the role of the line manager and also promoting the growth of coaching and mentoring. After an overview of mentoring and coaching, each will be considered in turn. The aim will be to develop an understanding of the use of the terms and of the different types of mentoring and coaching. We will explore the competencies of the mentor and the coach, and of the outcomes of mentoring and coaching. A key aspect of both mentoring and coaching is the nature of the relationship between the parties involved, which has important implications for the role of the manager and for the provision of organisational support for these activities.

Coaching and mentoring: an overview

The difference between coaching and mentoring

In spite of this increasing interest in mentoring and coaching, there remains a lack of consensus in the meaning of the terms. In part this reflects the range of activities involved as well as the variety of contexts in which they take place. Mentoring and coaching also share some important characteristics. They are relationships that facilitate the learning and development of those involved. While other 'developmental relationships' exist within organisations, such as relationships with colleagues, what distinguishes coaching and mentoring is an explicit focus on development. It is not surprising that many of the skills and techniques of effective mentoring and coaching are similar. Nevertheless there are important differences between the two activities, and the lack of clarity in terminology does not help a critical evaluation of their potential consequences for individuals and organisations.

Broadly speaking, coaching and mentoring may be distinguished primarily in terms of scope and duration, and also in terms of the relationship between the parties involved. Mentoring focusses on the longer-term development of the person being mentored, and may cover a wider territory. The mentor is typically seen as someone best outside a line relationship who also gains developmental outcomes from mentoring. On the other hand, coaching is usually seen as focussing on current performance improvement, and often involves a relationship between a line manager and a subordinate. At the same time there has also been a significant increase in the use of external consultants, particularly at the higher levels of organisations to provide coaching and mentoring.

The changing organisational context

Behind the growth of interest in mentoring and coaching lie a number of important changes within the internal and external context of the contemporary organisation. Together these have placed mentoring and coaching right at the heart of management, and at the focal point of strategy, of implementation, and of learning at the organisational, team, and individual levels. The most important developments may be summarised as follows:

- Increasing global competition and the recognition of the importance of social and intellectual capital as major sources of sustainable competitive advantage, and of the role of learning and diversity in their development.

- The increasing pace of change requiring mechanisms to facilitate behaviour change and to deal with the levels of stress generated by the change.

- Downsized, flatter, and more diverse organisations with less emphasis on hierarchies and a greater requirement for internal and external networking.

- The need to attract and retain talent at all levels coupled with an increased desire of employees for opportunities for enhanced individual growth and development.

- The changing patterns of careers and the emergence of a new psychological contract involving a reduced expectation of a long-term career with one organisation, and an emphasis on self-ownership of careers by employees, and on lifelong and self-managed learning.

- The changing nature of jobs, with reduced emphasis on performance against fixed job descriptions and increasing emphasis on broader roles with less clear boundaries.

- The need for the development of new skills coupled with a means of delivering 'just-in-time', focussed development for all levels of employee in a cost-effective manner.

- The changing role of the line manager, involving a shift from a 'controlling' to more 'participative' management style, and the increasing emphasis on 'leadership' and the need for 'soft skills' development.

- The devolution of key HR activities to the line, including recruitment, performance management, training and development and rewards.

Not only is the management and development of human resources seen as critical to organisational success but also the manager is increasingly the focal point of this process – the primary point of contact between an increasingly sophisticated employee and the organisation. Mentoring and coaching relationships have come to be seen as increasingly important means by which effective human resource management, and people development in particular, are achieved.

The changing context of human resource development

Mentoring and coaching are elements of an organisation's approach to human resource development (HRD). For Walton (1999), HRD is concerned with learning, and the management of learning within an organisation. As such it links to other aspects of human resource management (HRM) and in particular to reward and performance management as well as providing a framework for learning, education, training and development, and career development.

A wide range of techniques is available for an organisation to develop its people at all levels. These techniques may be classified in terms of whether they take place 'on-the-job' or 'off-the-job', or either (see Armstrong 2001):

- *on-the-job techniques*: demonstration, coaching, mentoring, job rotation/planned experience;

- *on-the-job or off-the-job techniques*: action learning, job (skill) instruction, question and answer, assignments, projects, guided reading, computer-based training, video, interactive video, and multimedia training;

- *off-the-job techniques*: lecture, talk, discussion, case study, role-playing, simulation, group exercises, group dynamics, T-groups, interactive skills training, assertiveness training, neuro-linguistic programming, distance learning, and outdoor learning.

A related distinction is that between 'formal' and 'informal' methods. The latter are typically, work-based, learner centred, experiential, often unplanned, incremental, and focussed on the immediate environment. Woodall and Winstanley (1998) argue that for 'the last 10 years work-related informal measures have been fashionable, and formal off-the-job development activities have on the whole been relegated to a secondary position'. Underlying this trend is an assumption that informal and work-based learning is more effective in achieving behaviour change for the individual learner. Furthermore, the latter part of the 20th century witnessed increasing concern with the nature of the learning process and, some would argue a misplaced obsession with learning styles (see e.g. Reynolds 1997). Mentoring and coaching have benefited from this shift from off-the-job training to on-the-job learning and a greater understanding of the processes by which adults learn. Table 12.1 provides an overview of the learning processes involved in methods of work-based development.

Table 12.1 An overview of work-based development methods

Method	Learning process
Learning from another person	
Coaching	Feedback, reflection, challenge
Mentoring and sponsorship	Support, advice, feedback, opportunity, challenge
Role models	Observation, reflection, imitation
Learning from tasks	
Special projects	Problem solving, taking responsibility, taking risks and making decisions, managing without mastering
Job rotation	Exposure to other cultures and points of view
Shadowing	Observation of tasks, new techniques, skills
Secondment	Exposure to other cultures and points of view
Acting up/delegation	Trial of new tasks and skills, challenge
Learning with others	
Task/forces/working parties	Strategic understanding, building awareness and confidence
Action learning	Problem-solving, interaction, influencing
Networking	Interaction and building awareness

Source: Woodall and Winstanley (1999).

The changing role of the line manager in HRD

Recent approaches to human resource management have supported the trend towards the decentralisation of key human resource activities to line managers. Increasingly line managers have local accountability for recruiting new employees, for managing and developing their performance, and agreeing rewards. An influential metaphor sees effective HRD as requiring a partnership between

Figure 12.1 Partners in development

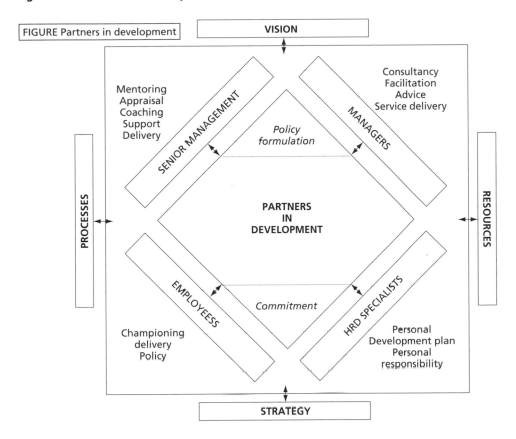

Source: Walton (1999).

senior managers, line managers, employees and HRD specialists. Walton's (1999) model identifies key aspects of the role of the line manager (Figure 12.1) as being to:

● champion HRD, by chairing committees, and resourcing HRD for example;

● deliver HRD learning activities;

● act as a central link in the HRD process, for example in performance management and appraisal related activities;

● provide a supportive learning climate;

● provide mentoring and coaching.

The line manager is key to the translation of strategy into performance, and mentoring and coaching are central to that process – they are key means by which strategy is turned into action, the learning organisation developed, and social and intellectual capital created. This model also suggests some issues for mentoring and coaching, particularly when conceived as a 'formal' activity or programme. These issues include the importance of senior management support, the role of HRD specialists in providing facilitation, consultancy, advice and service delivery, and the commitment of employees to the process.

In referring to the changing role and competences of the 'line manager' no distinction has been made between different roles or levels of line managers. However, it is interesting to compare the view of those (such as Hiltrop 1998) who see these changes in terms of generic roles and skills with others (such as Bartlett and Ghoshal 1997) who argue that while management roles and skills are changing, the implications of these changes will be different and top-level, senior, and operating levels. Nevertheless, all seem to agree that the future manager will require new skills, and that within the new skill set the ability to develop others, to facilitate, and to provide leadership for teams and individuals is likely to increase. The inevitable conclusion of these arguments seems to be not only that managers require coaching and mentoring skills to develop others, but that these are the key means through which their own skills, particularly of the 'soft' or 'inter-personal variety' will be best developed.

A theoretical framework for mentoring and coaching

There is no single or unified theory of mentoring and coaching. However a number of theoretical approaches provide useful insights. In addition to theories of learning considered in Chapter 11, these include:

- Lifespan psychology

- Social exchange theory

- Social cognitive theory.

Before we turn to a more detailed consideration of coaching and mentoring it will be worth briefly considering the contribution of these approaches.

Lifespan psychology

Lifespan psychology is concerned with the lifelong process of change. A wide number of models of development have been proposed, the characteristic of which is the identification of a number of stages in life through which individuals pass. One influential model in terms of mentoring is that of Levinson *et al.* (1978), who built upon Erikson's (1963) model the stages of ego development. Typically each stage has its own key issues and psychological tasks which must be accomplished in order that a person may pass effectively to the next stage of life. In Levinson's study of male development the mentor was someone whose role was to help a young adult enter the adult world. This focus on helping a person to accomplish major transitions in life and work often remains a distinctive characteristic of mentoring in comparison to coaching.

Social exchange theory

According to social exchange theory (Blau 1964) the basic paradigm is a two-person model of interaction, in which participants in the relationships are rational calculators weighing up the costs and benefits of exchange. They will commit effort to a relationship or exchange, based on an expectation that there will be a commensurate reward. This theory has been influential within mentoring literature in particular, for example in terms of understanding the willingness of senior managers to act as mentors. However it is worth noting that according to the developmental theory of Levinson *et al.* (1978) and Kram (1985) at certain stages in life, particularly in mid-career, managers may be particularly willing to act as mentors in order to pass on their knowledge and expertise.

Social cognitive theory

Social cognitive theory (SCT) and the concept of 'self-efficacy' have been derived from the work of Bandura (1997). Self-efficacy refers to an individual's belief in his or her ability to achieve a task or goal, and to a person's confidence that they can mobilise the necessary behavioural, cognitive, and motivational resources within a specific context. A person with low self-efficacy is more likely to fail in a task than someone with high self-efficacy – skill alone is not sufficient. Four main categories of experience have been identified as determining self-efficacy beliefs (see Stajkovic and Luthans 1998):

1 Enactive mastery experiences: that is, succeeding in a challenging task;

2 Vicarious learning: mastery modelling by means of observing competent individuals performing a task;

3 Social or verbal persuasion: by someone trusted and seen as competent;

4 Psychological arousal: the information someone gains from their own psychological and emotional states.

It would appear that SCT and 'self-efficacy' may help us to understand the processes by which mentors and coaches can help others not only to develop skills, but also to believe that they can achieve their goals.

Mentoring

Introduction

Mentoring is a relationship in which a more experienced and a trusted person provides support and guidance to another, especially through a period of transition and development. Mentoring relationships occur naturally and spontaneously. The first formal mentoring programme was launched in the USA in the

1930s (Douglas 1997) but it was not until the 1970s that organisational interest in mentoring grew rapidly.

Popular studies of business leaders indicated that many had received help from a mentor, and Levinson *et al.*'s classic (1978) study identified the mentor relationship as 'one of the most complex, and developmentally important' in the transition to adulthood. The mentoring relationships described by Levinson are typically voluntary and informal, often having a wide scope and an intense personal quality. The work of Kram (1985) has provided a seminal perspective on mentoring in organisations and the foundation for what has become known as the two-factor theory of mentoring:

> Mentors provide young adults with career-enhancing functions, such as sponsorship, coaching, facilitating exposure and visibility, and offering challenging work or protection, all of which help the younger person to establish a role in the organisation, learn the ropes, and prepare for advancement. In the psychosocial sphere, the mentor offers role modelling, counselling, confirmation and friendship, which help the young adult to develop a sense of professional identity and competence. (Kram and Isabella 1985:111)

The changing organisational context seems to have made the support and guidance from experienced others increasingly beneficial to individual employees as they build careers in a variety of organisations. Furthermore mentoring has provided organisations with a means of attracting, socialising, developing and retaining key employees, and ensuring that explicit and tacit knowledge is effectively transferred and embedded within the social network or the organisation. In the process, mentoring practice seems to have undergone a number of changes.

Types of mentoring

Mentoring relationships may be 'formal' or 'informal'. 'Informal' mentoring relationships develop spontaneously and often have a wide scope, covering a range of career development and psychosocial support functions. 'Formal' mentoring relationships are facilitated by an organisation, and may include both voluntary and assigned mentoring relationships (see Murray and Owen 1991). A related distinction is between 'classical' or 'primary' mentoring, emphasising longer-term, broader relationships covering both career and psychosocial functions, and 'secondary' mentoring, which emphasises short-term, less inclusive, career functions (see Chao and Walz 1992; Noe 1988).

'Formal' mentoring programmes are typically concerned with promoting secondary mentoring relationships, and may be promoted as a 'scheme' to achieve specific aims. These include graduate development in the case of Motorola and the representation of employees with disabilities in the Senior Civil Service. In both of these examples, mentees are able to select senior managers from within the organisation as mentors (IDS 2000). Mentoring schemes may demonstrate considerable variety in both form and objectives. One UK Building Society used external mentors to support its managers as they developed new competences in a period of rapid change (Conway 1998).

The Marketing Division of Procter and Gamble, USA, came up with an even more innovative solution. They already had a conventional mentoring programme for junior managers. However, the organisation noticed a problem with the retention and advancement of female managers in the early 1990s. The underlying issue was not that of pay or promotion, but rather that talented women managers were leaving the organisation because they did not feel valued in their jobs. A 'Mentor Up' scheme was developed to help male managers better manage issues specific to women and allow more junior women to develop quality relationships with senior management. Junior and middle-level female managers were selected to mentor their more senior managers. Over a two-year period, 'regretted losses' of women managers fell by 25 per cent to a level in line with male managers (Clutterbuck and Ragins 2002).

A difference in emphasis seems to have emerged between US mentoring practice and mentoring in a European context – although this difference should not be overstated. This difference is reflected in a distinction, between 'mainstream' and 'learning support' mentoring (see Gibb and Megginson 1993). Mainstream mentoring is focussed principally on the career development aspects of mentoring while the latter is more concerned with providing mentors to help in the achievement of specific goals such as developing competences, or achieving professional or vocational qualifications. An example of a 'mainstream' approach is the seen in the definition provided by Ragins and Scandura (1997). Mentors are defined as 'individuals with advanced experience and knowledge who are committed to providing upward support and mobility to their protégé's careers' – note the use of the term protégé. The Procter and Gamble mentoring scheme is interesting here because it focusses both on retention and the career advancement of participants.

An example of the alternative approach which stresses the role of mentoring as a support for learning and development is the definition of mentoring as 'off-line help by one person to another in making significant transitions in knowledge, work or thinking' (Megginson and Clutterbuck 1995). In these contexts the term 'mentee' is often preferred to that of protégé. An example of a mentoring programme aimed at developing competence is found in the Scandinavian airline, SAS. This voluntary scheme is aimed at helping to develop future leaders by providing them with support, and enabling them to widen their networks and knowledge of the organisation. However, even though the focus of this scheme is the development of leaders, or rather helping leaders to develop themselves in order to meet the needs of the organisation, it may in practice be difficult to distinguish between career and other developmental purposes.

A more or less universal trend, as in the case just mentioned, seems to be the facilitation of shorter-term, focussed relationships, available to a more inclusive range of employees in an organisation, and the recognition that mentoring is one of a number of possible developmental relationships. Other challenges to more traditional views of mentoring include Caruso's (1992) conceptualisation of mentoring as an 'open' and dispersed activity in which an individual gains support from a variety of individuals and other sources – including peers, line managers and other mentors. Recent research also points to the importance of networks of developmental relationships for career development (see Higgins and Kram 2001; Higgins and Thomas 2001). Downsized, flatter and rapidly changing organisations have fewer potential 'hierarchical' mentors available to mentor others. These are probably factors in the increasing interest in 'peer' mentoring between partners of equal status (McDougal and Beatty 1997), as well as in upward mentoring as in the Procter and Gamble 'mentoring up' example.

However, in spite of these new areas of interest, mentoring is still seen primarily as a paired relationship in which a more experienced person provides support and guidance to another. The objectives and context of mentoring relationships may vary, and one and the same individuals may be involved in a number of mentoring relationships – either simultaneously or serially and possibly as a mentor and as a mentee at the same time.

The mentoring relationship

The value and outcomes of all kinds of mentoring are significantly dependent upon the quality of the relationship – defined in such terms as openness, closeness, supportiveness and helpfulness (see Shockett and Haring-Hidore 1985). Relationship quality is affected by a number of factors.

A critical factor is the frequency and amount of contact between mentor and mentee. In addition the duration of the relationship and the diversity between the mentoring pair seem important. The typical 'secondary' or 'learning support' mentoring relationship may last no more than a year or two. In contrast the informal 'mainstream' or 'classical' mentoring relationships may last as long as 10 years or more in some cases (see Kram 1983). There is some evidence that the greater the diversity in terms of power, gender, race, personality, or learning styles, the less mentoring is received. However, diversity in a mentoring relationship may also be a means of promoting learning and development opportunities. Individuals may benefit from multiple mentoring relationships with differing levels of diversity, rather than relationships with minimal diversity.

Critical to all mentoring relationships is confidentiality. Even 'formal' mentoring relationships require some informality together with a risk-free environment to discuss issues 'off the record'. Trust and rapport lie at the heart of successful mentoring relationships and a high level of personal disclosure will be required on both sides. Successful mentoring relationships also require a holistic and long-term perspective of the needs of the mentee. This may be more difficult to achieve where mentor and mentee are in a line relationship, given pressures on line managers to focus on short-term organisational objectives.

Kram (1983) identified four phases of the mentoring relationship (initiation, cultivation, separation, and redefinition) and argued that mentor and mentee have different needs at different stages in the relationship, as well as at different stages in their lives and careers. Evidence for such stages, and for differing functions and types of mentoring at these stages, is inconclusive. Mentoring relationships in practice reveal significant diversity. They do not exist in isolation, and are influenced both by internal dynamic issues, and by external factors. Thus whilst some mentoring relationships will come to an end when the mentee or protégé outgrows the mentor, others may end for dysfunctional reasons such as jealousy, dependency, and lack of support or unrealistic expectations, or because of physical separation (see Ragins and Scandura 1997).

Developments in remote working and the Internet have promoted an interest in the possibility of e-mentoring. While asynchronous communication may offer advantages in promoting reflection and encouraging more open relationships, the reduction in sensory cues may entail that it takes longer to develop a relationship of trust than face-to-face relationships. Therefore, there may be greater need to support such relationships with appropriate training and matching processes, and a face-to-face meeting at the outset of the relationship may be helpful.

Research into what happens in mentoring sessions, as opposed to their outcomes, is relatively limited – in part due to the fact that the mentoring relationship is confidential. Furthermore there seems to be a significant variation in practice and there are few general guidelines that may be offered in terms of the frequency of meetings and their duration. For example, regular meetings, perhaps weekly or fortnightly at the outset, and lasting between 30 minutes and an hour, will be helpful. There will be other occasions when a mentoring conversation may last just a few short sentences during a telephone call. Each mentoring pair will need to agree its own requirements and boundaries. For many it can be helpful to agree a mentoring 'contract' at the outset – whether as a 'written down' or a psychological contract – and Figure 12.2 identifies some useful areas for discussion and agreement.

Figure 12.2 A mentoring contract

- Goals and learning outcomes
- Ground rules and parameters
- Meetings and availability
- Dealing with issues that may arise
- Criteria for success and completion
- Time frame and closure of relationship
- Checkpoints and evaluation.

The variation in mentoring conversations also means that it may be difficult to provide a generic model for a mentoring session. In Section 5.2 the GROW model will be introduced as a model of coaching, and such models could find application for mentoring too. Another useful framework is Clutterbuck and Megginson's (1999) model of 'Personal Reflective Space' (Figure 12.3). Here a mentoring session is an opportunity to take time out of the ceaseless flow of

Figure 12.3 The dynamics of reflective space

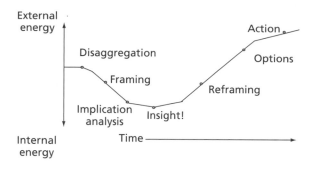

Source: Clutterbuck and Megginson (1999).

activity, to look inwards and reflect and to explore issues and implications, to gain insight and look at issues in a different light before identifying options and actions. The mentor is a facilitator of this process, primarily through skilled questioning.

Mentor competencies, selection and development

The commitment and competence of the mentor is critical to the success of the mentoring relationship – and the selection of mentors is a key success factor for formal mentoring. Whilst the traditional mentor is typically seen as someone in mid-career, mentoring is valued at a wide range of ages – both from the view of the mentor and mentee. From a social exchange perspective, anticipated costs and benefits are important in the willingness to mentor. Evidence suggests that those who have previously been mentored are more likely to see potential benefits from mentoring, and fewer costs and barriers – hence current mentees may be willing potential mentors. The introduction of mentoring needs to be accompanied by effective briefing to minimise perceived costs. Intrinsic rewards, and recognition, may well be more appropriate than extrinsic reward for a mentor.

The competence of the mentor will depend in part on the functions or objectives of mentoring, and also on the needs of the mentee. There seems to be widespread agreement that the primary role of a mentor is that of a facilitator and not a supervisor. However, there is no consensus as the roles a mentor may fulfil. Table 12.2 identifies different mentoring roles that have been identified.

Given that there is no consensus on the definition, roles, and functions of mentoring it is not surprising that there is no common agreement on specific mentor competencies. However the following characteristics seem to be important:

- relevant job experience
- organisational knowledge
- personal credibility

Table 12.2 The roles of the mentor

Kram (1985)	Daloz (1986)	Gibb and Megginson (1993)	Clutterbuck and Megginson (1999)
Career functions:			
Exposure and visIbIlIty	Support	Helping improve performance	Sounding board
Sponsorship	Challenge		Critical friend
Protection	Vision	Helping career development	Listener
Coaching			Counsellor
Challenging assignments		Being a confidential counsellor	Career advisor
			Networker
		Sharing knowledge	Coach
Psychosocial functions:			
Counselling			
Acceptance and confirmation			
Role modelling			
Friendship			

- self-awareness

- job satisfaction

- communication skills (including skills in listening, questioning, summarising, and providing feedback)

- interpersonal sensitivity

- willingness to be involved in developing others

- willingness to share learning.

The core skills of coaching and mentoring are similar, although the role of the mentor requires a greater emphasis on the development of relevant experience and organisational knowledge. A mentor's development may therefore require an extended period. In addition to providing background briefing, mentor training within a formal mentoring programme may be helpful in refining particular skills, or providing specific tools and techniques, but it is probably better to select mentors who already have most if not all the appropriate qualities.

Establishing a formal mentoring programme

An organisation wishing to benefit from mentoring has a choice between creating a supportive climate for informal relationships, or establishing a formal programme. Much recent interest relates formal mentoring relationships, which may be particularly important for more junior employees. Formal, or 'facilitated' mentoring is 'a structure and series of processes designed to create effective mentoring relationships, guide the desired behaviour change of those involved, and evaluate the results for the protégé, the mentors and the organisation' (Murray and Owen 1991). Formal programmes may take a number of forms and have, as we have seen, been developed for a variety of purposes including:

● Graduate development

● Professional development

● Support for qualification programmes

● Inducting new employees

● Developing disadvantaged groups

● Change management.

Evidence as to the comparative effectiveness of formal and informal mentoring is not conclusive but research suggests that informal relationships may offer a wider range of career related and psychosocial functions than formal relationships (Noe 1988; Chao and Walz 1992). There is also evidence to suggest that where mentees are involved in the selection of mentors, satisfaction with both mentor and the relationship will be greater. Accordingly, provided that mentors and mentees in formal relationships are involved in the choice of partner, meet regularly, clarify their expectations, and develop an open and trusting relationship, they will probably be able to achieve comparable levels of benefits as those in effective informal relationships.

Informal mentoring avoids some of the costs of formal mentoring in terms of time and administration, and the need to adapt systems such as appraisal and reward. It may also be more appropriate for senior managers in an organisation, who have a greater need for access to networks than for guidance – external mentors may be a preferred option for newly appointed senior executives. Informal mentoring may be promoted by providing opportunities for frequent interaction between potential mentors and mentees, and by promoting an open and collaborative organisational culture. However, informal mentoring is inherently more difficult to control, and it is influenced by the willingness and ability of mentees to initiate mentoring relationships – it may, therefore, not reach those individuals and groups who would most benefit from mentoring.

A formal mentoring programme is more likely to be successful if it has:

● Clarity of objectives which fit with organisational culture and strategy, and other development initiatives and processes;

● Commitment of all key stakeholders;

● Clarity of roles and responsibilities;

● Ongoing support and resources, including programme management and administration;

● Arrangements for selecting, briefing, matching, and introducing mentors and mentees, preferably on the basis of voluntary participation;

● Recognition that each relationship is able to agree to its own objectives within the context of overall programme objectives;

● Arrangements for terminating relationships, whether on achievement of objectives or in the event that a relationship is dysfunctional;

● Evaluation at both programme and relationship levels, using a range of approaches and both hard and soft data;

● Continuous development of the programme to meet the needs of all stakeholders.

The benefits and problems of formal mentoring

A recent summary of the main potential benefits and problems of formal mentoring is provided in Table 12.3, and most if not all the outcomes could also be applicable to informal mentoring relationships.

Table 12.3 Benefits and drawbacks of formal mentoring relationships

	Major benefits	Potential drawbacks
For organisation	1 Development of managers in the organisation 2 Reduced turnover 3 Increased organisational commitment 4 Low costs or cost-effectiveness associated with formal mentoring programmes 5 Improved organisational communication	1 Lack of organisational support 2 Creation of a climate of favouritism 3 Difficulties in co-ordinating programmes with other organisational initiatives 4 Costs and resources associated with overseeing and administering programme
For mentee/ Protégé	1 Career advancement 2 Personal support 3 Learning and development 4 Increased confidence 5 Assistance and feedback	1 Neglect of core job 2 Negative experiences 3 Unrealistic expectations 4 Overdependence on relationship 5 Role conflict between boss and mentor
For mentor	1 Personal fulfilment 2 Assistance on projects 3 Financial rewards 4 Increased self-confidence 5 Revitalised interest in work	1 Lack of time 2 Lack of perceived benefits 3 Lack of skills needed for mentoring role 4 Pressure to take on mentoring role 5 Resentment of protégés

Source: Douglas (1997).

Coaching

What is coaching?

If the origin of mentoring lies more in the role of 'elder statesman' or the 'wise and trusted counsellor', the origin of coaching in management seems to be derived from the 'private tutor' or the 'sports coach'. As is the case with mentoring, there is no agreed definition of 'coaching', but definitions typically focus on performance improvement as in the following examples:

> Coaching is the art of facilitating the performance, learning and development of another. (Downey 2001)

> Coaching is meant to be a practical goal-focused form of personal, one-to-one learning for busy executives and may be used to improve performance or executive behaviour, enhance a career or prevent derailment, and work through organisational issues or change initiatives. Essentially, coaches provide executives important feedback that they would normally never get about personal, performance, career, and organisational issues. (Hall *et al.* 1999)

> Coaching is 'a relationship that focuses on improving both skills and behaviour in pursuit of better individual and organisational performance'. (Malone 2001)

While the focus of mentoring is on the development of the mentee throughout his or her life or career, the focus of coaching is on the results of the job, exploring problems and providing opportunities to develop new skills. It seems to focus more on specific issues and activities than mentoring. It should also be more time-bounded than a mentoring relationship (Hall *et al.* 1999). Mentoring relationships tend to broader, to rely more upon the experience of the mentor and may also include some coaching activity. An interesting recent development is that 'coaching' seems to be the preferred term for the support provided to more senior managers, rather than 'mentoring'.

Coaching activity, as in the case of KPMG or ICI for example, is often seen as integral to management (Parsloe and Wray 2000). This view is exemplified by Larry Bossidy, CEO of Honeywell, and previously of Allied Signal, for whom the best opportunities for coaching are real-time business situations, and that every meeting is a coaching opportunity.

Models of coaching

There are two main forms of coaching, depending on the skill level and motivation of the person being coached:

1 'Demonstration and practice' models

2 'Goal-focussed' models.

Demonstration and practice (the coach as instructor)

This is perhaps the more traditional model of coaching, and more appropriate for an inexperienced person seeking to develop specific skills under the guidance

Figure 12.4 The practical spiral

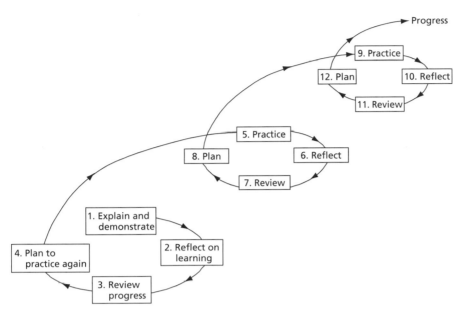

Source: Parsloe and Wray (2000).

of an accomplished performer. One technique is the 'Practice Spiral' of Parsloe and Wray (2000) (Figure 12.4).

This model, which involves the concept of the 'learning cycle' (see Kolb 1984; Honey and Mumford 1986), comprises a series of connected cycles of performance and learning commencing with the demonstration of a skill or activity by the coach. This approach is 'hands-on'. The coach not only demonstrates a particular skill, but also explains how it is done, and why it is important. The learner then has an opportunity to reflect on the experience in a systematic way and to review overall progress towards an agreed goal. Finally, the coachee plans to practise the skill. At this point the new cycle commences, and practice is followed by periods of reflection, review and planning, each at higher levels of performance. Throughout the process the coach will use observation and questions to assess both performance and understanding and provide feedback and motivation. Practice sessions allow the coachee to move from a 'risk-free' environment where mistakes can be made to real-life situations, where actual performance may be evaluated.

Goal-focussed models (the coach as consultant)

A second approach aims to help a coachee to identify ways to solve their own issues or achieve their own goals. This 'hands-off' approach is more suited to the more experienced employee. Such methods have been used in high-level sports coaching. One approach is Schein's (1988) model of 'process consulting' defined as 'a set of activities on the part of the consultant that help the client to perceive, understand, and act upon the process events that occur in the clients environment'. Another very influential approach is the GROW model (Figure 12.5) which provides a structure for a coaching session.

Figure 12.5 The GROW model

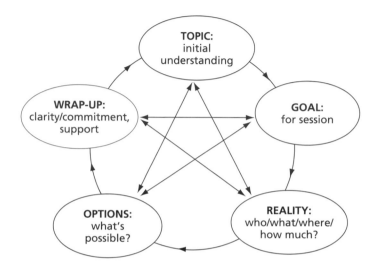

Source: Downey (2001).

The process begins with the coach seeking an understanding of the issue and the goal that the coachee wishes to work with. The role of the coach is to help the coachee to gain a better understanding of this issue, its 'reality', the options open to the coachee, and then to commit to a specific course of action. The key point about this model is that the role of the coach is fundamentally non-directive. Listening and questioning are key activities for the coach in this process – not instructing.

Coaching relationships: the practice of coaching

The quality of the relationship and the development of trust and rapport are equally important in coaching as in mentoring relationships. While coaching relationships or interventions tend to be of short duration and or focussed around the development of discrete skills or the achievement of specific goals, it should also be remembered that where the coach is the line manager the coaching relationship will be ongoing.

The frequency and duration of coaching meetings will depend on circumstances. A coaching intervention could take place as a 'one-off' event, or comprise a series of meetings. Typically such a series could involve between three and six meetings – including an initial session to agree expectations and goals, followed by a series of coaching meetings, with a final review meeting. In a longer programme a mid-point review meeting could be helpful. Each meeting will typically last between 30 minutes and 2 hours, but again this will vary on the situation. At the start of a relationship the meetings may be weekly or fortnightly, and then move to fortnightly or monthly.

Coaching activity may address a range of issues that may vary depending on the level of the coachee. Table 12.4 identifies the issues addressed in a recent study of executive coaching in ascending order of difficulty, with level one the highest.

Table 12.4 Issues covered in executive development

Level 1	Level 2	Level 3	Level 4
● Improving and managing interpersonal relationships with boss, senior managers ● Listening, being more personal, warm, open ● Implementing layoffs ● Relations with external partners ● Varying voice intensity (especially for women)	● Improving interpersonal relationships with teams, peers ● Meeting management skills ● Personal style, behaviours ● Appearance ● Influencing; team building; upward communication; dealing with employees; role definition; limits of own and others' responsibilities	● Learning the language of others, 'hot buttons' (e.g. 'loyalty') so others can hear you ● Planning for layoffs ● Planning for performance reviews, goal setting ● Career planning ● Presentation skills ● Transitions, entry; process improvement ● 360° feedback ● Validation of strengths ● Developmental action planning	● Assessing staff needs ● Setting priorities ● Writing skills

Source: Hall *et al.* (1999).

The manager as coach and leader

Coaching is increasingly seen as an integral element in the role of the manager. The key process that incorporates coaching within a line manager's ongoing activity is that of performance management as is illustrated in Figure 12.6. Effective performance management is achieved though the ongoing interaction of manager and employee, rather than considered as an annual, or even quarterly activity linked to appraisal. There is evidence that the inclusion of coaching activity within performance management by line managers or supervisors who engage in an ongoing dialogue with employees about how to achieve effective performance will be more effective than simply measuring performance relative to a set of pre-established behaviours or goals (Gittell 2000).

Performance management is also the activity that links employee performance to business strategy and all other elements of the organisation's approach to HRM. Hence the relationship between line manager and employee becomes critical to organisational performance. This will mean that for a line manager to provide effective coaching support to subordinates, an open and trusting relationship must be maintained at all times. Whilst this is a function of the individual relationship,

Figure 12.6 Performance management cycle

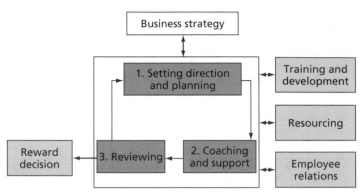

Source: Beardwell and Holden (2001).

it will be difficult to achieve if the wider organisational climate is not transparent and open.

Coaching activity within an ongoing performance management framework provides a key means by which a line manager may develop the skills of their people, as well as their self-efficacy perceptions. The line manager as coach can (see Malone 2001):

● challenge destructive thinking and establish constructive thought patterns;

● provide intentionally creating opportunities for employees to be successful at undertaking new activities, reinforcing success and building confidence, without putting them into situations where success is unlikely;

● provide opportunities to observe other competent employees being successful and receive positive reinforcement;

● provide realistic encouragement;

● encourage employees to take good care of themselves physically and to reduce their stress levels;

● be clear about expectations and standards.

It would also be a mistake to see coaching as only to do with one aspect of management. It links directly to leadership, change management, and strategy. As Larry Bossidy, CEO of Allied Signal said in 1995, 'strategies are intellectually simple; their execution is not' (Tichy and Charan 1995). Behaviour change at the individual level is the basis of organisational change. Senior or middle managers in particular have an important role in linking the top level leaders and visionaries in an organisation with operating level managers and entrepreneurs. That link is encapsulated in coaching and people development (Bartlett and Ghoshal 1997). For Lyons 'with the right conditions in place coaching is organisational transformation; coaching is team development; coaching is strategy in motion' (Lyons *et al.* 2000). Such arguments suggest that coaching is not so much a discrete management activity, but a style of management, promoting greater involvement and participation.

Interestingly though it is worth noting an alternative view that coaching may not be the only appropriate management style. The choice of an appropriate style will depend upon a variety of situational factors including the levels of a team member or subordinates competence and commitment (see, e.g. Hersey and Blanchard 1982). At times a manager may need to be directive while other occasions will permit a more strictly coaching approach, which seeks develop both the skill and commitment of others and allow effective delegation.

Selecting and developing coaches

Identifying the key skills of the coach is relatively uncontroversial, although different writers express these skills differently. Three examples are provided in Table 12.5.

Table 12.5 Key coaching skills

Woodall and Winstanley (1998)	Hillman *et al.* (1990)	Downey (1999)
<ul><li>observation</li><li>active listening</li><li>discussion</li><li>challenge</li><li>questioning</li><li>delegation</li><li>timing (setting time aside)</li></ul>	<ul><li>attending</li><li>reflecting</li><li>exploring</li><li>self-disclosing</li><li>accepting</li></ul>	(a spectrum of skills from the directive to non-directive)<ul><li>telling</li><li>instructing</li><li>giving advice</li><li>offering guidance</li><li>giving feedback</li><li>making suggestions</li><li>asking questions to raise awareness</li><li>summarising</li><li>paraphrasing</li><li>reflecting</li><li>listening to understand</li></ul>

Behind the effective use of these skills, particularly given the importance of building self-efficacy, are the importance of attitudes and beliefs that support the development of others. Some recent research indicates that there may be a positive relationship between certain aspects of personality, and in particular levels of agreeableness and openness to experience, and preference for participative management styles (Stevens and Ash 2001). The implication of this research is that whilst skill training and development may be important, those organisations for which a participative management style and coaching is critical may wish to consider the selection of coaches in terms of greater personality fit.

A further factor in terms of selecting coaches is the choice between internal and external coaches. Particularly at senior levels there has been a significant growth in the use of the latter as 'executive coach'. This decision will involve a trade-off between anonymity, objectivity, impartiality, and new ideas versus organisational knowledge, cost, and availability. Accordingly external coaches are more likely to be appropriate for senior executives, particularly when new in post.

Future considerations

Interest in mentoring and coaching activity is likely to increase because coaching and mentoring seem to address a number of key issues of the moment to do with developing people, performance, and organisations. Coaching and mentoring skills are increasingly seen as key aspects of the essential toolkit for managers, both as a means of developing others and of developing themselves and their careers.

A number of new trends may become evermore important. The first is that there is likely to be an increasing focus on the development of a network of supporting relationships – a developmental constellation – in order to promote valued career and learning outcomes. This will broaden the current tendency to focus on a relatively few relationships. In addition to face-to-face mentoring and coaching activities, there is likely to be an increasing interest in virtual mentoring and coaching relationships. As virtual teamworking and remote working increase, and as familiarity with electronic communication grows, virtual mentoring and coaching relationships are likely to become more commonplace.

At the same time an organisation wishing to introduce or support coaching and mentoring activity needs to be clear about the resources and commitment success requires. Evidence as to their potential effectiveness seems to be growing. However it is worth bearing in mind that they remain relatively new techniques, that definitional confusion exists, and that research on both mentoring and coaching is still relatively limited in some areas such as executive coaching (see Schuler and Jackson 2000; Berglas 2002).

The theme developed in this chapter is that coaching and mentoring may provide effective means of on-the-job development and performance improvement. However, it is important for an organisation to identify the contribution of different employees to the creation of value and to develop its HR architecture accordingly (Lepak and Snell 1999). It is possible that an organisation will decide that the level of support of coaching and mentoring should vary across categories of employee.

Where mentoring and coaching is considered to be of value it will be essential to develop a supportive organisational culture and to develop and reward effective role models, at all levels in the organisation.

Further reading and references

Armstrong, M. (2001) *A Handbook of Human Resource Management Practice*, London, Kogan Page.

Bandura, A. (1997) *Self-Efficacy: The Exercise of Control*, W.H. Freeman & Co.

Bartlett, C.A. and Ghoshal, S. (1997) 'The myth of the generic manager: new personal competencies for new management roles', *California Management Review*, Vol. 40, No. 1, pp. 92–116.

Berglas, S. (2002) 'The very real dangers of executive coaching', *Harvard Business Review*, June, pp. 86–92.

Blau, P. (1964) *Exchange and Power in Social Life*, New York, Wiley.

Bossidy, L. (2002) 'The art of good coaching', *Chief Executive*, Vol. 178, pp. 16–17.

Caruso, R.E. (1992) *Mentoring and the Business Environment: Asset or Liability*, Aldershot, Dartmouth.

Chao, G.T. and Walz, P.M. (1992) 'Formal and informal mentorships: a comparison on mentoring functions and contrast with nonmentored counterparts', *Personnel Psychology*, Vol. 45, pp. 619–36.

Clutterbuck, D. and Megginson, D. (1999), *Mentoring Executives and Directors*, Oxford, Butterworth-Heinemann.

Clutterbuck, D. and Ragins, B.R. (2002) *Mentoring and Diversity*, Oxford, Butterworth-Heinemann.

Conway, C. (1998) *Strategies for Mentoring: A Blueprint for Successful Organizational Development*, New York, John Wiley & Sons.

Daloz, L.A. (1986) *Effective Teaching and Mentoring: Realizing the Transformational Power of Adult learning Experiences*, San Francisco, Jossey-Bass.

Douglas, C.A. (1997) *Formal Mentoring Programs in Organizations: An Annotated Bibliography*, Greensboro, Center for Creative Leadership.

Downey, M. (2001) *Effective Coaching*, London, Texere.

Doyle, M. in Beardwell, I. and Holden, L. (2001) *Human Resource Management: A Contemporary Approach*, Harlow, Pearson Education.

Erikson, E. (1963) *Childhood and Society*, New York, Norton.

Gibb, S. (1994) 'Evaluating mentoring', *Education and Training*, Vol. 36, No. 5, pp. 32–39.

Gibb, S. and Megginson, D. (1993) 'Inside corporate mentoring schemes: a new agenda of concerns', *Personnel Review*, Vol. 22, pp. 40–54.

Gittell, J.H. (2000) 'Paradox of coordination and control', *California Management Review*, Vol. 42, No. 3, pp. 101–17.

Hall, D.T., Otazo, K.L. and Hollenbeck, G.P. (1999) 'Behind closed doors: what really happens in executive coaching', *Organizational Dynamics*, Winter, pp. 39–53.

Hersey, P. and Blanchard, K. (1982) *Situational Leadership: A Summary*, University Associates, San Diego, CA.

Higgins, M.C. and Kram, K.E. (2001) 'Reconceptualizing mentoring at work: a developmental network perspective', *Academy of Management Review*, Vol. 26, No. 2, pp. 264–88.

Higgins, M. and Thomas, D. (2001) 'Constellations and careers: toward understanding the effects of multiple developmental relationships', *Journal of Organizational Behavior*, Vol. 22, pp. 223–47.

Hillman, L.W., Schwandt, D.R. and Bartz, D.E. (1990) 'Enhancing staff members' performance through feedback and coaching', *Journal of Management Development*, Vol. 9, No. 3, pp. 20–28.

Hiltrop, J.-M. (1998) 'Preparing people for the future: the next agenda for HRM', *European Management Journal*, Vol. 16.

Honey, P. and Mumford, A. (1986) '*Using Your Learning Styles*', Honey, Maidenhead, UK.

Incomes Data Services (2000) 'Mentoring', *Study No. 686*.

Kolb, D. (1984) *Experiential Learning*, Englewood Cliffs, NJ, Prentice-Hall.

Kram, K.E. (1983) 'Phases of the mentor relationship', *Academy of Management Journal*, Vol. 26, No. 4, pp. 608–25.

Kram, K.E. (1985) '*Mentoring at Work: Developmental Relationships in Organizational Life*, Scott Foresman & Co.

Kram, K.E. and Isabella, L.A. (1985) 'Mentoring alternatives: the role of peer relationships in career development', *Academy of Management Journal*, Vol. 28, No. 1, pp. 110–32.

Landsberg, M. (1997) *The Tao of Coaching*, London, HarperCollins Business.

Lepak, D. and Snell, S. (1999) 'The theory of human resource architecture: toward a theory of human capital allocation and development', *Academy of Management Journal*, Vol. 24, pp. 31–48.

Levinson, D.J, Darrow, C.N., Klein, E.B., Levinson, M.A. and McKee, B. (1978) *Seasons of a Man's Life*, New York, Knopf.

Lyons, L. in Goldsmith, M., Lyons, L. and Freas, A. (2000) *Coaching for Leadership*, San Francisco, Jossey-Bass Pfeiffer.

Malone, J. (2001) 'Shining a new light on organizational change: improving self-efficacy through coaching', *Organizational Development Journal*, Vol. 19, pp. 27–36.

McDougall, M. and Beatty, R.S. (1997) 'Peer mentoring at work: the nature and outcomes of non-hierarchical developmental relationships', *Management Learning*, Vol. 28, pp. 423–37.

Megginson, D. and Clutterbuck, D. (1995) *Mentoring in Action*, London, Kogan Page.

Murray, M. and Owen, M.A. (1991) *Beyond the Myths and Magic of Mentoring: How to Facilitate an Effective Mentoring Program*, San Fransisco, Jossey-Bass.

Noe, R.A. (1988) 'An investigation into the determinants of successful assigned mentoring relationships', *Personnel Psychology*, Vol. 41, pp. 457–79.

Parsloe, E. and Wray, M. (2000) *Coaching and Mentoring: Practical Methods to Improve Learning*, London, Kogan Page.

Ragins, B.R. and Scandura, T.A. (1997) 'The way we were: gender and the termination of mentoring relationships', *Journal of Applied Psychology*, Vol. 82, No. 6, pp. 945–53.

Reynolds, M. (1997) 'Learning styles: a critique', *Management Learning*, Vol. 28, pp. 115–33.

Roberts, I. in Beardwell, I. and Holden, L. (2001) *Human Resource Management: A Contemporary Approach*, Harlow, Pearson Education.

Schein, E.H. (1988) *Organisational Psychology*, Englewood Cliffs, NJ, Prentice-Hall.

Shockett, M. and Haring-Hidore, M. (1985) 'Factor analytic support for psychosocial and vocational mentoring functions', *Psychological Reports*, Vol. 57, pp. 627–30.

Schuler, R.S. and Jackson, S.E. (2000) *Managing Human Resources: A Partnership Perspective*, Cincinnati, South-Western College Publishing.

Stajkovic, A.D. and Luthans, F. (1998) 'Social cognitive theory and self-efficacy: going beyond traditional motivational and behavioural approaches', *Organizational Dynamics*, Spring, pp. 62–74.

Stevens, C.D. and Ash, R.A. (2001) 'Selecting employees for fit: personality and preferred management style', *Journal of Managerial Issues*, Vol. 13, No. 4, pp. 500–17.

Tichy, N.M. and Charan, R. (1995) 'The CEO as coach: an interview with allied signal's Lawrence A. Bossidy', *Harvard Business Review*, March–April, pp. 68–78.

Turban, D.B. and Dougherty, T.W. (1994) 'Role of protégé personality in receipt of mentoring and career success', *Academy of Management Journal*, Vol. 37, No. 3, pp. 688–702.

Waldroop, J. and Butler, T. (1996) 'The executive as coach', *Harvard Business Review*, November–December, pp. 111–17.

Walton, J. (1999) *Strategic Human Resource Development*, Harlow, Pearson Education Limited.

Woodall, J. and Winstanley, D. (1998) *Management Development: Strategy and Practice*, Oxford, Blackwell Business.

Concluding comments:
the new HR agenda

The question of whether there is a new agenda for human resource management has been one of the underpinning themes of this book. To what extent are we now genuinely at a crossroads in terms of managing people within organisations? There is no doubt that the nature of the organisational context is changing and in this book we have endeavoured to indicate some of the most important changes. However, change itself is not new and does not of itself give rise to a new agenda.

We have pinpointed some aspects of the HR agenda from the latter part of the 20th century, which continue to exert a powerful influence on people management. Accordingly the need to manage performance, to promote effective reward processes and to encourage learning and development within organisations, as well as to promote greater interlinkage between these key levers of HR, remains critical. In addition, a stress on the importance of the strategic deployment of human resource management and on the critical role of the line manager are themes which are as relevant today as they have been for the last decade or more. This being the case, what is different now?

Some new themes in the HR agenda are explored in this book. For example, emotional intelligence has emerged as an important factor in individual and organisational performance and a focus for developing the individual and for leadership development within organisations. The rise of virtual organisations and team working and the greater importance of demonstrating social responsibility within the context of stakeholders and the wider community are also new themes in human resource management. The notion of organisational reputation is linked to another emergent theme, that of the need to develop an employer brand that helps an organisation to recruit, engage and to develop its people capability. This represents something of a new emphasis for human resource management. Not only is it important to ensure that human resource policies and practices are linked to business objectives and aligned with each other; this internal focus must now be balanced by a greater understanding of the external context. The psychological contract, a notion that has become of fundamental importance to the understanding of behaviour within organisations, begins to be formed before an individual joins an organisation, and the development of an employer brand will be an important aspect in securing the people capabilities an organisation needs in an increasingly competitive environment.

A number of new perspectives on the established HRM agenda have also been highlighted. The need to demonstrate the impact of HR on the organisational bottom-line remains vital for the profession, and for the individual HR manager. However, there is now compelling evidence that this impact can be demonstrated. In addition, this confidence is reflected in the development of approaches seeking to quantify the value of human capital for an organisation.

There are also differences in emphasis in the traditional key levers of human resource management and especially in the management of performance, rewards and learning and development. The importance of linking these elements such that they may be seen as different aspects of a central process which negotiates the ongoing deal between an organisation and the individual and which delivers performance and capability on the one hand, and the total rewards consistent with an individual's psychological contract on the other, is becoming more critical. Performance management is becoming more focused on developing capability and culture change, whilst reward management is seeking to promote greater involvement from stakeholders along with greater flexibility and openness. Performance and reward management processes, alongside the learning and development processes within organisations, are seen as means to manage increasingly diverse talent and to develop new career structures choices for employees and leadership capability.

These approaches understand the need to consider the role of expectations and commitment, and indeed trust, for the individual within an organisation. At the same time the HR professional needs to focus on delivering and measuring performance, and on providing evidence as a basis for developing policies and processes. The new HR agenda in this sense represents an innovative combination of 'hard' and 'soft' approaches. To succeed in this environment the HR professional needs to develop personal credibility and professional competence. There is no single role for the HR function or the HR manager. Rather the HR professional needs to build even closer links to the business and to adapt his or her approach to those needs.

The last words in this book should be reserved for the role of the line manager. There is little doubt that the individual line manager is the lynchpin for business performance and success, and is the primary medium through which an organisation implements its HR policies and practices. The line manager has a critical role in making the organisation a compelling place to work – or indeed the opposite. In the current context of work the line manager now has a greater responsibility to develop him or herself, and to develop others through coaching and mentoring activities. The line manager is at the fulcrum of turning business and HR strategy into performance. This position implies that the line manager must more than ever understand the HR context and content within the organisation, and be able to identify the key levers that drive individual and team performance. At the same time the organisation, and particularly the HR function, has a greater responsibility to provide support and development to promote the development of individual line managers and the capabilities of an organisation's human resource capability.

Index